Queen of the Burglars

Queen of the Burglars

*The Scandalous Life
of Sophie Lyons*

SHAYNE DAVIDSON

Exposit

Jefferson, North Carolina

Library of Congress Cataloguing-in-Publication Data

Names: Davidson, Shayne.
Title: Queen of the burglars : the scandalous life of Sophie Lyons /
Shayne Davidson.
Description: Jefferson : Exposit, 2020. | Includes bibliographical
references and index.
Identifiers: LCCN 2020027082 |
ISBN 9781476682549 (paperback : acid free paper) ∞
ISBN 9781476640549 (ebook)
Subjects: LCSH: Lyons, Sophie. | Swindlers and swindling—United
States—Biography. | Thieves—United States—Biography.
Classification: LCC HV6692.L96 D38 2020 | DDC 364.16/2092 [B]—dc23
LC record available at https://lccn.loc.gov/2020027082

British Library cataloguing data are available

ISBN (print) 978-1-4766-8254-9
ISBN (ebook) 978-1-4766-4054-9

On the cover: Sophie Lyons in a photograph
from the New York City Rogues' Gallery, 1886

Printed in the United States of America

Exposit is an imprint of McFarland & Company, Inc., Publishers

Exposit

Box 611, Jefferson, North Carolina 28640
www.expositbooks.com

Table of Contents

Table of Contents

Acknowledgments

I am indebted to the staff at the Library of Michigan. The archivists there have done an incredible job of preserving and indexing the voluminous criminal records from 19th-century Detroit. They helped me locate Sophie's Detroit criminal records and the appeal of her will. Without those resources this book could not have been written.

I appreciate the assistance I received from the staff at the London Metropolitan Archives in London, England, and the Surrey History Centre in Woking, England. Staff there located the records related to some of Madeline Belmont's hospitalizations.

The New York State Archives in Albany gets my thanks for locating the reformatory records of George Lyons and the prison records of Jim Brady.

Thanks to Jerry Kuntz for sharing with me the records of the Pinkerton Detective Agency held at the Library of Congress.

I am very grateful for the excellent editorial assistance I received from Jen Tebbe.

To my friends Anne DeMarinis and Melanie Killen go my thanks for their willingness to listen to my concerns and for their sage advice.

Last but definitely not least, I thank my husband, John Fink. He accompanied me on many research trips and he carefully held down yellowed, curling papers while I photographed them. He listened to more stories about Sophie Lyons than anyone without a substantial interest in crime history should ever have to hear. With his patience and support, he is my rock.

Preface

One of the most renowned professional criminals in 19th-century America was a woman named Sophie Lyons. In 1913 she published a book about her life titled *The Amazing Adventures of Sophie Lyons, Queen of the Burglars, or Why crime does not pay.* (The title was shortened to *Why Crime Does Not Pay* for the hardbound edition of the book.) It's filled with entertaining anecdotes about crime, stories of her adventures, and the escapades of her friends and lovers. Some of the book's more sensational stories were even published in newspapers as stand-alone articles.

Sophie was a con woman, among other things, and the stories she told about her life were generally a little truth woven together with a pile of lies. After she died, the press regurgitated Sophie's exaggerations and fantasies. Ultimately so much questionable information was written about Sophie's life and crimes that I wondered whether it would be possible, nearly 100 years after her death, to research her background and discern the true story of her unconventional life.

I began my research by creating a family tree for Sophie from genealogical sources such as the U.S. Census and records of births, immigration, marriages, and deaths. While I was in the process of making the family tree, I noticed the listing of a book for sale at a rare bookshop in Detroit: a first edition of *Professional Criminals of America* by Thomas Byrnes.

Byrnes, a poor Irish immigrant, grew up in the notorious Five Points slum in lower Manhattan. In 1863, when he was 21 years old, he joined the police force and rose quickly through the ranks. New York City centralized its detectives under one roof in 1882 and the following year Byrnes was appointed the head of the Detective Bureau. Three years later he published his magnum opus, *Professional Criminals of America*. The book contains photos and biographies of 204 seriously bad men and women, including Sophie.

1

As it turns out, the first edition for sale in Detroit once belonged to someone named Florence L. Bower. Florence had written her name in neat script in the front of the book. Because Sophie's family tree was fresh in my mind, I realized that the book had probably belonged to Sophie's oldest daughter, Florence Lyons Bower. It was such a bizarre coincidence that I felt compelled to go to the shop. Once there, I carefully looked over the book, decided it was legit, and purchased it.

Around 1877, Sophie moved from New York City, where she'd spent much of her childhood, and established a home base in Detroit, which was where Florence lived the majority of her life. Although they'd been estranged for years, Sophie reached out to Florence shortly before she died, in 1924, and told her that she'd made a new will. The updated document specified that many of her household possessions and some of her real estate were earmarked for Florence.

It's entirely possible that my copy of *Professional Criminals of America* once belonged to Sophie and Florence inherited it. After all, it contains a number of notations in a hand other than Florence's. In the section near Sophie's photo and biography, the pages have been so well perused that the binding is loose and falling apart. My copy of the Byrnes book and some of the notations in it became an inspiration for this book.

Additional discoveries followed on the heels of finding Florence's book. For example, I purchased a rare photograph of another of Sophie's daughters, Lotta Belmont, on eBay. I also found that some of the original court records related to Sophie's life and crimes in Detroit have survived. These materials—some of which are now almost 140 years old—have been archived at the Library of Michigan in Lansing.

News stories written as close to the time and place of a particular event or crime provided the information I found to be the most reliable. Reporters from the *Detroit Free Press* attended Sophie's many hearings and trials in the 1880s, and they took shorthand of witness statements. Those notes evolved into articles that often included lengthy verbatim testimony.

One document that proved to be a gold mine of information was the appeal of Sophie's estate to the Michigan Supreme Court. This document holds more clues about her life than anything else. It includes two depositions from Florence, along with depositions from many of Sophie's closest friends in Detroit and some of her tenants. These people knew her for many years and recounted their personal recollections of her in their depositions.

Not surprisingly, given its subject, the appeal is an unusually eccentric document. Folded in between several hundred pages of depositions is a complete paperback copy of Sophie's memoir. It was included to demonstrate that her mind was unstable when she wrote her will. The executor of her estate decided that the cost to have a court reporter transcribe the book would be prohibitively expensive, so the paperback edition was bound in with the other documents. When I showed it to the archivists at the Library of Michigan, they commented with amazement that they'd never seen anything like it. Sophie likely would have enjoyed knowing she'd broken the rules, even after death!

Before I began writing, I created a timeline of Sophie's life, starting with events from the family tree and adding in events from court records, newspaper stories, the appeal of her will, and other sources. This 21-page timeline revealed a life jam-packed with love affairs, marriages, and childbirths, as well as crimes spread across the globe. I knew I'd end up writing about Sing Sing Prison and the Detroit House of Correction, but there were surprises along the way, such as when I uncovered links to Bethlem (aka Bedlam) Asylum and to several workhouses in London.

Sophie Lyons masked her fascinating life story with lies and half-truths. I hope my book lays those false tales to rest as it introduces you to the real-life story of the woman who proudly called herself the Queen of the Burglars.

Aliases and Nicknames

Sophie Van Elkan Lyons:

Louisa Andress
Mrs. F.H. Brody
Ella Dramach
Sophia DeVarney
Rose Devine
Sarah English
Julia Kelso
Sophie Levy
Susan Lockwood
Kate Lorangie
Kate Loranger
Sophie Lorens
Kate Lucas
S. E. Lucas
Sarah Lyons
Sophia Monacky
Fanny Owings
Sarah Richardson
Harriet Smith
Jane Smith
Sarah Smith
Louisa Sylvan
Mary Walton
Catherine Williams
Kate Wilson

Morris Harris:

"Morrie" Harris
Frank Lewis
Wolf Levy
? Moore
John Norris
Wolf Undelsy

Edward Lyons:

"Ned" Lyons
Alexander Cummings
Robert E. Hapgood
George Jackson
George F. Lenning
Edmund Lyons
James F. Richardson
Edward T. Sanman

James Brady:

"Albany Jim" Brady
"Big Jim" Brady
James Morrison
Oscar D. Peterson
Charles Robinson
George Woods

William James Burke:

"Billy the Kid" Burke
"Flash Billy"
Charles Bates
William Brady
W. H. Burton
Frank Lackrose
George Moore
Charles H. Page
John Petrie
Frank Smith
James William Taylor

Introduction:
The Queen of the Burglars

Sophie Lyons lived a life filled with excitement, danger, and tragedy. Her career as a thief began when her parents taught her how to steal—and forced her to do it using physical violence.

As it turned out, Sophie was unusually good at being a thief, particularly as a pickpocket. Her career blossomed when she hit her teen years and continued as she grew older. Crime was her source of income for decades. Picking pockets and shoplifting were mainstays; as time went on she added swindling, blackmail, and bank robbery to her resume. Unlike most of her male counterparts, Sophie was good at managing money and ended up with a fortune. That wealth was built partly through real-estate investments, but the foundation of her business was the money she'd "earned" through various criminal activities.

As a young woman, Sophie's beauty and magnetism made her the toast of criminal circles, and her daring and nerve helped her get out of numerous challenging situations. Confident and striking looking, she attracted the romantic attentions of many men. She robbed banks, married bank robbers, seduced wealthy men (then blackmailed them), escaped from Sing Sing Prison, ran with a gang of thieves in Detroit, and committed crimes on two continents.

In her later years, Sophie's business acumen and perseverance allowed her to reinvent herself as a property owner, author, and prosperous citizen of Detroit. But it wasn't easy for her to live down her reputation as a criminal. She was feared, hated, and maligned by policemen across America long after she'd hung up her burglar's tools.

A Tip-Top Criminal

Sophie's notoriety reached sensational proportions when she found herself among the 18 women profiled in a publication that sent shivers down the spines of America's most successful criminals. Thanks to New York police inspector Thomas Byrnes' 1886 book *Professional Criminals of America*, 204 of the country's top criminals could no longer hide easily behind disguises and aliases. Byrnes had included photographs, aliases, and brief criminal biographies, making them something they never wanted to be: recognizable. (Three of Sophie's four husbands were also included in the book. Ned Lyons and William "Billy" Burke had photos in addition to their bios; James "Big Jim" Brady simply had a biography and list

of aliases because Byrnes didn't have a mug shot of him.)

Despite being good at the crime game, Sophie was arrested, convicted, and imprisoned multiple times. She parted company with three husbands, two of whom had also made substantial fortunes through criminal means but had squandered it all by the ends of their lives. Adding to her personal problems was the fact that she suffered from mood swings and uncontrollable rages, possibly a result of being abused by her family as a child.

One might think this history, combined with Sophie's profession, would have led her to avoid having children. The opposite proved true: She had seven documented children and claimed to have had as many as 10.[1] Several of her children preceded her in death, including a

Thomas Byrnes was a legendary New York police inspector. His innovative book, *Professional Criminals of America*, included photographs and biographies of the criminals he thought were the most dangerous threats to society. Sophie's photograph and bio were included in the book. New York police commissioner Theodore Roosevelt later ousted Byrnes from the force amid allegations of corruption.

son who died in prison before he turned 21. Others attempted to get as far away from their notorious mother as possible, such as Sophie's favorite son, who went so far as to change his name, enlist in the military, and move to the West Coast.

An Inventive Author

In 1913, Sophie published her memoir, *Why Crime Does Not Pay*. She described on the title page of the paperback version as "the most famous and successful criminal of modern times, who made a million dollars in her early criminal career." Nonetheless she focused many of her tales not on herself but on the adventures of infamous people she'd known, such as Fredericka "Marm" Mandelbaum, Max Shinburn, Eddie Guerin, and Adam Worth. Despite her personal acquaintance with these individuals, Sophie relied heavily on newspaper reports of their escapades, plus a liberal dose of imagination, when writing their "true" stories. She also copied some of her information straight out of Byrnes' *Professional Criminals of America*.

Of course, she couldn't dampen her constant desire to be the star of the show, so she inserted herself into certain events, including ones she couldn't possibly have participated in because she was either in jail or prison at the time they occurred. In other situations when she *was* present, such as an attempted bank robbery in Mt. Sterling, Kentucky, she changed so many details that the book version of the story shared few similarities to the actual event.

One example of how Sophie lied in her book was her claim that she was involved in a clever investment swindle with another criminal who at the time used the alias Carrie Morse. Authorities also knew this woman by her married name: Marion LaTouche.[2]

LaTouche was a cunning professional criminal whose ingenuity Sophie doubtlessly admired. Consequently, she wrote that she once bumped into LaTouche in New York. She claimed LaTouche recognized her and requested she become a partner in the "Ladies' Investment Bureau" on West 37th Street that LaTouche planned to open.[3]

Here's how the scheme worked: During most of the 19th century society frowned upon the notion of a woman working as a stockbroker and it was difficult for women to invest in the stock market. Generally they had to rely on men, who took large commissions, to invest for them.[4] Many women knew there was good money to be made in the market, and LaTouche took advantage of this in her swindling plots. She told her victims she'd found a way to make stock-market investments and had opened a women-only investment bureau. She then lured naive women into handing over their money by offering them ridiculously high rates of return on investments made through her bureau.

Sophie claimed LaTouche asked her to play the role of "Celia Rigsby," the investment bureau's president. As such, her job was to convince the dupes to place their money in LaTouche's crooked hands.[5] She claimed LaTouche outfitted her with a lavish apartment and beautiful clothes in order to trick gullible women into believing she'd become wealthy by investing with Mrs. Morse.

The whole operation was a scam and there was no investment bureau. LaTouche had rented a space that served as a front for her set-up and made it look like a bank. Sophie claimed that things went smoothly for a time, but after some investors were frustrated in efforts to collect their money, the police began an investigation and uncovered the scheme. Sophie claimed she only just managed to avoid arrest by absconding to her hotel and making a dramatic escape down a rope thrown out a back window.[6] She insisted, incorrectly, that LaTouche was never caught either.

The swindle did actually occur, more or less as Sophie described it, but no Celia Rigsby character was involved because LaTouche was fully capable of reeling in her victims by herself. However, she didn't manage to avoid arrest and was ultimately convicted and sentenced to prison for tricking her victims—many of whom were working-class and could ill afford to lose their capital—out of their money.[7] Sophie couldn't possibly have been involved in the scam because it occurred in 1882, when she was on trial for grand larceny in Michigan.[8] Sophie wound up convicted of the charge and was sent to prison in Detroit.[9] Even someone as clever as she couldn't be in two places at once.

Sophie also wasn't willing to put herself in the position of facing charges for past misdeeds, so she purposely omitted dates and kept details about her past crimes sketchy. She admitted that her criminal career had taken a heavy toll on her personal life, but she blamed most of her failures on her husband, Ned Lyons, whom she hated by that point. She never mentioned her three other husbands, one of whom, Billy Burke, was still an active criminal when the memoir was released.

Before *Why Crime Does Not Pay* came out in book form, some of its chapters were published as stand-alone stories in newspapers across the country. Thanks to Sophie's expertise at spinning tales and running cons, the public ate them up and soon—for a time, anyway—Sophie was known more for being an author than for being a criminal. (Her book's success even led to other memoirs authored by "reformed" criminals during the early 20th century.)

Despite the fact that the mantra "crime doesn't pay" is repeated over and over in her book, it's clear Sophie's comment was tongue in cheek. In the long run, crime didn't pay for many of her pals, but that was only because of foolish, risky, or just plain stupid decisions they'd made after successfully getting rich by committing crimes. In Sophie's opinion, if they'd made smarter decisions, they could have kept their ill-gotten gains and done quite well for themselves, just like she had.

A Tortured Soul Trying to Give Back

Sophie persisted with crime and was better at it than most of her male colleagues. As one news article noted about her second husband, "Lyons owed many of his escapes to her. But his criminal record paled before hers. She was not a specialist. Anything from blackmail to small shoplifting was in her line."[10]

During the last two decades of her life, Sophie was known as a benevolent figure in her community. She made visits to people in jail and spent some of her money to try to help people in prison. She even left instructions in her will that she wanted most of her estate to be used to establish a home for prisoners' young children.

Sophie's public demonstrations of philanthropy hid something darker—likely an untreated mental illness influenced by the abuse she suffered as a child. Over the years, angry emotional outbursts alienated Sophie from her friends and family, including all of her surviving children.

After Sophie died, newspapers and magazines published articles about her life and crimes. The so-called "facts" related in them often weren't accurate, partly because Sophie had given lots of newspaper interviews in which she had lied or twisted the truth so effectively that reporters didn't question the veracity of her tales. As time went on, these news stories about Sophie were repeated and modified until they contained but a grain of truth under a mountain of baloney. They even led to a movie based loosely on her life called *The Notorious Sophie Lang*, starring Gertrude Michael as the glamorous jewel thief.

One fact is clear: Sophie Lyons was a deeply flawed and damaged woman who defied gender stereotypes and lived a wildly unconventional life at a time when women were expected to shut up, stay at home, and mind the children. This book reveals the fascinating story of her life, as well as its tragedies.

1

A Thief Since the Cradle

All during my early childhood I did little but steal, and was never sent to school. I did not learn to read or write until I was twenty-five years old. If my stepmother brought me to a place where many persons congregated and I was slow in getting pocketbooks and other articles, she would stick a pin into my arm to remind me that I must be more industrious. If a pin was not convenient she would step on my toes or pinch me when occasion made her think I was in need of some such stimulant.
—Sophie Lyons, *Why Crime Does Not Pay*

The day after Christmas 1855, a sailing ship by the name of *Von Stein* arrived in New York Harbor from Bremerhaven, a port city along the North Sea coast of Germany. Most of the passengers, including a little girl named Sara "Sophie" Van Elkan, traveled in steerage on the cheapest ticket.[1]

Four days before the boat landed, Sophie turned eight, but there were no presents or sweets to celebrate her birthday. An unusually pretty child with gray eyes and long, curly brown hair, she clung tightly to the hand of her six-year-old brother, Meyer, as they made their way down the gangplank to dry land. They stayed close to their older brother, 10-year-old Gerson, and their cousins Caroline, 14, and Brune Simon, 11. Exhausted, hungry, dirty, and cold, they were anxious to get off the ship yet happy to have made it alive to the country they hoped to call home.

Once ashore, the Van Elkan children stood outside with their fellow passengers, some of whom they'd gotten to know well during their miserable weeks of travel packed together in the lowest deck. After what seemed like an eternity, the children entered the doors of the immigrant landing depot, an enormous, oval-shaped building at the southern tip of Manhattan that served as America's new immigration center. Originally

IMMIGRANTS LANDING AT CASTLE GARDEN.—DRAWN BY A. B. SHULTS.

This wood engraving shows the scene Sophie might have encountered as a child when she came ashore at the immigrant landing at Castle Garden in New York. Library of Congress.

built as a military fort in the early 19th century and later used as an entertainment venue, it now saw Irish and German newcomers to America pouring through its doors every day.[2]

As soon as federal immigration officials determined the children were free of disease, they were allowed to enter the country as newly minted American citizens.[3] They then headed north on the crowded streets of Manhattan to locate their parents, Jacob and Friedericke, who were living somewhere on the city's Lower East Side.

The Van Elkan Family

As an adult, Sophie always claimed she was born in New York, but she was actually born in the southern Bavarian town of Lauben.[4] She also said that her father, Jacob Marcus Van Elkan, was born in Holland; that statement, though still inaccurate, was closer to the truth. Jacob was born near the North Sea in Aurich, in the East Frisian region of Lower Saxony (a German state). After the forces of Napoleon I defeated the Prussian army in 1808, Aurich became part of the Kingdom of Holland. However, by the time Jacob was born on April 6, 1820, Napoleon had been defeated, and Aurich belonged to the Kingdom of Hanover.[5]

Around 1844, Jacob married Friederike Levy and was working as a "handlesmann," a self-employed merchant or trader.[6] At a time when most Germans tended to live in or close to the places where they were born, Jacob clearly traveled with his family because three of his children, including Sophie, were born more than 500 miles south of his birthplace.

The Van Elkan family was Jewish. From the earliest times, Jews weren't allowed to be citizens of any German state. By the Middle Ages, a system known as Schutzjude allowed Jews to stay as resident aliens under the protection of the head of the state in which a family lived.[7] Jacob acquired this protected status for his family, but it was dependent on him paying Schutzgeld (protection money) annually.

By the 1840s discrimination based on religion, along with wars and famine, had made life miserable for Jews in German states. Many, including Jacob, were willing to risk the hazardous trip to America in order to escape.

Accompanied by their infant Mary, Jacob and Friederike made the journey to America a year and a half before Sophie, Meyer, Gerson and their cousins did. They traveled on the *Gesine*, which sailed from Bremerhaven and arrived at New York on May 20, 1854.[8] Jacob's occupation was listed as "merchant" on the ship's manifest.

Soon after arriving in the United States, Jacob saved enough money by peddling wares from a cart to pay the passage for Sophie, her brothers, and their cousins. Caroline and Brune Simon were the children of his brother, Simon Samuel Van Elkan, who'd lost his wife in 1844 and remained in Aurich until his own death in 1862.[9]

By 1857 the Van Elkans lived at 48 Columbia Street, just a few blocks from the East River in Kleindeutschland (Little Germany), located within Manhattan's Lower East Side.[10] With the largest German-speaking population in the world outside of Berlin and Vienna, Kleindeutschland was a bustling neighborhood full of beer halls, oyster saloons, grocery stores, theaters, and small family shops.[11]

Life was hectic in Kleindeutschland, and privacy was nonexistent. The Van Elkans would have lived in a two- or three-story wooden row house subdivided to hold several families per floor. Because indoor plumbing connected to sewer lines wouldn't have been available, residents would have used a chamber pot or a smelly outhouse for relieving themselves.[12] Water had to be brought into the apartment from the yard, making home bathing a rare event. Public bathhouses, such as one located more than a mile east on Mott Street, were more likely where the family did their washing up.[13]

Sophie's Maternal (and Criminal) Influences

Sophie's mother's background is a bit of a mystery, but it's one that plays a significant role in her life story—particularly her early start in crime. According to the passenger record from her voyage to America, Friederike was born in Germany in 1826.[14] Yet on the 1860 federal census, Sophie's mother was recorded as a woman named Mary who was born in Bremen around 1819.[15]

Because new immigrants to America often changed their first names to ones that sounded less foreign, it's possible Friederike changed her name to Mary, a moniker that would have rolled off American tongues more easily. Additionally, the discrepancy in her age may have occurred because language-related communication problems sometimes prevented birth years from being recorded accurately on 19th-century censuses (along with the fact that many people were illiterate and unsure of their birth year). It's also possible Friederike died before 1860 and her death wasn't documented. In this case, Jacob may have taken a second wife named Mary, though there's no record of a second marriage for Jacob during this time.

What we do know is that in a news article about her life published in Joseph Pulitzer's *The World* newspaper in 1896, Sophie wrote that it was her *mother* who taught her to steal and compelled her to become a thief, though she also laid some of the blame at her father's feet. "Those who were cruel to me were my parents, and I cared for them very much in spite of the home and the abuse I had."[16] By the time she penned her memoir in 1913, Sophie was adamant that it was her *stepmother* who had abused her, taught her to steal, and punished her when she wasn't successful.

Whether it was Sophie's biological mother or her stepmother who guided her early criminal career, Sophie actively sought to distance her-self from criminality theories that were popular in the late 19th and early 20th centuries. According to Italian-born criminologist Cesare Lombroso, crime was hereditary, and certain people were "born criminal." In her memoir, Sophie bridled at the idea that criminality was inborn and insisted that her crimes weren't caused by inherent tendencies but rather by the training she received from her evil stepmother, a woman to whom she wasn't biologically related. Nurture, not nature, Sophie insisted, had launched her into a life of crime.

Details about these first crimes—and Mary's part in them—abound in Sophie's book. For example, Mary dressed the pretty little girl in a different outfit every day before the two of them went out to "work." This kept Sophie from being easily recognized in an era when poor people rarely had a change of clothing. Big crowds were another requirement for Mary's larcenous plans. The pair often went to the large New York department stores to shoplift and to the ferry station in Jersey City, New Jersey, to pick the pockets of ferry riders.

Another favorite hunting ground was Barnum's American Museum, located at the corner of Broadway and Ann Street in lower Manhattan. As curious onlookers gawked at showman P.T. Barnum's collection of exhibits, little Sophie picked their pockets while Mary waited outside. If Sophie emerged with less than what Mary expected, she got a pinch and was sent back in. If she got lazy and refused to cooperate, she got a beating from Mary or her cousin Brune Simon.[17]

> Finally, I was told that money was the really valuable thing to possess, and that the successful men and women were those who could take pocketbooks…. I was taught how to open shopping bags, feel out the loose money or the pocketbook and get it into my little hands without attracting the attention of my victims. In those days leather bags were not common—most women carried cloth or knitted shopping bags. I was provided with a very sharp little knife and was carefully instructed how to slit open the bags so that I could get my fingers in.[18]

Using a child to commit crimes was a devious way for an adult to reap the benefits of theft while trying to avoid going to jail, but it was also morally reprehensible. That apparently mattered little to Mary, whom Sophie recalled as an abusive parent and a hideous role model.

> Memories of my childhood recall nothing but cuffs, blows and harsh words. I never knew a mother's caress, never knew what it was to be folded in loving embrace to a mother's breast. Even now I have on my arms scars made by a red-hot poker with which my mother sometimes punished me. Never once did I receive a word of endearment. Every day I was cursed.[19]

Oddly enough, young Sophie experienced more love and care from law enforcement than she did from her own family. One of her earliest memories was of being carried to the station house in the arms of a detective after he had just arrested her.[20] The policeman gave her candy and let her play—unlike at home, where it was either work or punishment if she didn't produce the goods. Unsurprisingly, Sophie enjoyed the experience! This sad glimpse into Sophie's childhood sheds light on the complicated and conflicted relationships she had with some of the policemen and detectives who arrested her as an adult.

Surrounded by Criminals

Before the 1860 census recorded the Van Elkans, the family dropped Van from its surname and altered the spelling of Elkan to Elkin or Elkins.[21] Additionally, Gerson changed his name to George, Brune Simon started going by Samuel (his father's middle name), and Caroline began using the alias Pauline Walton.[22] Sophie's cousins, as well as Jacob and Mary, were all convicted of crimes and incarcerated in New York prisons at various points in the mid–19th century.

Meanwhile, Sophie's brothers, George and Meyer, were untraceable after 1860. A baby named Sarah joined the family in 1860, but evidently she died in early childhood. It appears that Sophie's younger sister, Mary, was her only sibling who lived to adulthood. Mary was never convicted of a crime. She married William Rohrs in New York, raised four daughters, and died in Brooklyn in 1926.[23]

According to the *New York Tribune*, Jacob was arrested in September 1859 after being accused by two police officers of committing perjury.[24] Evidently the officers suspected him of grand larceny and arrested him, but the charges didn't hold up and were dropped. Jacob then went before the police commissioners and claimed the officers had tried to blackmail him. The officers responded by accusing Jacob of perjury. New York was rife with Tammany Hall corruption at the time, making it likely that Jacob was arrested because he foolishly refused to pay the officers a bribe to turn a blind eye to his criminal activities.

By 1860 Jacob had stopped peddling and opened a clothing store.[25] Known in police circles as "old Elkin the fence," Jacob sold some of the items stolen by his family members inside his New York store. Two years later, Jacob and Samuel were sentenced to prison for a year and six months, respectively, on a conviction of conspiracy to have a man indicted for larceny.[26]

Sophie's memoir, however, reinvents her father as a good man who went off bravely to fight in the Civil War. She claimed that while her father was away from home serving his adopted home country, her stepmother forced her to become a thief. Her father was supposedly unaware of what transpired while he was gone, but this was certainly a lie because Jacob didn't join the New Jersey Infantry until April 5, 1865, four days before the war ended. He may well have signed up simply to collect the $300 enlistment bounty rather than out of feelings of patriotism, especially considering he mustered out of the army just three months later.[27]

As for the women of the family, while under the alias Pauline Walton, Caroline was described as a "young looking woman, wearing a bloomer and a bright colored shawl" when she was charged with stealing $170 from a soldier in February 1864 (so much for the alleged family loyalty to the Union cause).[28] The judge in her case gave her a chance to return the money and avoid a prison sentence, but she insisted she wasn't guilty of the crime and claimed another female prisoner in the jail had taken the man's cash. The judge replied, "You bear a pretty bad character, Pauline, and the sentence of the Court is that you be confined to the State Prison for two years."[29]

Mary Elkin served at least three terms in Sing Sing prison. She was sentenced to five years there on October 16, 1867, for attempted grand larceny.[30] (Given that most people served between half and two-thirds of their sentence, she likely didn't serve the full five years.) In 1872 she was sent to Sing Sing again for retrieving a valuable stolen diamond pin and an earring she'd left with one pawnbroker and then selling them to another pawnshop.[31] As she was taken to the cells, Mary, who was described in the newspaper as "well known in the police records as a pickpocket and shoplifter," screamed and protested her innocence. (Jacob and Caroline were also involved in this particular scheme, but the charges against them couldn't be proven and were dropped.) In November 1876, Mary was sent to Sing Sing again, this time under the alias Julia Keller, for a term of five years for committing grand larceny.[32]

For her part, Sophie was convicted of burglary at the age of 12 and incarcerated in the House of Refuge, a prison for young offenders on Randall's Island near New York. The details of her crime and the length of her sentence are lost to history, but we know she was an inmate on the island because she was listed on the 1860 census as residing at Randall's Island.[33]

She also discussed her confinement there in her memoir. This was one of Sophie's earliest imprisonments in a long list that would stretch over the next 40 years.

Lessons from the House of Refuge

Randall's Island is a rounded rectangle of land separated from the surrounding city by three different bodies of water. A narrow waterway called the Bronx Kill divides it from the Bronx to the north, the Harlem River cuts it off from the rest of Manhattan to the west, and the East River delineates it from Queens to the east. In the 19th century the location of Randall's Island made it the perfect spot for New Yorkers to dump their youngest offenders and other undesirables. However, it wasn't always home to the House of Refuge.

The first institution of its kind in America, the House of Refuge opened at Broadway and 23rd Street in 1825 as a reform school for juvenile delinquents. As New York real estate increased in value, the House of Refuge relocated to Randall's Island in 1854.[34] There it joined an orphanage, a poorhouse, a hospital, and burial grounds for the indigent.

The children at the House of Refuge were referred there either by the judicial system or at the request of their desperate parents. They were supposed to be between the ages of eight and 17, but some had been given long terms that kept them there until they were 20.[35] When Sophie arrived in 1860, a female department had only recently been added.[36] Most of the approximately 500 boys and 100 girls at the House of Refuge were in their mid- to late teens, making her one of the youngest residents. The majority had been convicted of vagrancy or petty larceny, though a few had been charged with arson and manslaughter.[37] Sophie's crime of burglary was one of the more serious offenses.

In her memoir, Sophie claimed she played with the assistant superintendent's daughters, but it's unlikely he would have allowed his middle-class children to mix with any of the lower-class inmates incarcerated at the facility. In reality, playtime at the House of Refuge was minimal, and corporal punishment was imposed on any child who broke the rules. Whipping, solitary confinement, and leg irons were used on children who didn't comply.[38] The food was said to be better than what the laboring classes generally got at that time, both in quality and quantity, but that wasn't really anything to brag about given the austerity of 19th-century penal institutions.

While Sophie was at the House of Refuge, she would have been trained in washing, cooking, sewing, and the making of clothing and bedding (which was used by the institution's inmates). If properly learned, these life skills would allow her to find employment in poorly paid jobs on the lowest rungs of society after she was released. The *New York Times* bluntly described what the graduates of the House of Refuge could expect out of life: "They may and can become honest, upright, conscientious and hard-working laborers and mechanics ... but very few of them will ever attain exalted station."[39]

SOPHIA LEVY.

This undated engraving of Sophie was made from a rogues' gallery photograph (known today as mug shots) for New York City detective Philip Farley's book *Criminals of America*. It is the earliest portrait of Sophie and the photograph it is based on no longer exists.

An unusually bright child, Sophie undoubtedly learned an important lesson at the House of Refuge: Crime could provide a path to a better income and lifestyle than could be achieved through the kind of honest work available to someone like her.

Leaving Her Family

By 1861, Sophie had been released from the House of Refuge. With most of her family coping with their own legal problems, she was ready to strike out on her own. Her family had provided her with some basic criminal skills, but now it was up to her to decide whether she wanted to develop those skills or go straight. Her September 1861 conviction for picking pockets alongside a boy named Louis Minot reveals she pretty quickly chose the crooked path.[40] Not quite 14 years old, she received a two-month sentence at the penitentiary on Blackwell's Island, located in the East River.[41]

When she was about 15, Sophie married her first husband, a German Jew named Morris (or Maurice) Harris, better known as Morry.[42] Born around 1842, Harris had immigrated to America and settled in New York by 1860. At that time, Harris boarded with a cigar dealer named Joseph Cohen in Manhattan. Sophie may have met him through her cousin Samuel, who was learning the cigar-making trade.[43] Harris' legitimate occupation was as a shoemaker, but he spent more of his time picking pockets than working shoe leather. By 1860 his photograph was in the New York City Police Department's Rogues' Gallery, and he'd done some time in the penitentiary.[44]

MOORE, alias LEVY—Husband of SOPHIE LYONS.

GENERAL SNEAK AND SHOPLIFTER.—Age 33 years; height 5 ft. 5¼ in.; weight 145 lbs.; well built; complexion dark;· eyes hazel; hair black; features short; left wrist has been broken and is badly scarred; both little fingers partly stiff. Has done time in Ohio Pen.

This undated engraving created for *Grannan's Pocket Guide to Noted Criminals* may show Sophie's first husband, Morris Harris. Harris used the alias Wolf Levy when he was sent to Sing Sing in 1898. Written by Cincinnati detective Joseph Grannan, the book was small enough to fit in a policeman's coat pocket.

When he was sent to prison for burglary in 1898, Harris was incarcerated under the name Wolf Levy.[45] The inspiration for this alias may well have come from Sophie, who used her mother's surname, Levy, early in her criminal career.[46] Although Harris may have used Sophie's alias, the marriage between them didn't last long—by the time she was 17 they had split up.

Sophie's skill as a pickpocket helped her move up rapidly in Gotham's burgeoning underworld. While still in her teens, she joined a cadre of other New York–based criminals. The group included a well-known pickpocket, Kate Gorman, and her future husband, an accomplished bank robber named John "Red" Leary.[47] Another new pal was a dashing bank burglar, Edward Lyons, known to his friends as Ned. Eight years her senior, Ned and Sophie fell madly in love. Ned was the man whose surname she would eventually become known by throughout the world. The pair became partners in crime and in life, at least for a while.

2

From Motherly Trauma to Motherhood

I shall never forget the atmosphere of "Mother" Mandelbaum's place on the corner of Clinton and Rivington Streets. In the front was the general store, innocent enough in appearance; and, in fact, the goods were only part stolen, and these of such a character that they could not possibly be identified. "Mother" Mandelbaum led a life that left her open to many dangers from many different directions. Every member of the underworld knew that stolen goods of great value were constantly coming into her resort and from time to time schemes were devised to plunder the famous old "fence."
—Sophie Lyons, *Why Crime Does Not Pay*

By the time she was in her late teens, Sophie had found a new mother—one who wouldn't poke her with pins, step on her toes, or burn her with hot pokers. She had found Fredericka Mandelbaum, one of the most adept and well-known criminals of mid– to late 19th-century New York City. Her friends and enemies alike knew her as Marm. Sophie fondly called her Mother.

Mandelbaum was born Fredericka Henriette Auguste Wiesener in the German city of Kassel on March 25, 1825.[1] She married Wolfe (who went by the name "William" in America) Mandelbaum in her native land and immigrated with him to America.[2] The couple arrived in New York sometime before 1860 with nothing in their pockets, but thanks to Fredericka's business sense, she and her husband were able to build an empire around fencing stolen goods.[3] Wolfe died in 1875 and Fredericka continued to run the business with her children and several trusted employees.[4]

George W. Walling, a police officer who became New York's chief of police during Mandelbaum's reign as a fence, never could manage to lock her up. He despised her as a result and had some choice words to describe her looks and her criminal operation in his 1887 book, *Recollections of a New York Chief of Police.*

> She was a woman above the middle height, sufficiently corpulent to be easily caricatured, who never, possibly, had enough of coquetry to indulge in corsets, with a large mouth and thick lips. But she was shrewd, careful, methodical in character, and to the point in speech. Wary in the extreme, she never admitted any one unknown to her and unvouched for beyond the precincts of the little dry goods store. Once the entrée given by a hint, note or personal recommendation from any one she depended on, and the little wing of her establishment was wide open to him or her.
>
> Her methods were extraordinarily simple. She kept what appeared to be a thriving dry goods and haberdashery shop, at No. 79 Clinton Street. The house was rated as "fourth class" by the insurance company, being possibly one-sixth brick and five-sixths wood. It was a straggling, ill-built, yet curious looking building, more pretentious at its angle with Rivington Street than at any other. This angle was the business concern which concealed the real occupation of its owner. Sprawling away from this angle down Clinton Street was the actual business part of the establishment. This was a two-story, clapboarded wing, some twenty-five feet long. On the first floor was one of the best furnished apartments in this city, a room the like of which was not to be found anywhere in the region known as Klein Deutschland, or Little Germany.

Fredericka Mandelbaum, known as Mother or Marm, was a German immigrant to America and one of the most well-known dealers in stolen goods during the 19th century. She was arrested in 1884 but jumped her bail and fled to Canada, where she died in 1894. This drawing of her is from George Walling, *Reflections of a New York Chief of Police* (New York: Caxton Book Concern, 1887). No photograph of Mandelbaum has survived.

Lessons from Mother Mandelbaum

By the time Sophie met her in the mid–1860s, Mandelbaum's reach extended to big cities on the East Coast and in the Midwest. Although the majority of the "swag" she fenced came from New York, some of the silks and other valuables she sold had been stolen from Philadelphia, Boston, and even as far away as St. Louis, Missouri. Eventually her reputation as a fence extended beyond the United States to Canada, Mexico, and Europe.[5]

The key to her success? Mandelbaum was too cunning to ever dip her own hand into someone's pocket. She never burgled any jewels or slid a bolt of silk off a store shelf into a shoplifter's bag. Instead, she relied on those under her protection and tutelage to do her dirty work, and she paid them well in return. She was therefore able to truthfully say she'd never stolen a thing. Rather, she "attained a reputation as a businesswoman whose honesty in criminal matters was absolute," while at the same time making a fortune off her gang of pickpockets and shoplifters.[6]

New York City was permeated by corruption and graft and Mandelbaum paid hefty bribes to the police in order to protect her protégés, including Sophie. If any of her gang ended up in court, she hired the best lawyers to make sure they stayed out of prison.[7] Avoiding jail was critical for anyone who made their living as a criminal, and it was well known that Mandelbaum paid the famous New York City law firm Howe and Hummel a $5,000 yearly retainer to keep those who sold to Mandelbaum free to steal another day.[8] If one of her pickpockets, shoplifters, or burglars was caught red-handed and needed bail, she paid it—and then charged the unfortunate crook a high interest rate for the service. Not only did this arrangement allow the crooks to get back to work quickly, it kept them in dear Marm's debt.

Police Chief Walling's book provides a thorough description of how Mandelbaum ran her business. He also implied that Mandelbaum's right-hand man, a German named Hermann Steid, was her lover after her husband died.

> On the shelves of the store where the ostensible business of the concern was conducted were displayed the usual assortment of dry goods suitable to the needs of the neighborhood. The attendants were usually Mrs. Mandelbaum (the presiding deity), one of her two daughters, a hired shop-woman, and the successor to the Hon. William Mandelbaum (her late and lamented spouse), Hermann Steid, a stalwart looking man, with curling blonde hair. Mrs. Mandelbaum, thanks to her business capacity, could have easily earned an excellent living simply by keeping a dry goods establishment. She preferred "minting" money by dealing with thieves.

Mandelbaum stayed behind a barred window in her shop. From that vantage point she could view the comings and goings but remain beyond the reach of easy arrest. She even installed a dumbwaiter hidden behind a false chimney in a fireplace where small items could be stashed quickly when the need arose.[9] Many of the supposedly honest shopkeepers who purchased from Mandelbaum knew they were buying stolen goods, but the profits were so large they didn't care.

According to Sophie, Mandelbaum "developed a system for scattering her stock so that her New York headquarters never contained a very large amount of stolen goods. She kept her employees busy melting down gold and silver and disguising jewelry. Others ferreted out supposedly honest merchants who were willing to buy her wares with no questions asked."[10] Sophie noted that of all the things brought into the shop, diamonds were Mandelbaum's favorite. She loved them because they were imperishable, easily hidden, always in demand, and difficult to recognize after the gem was removed from its setting (as was her practice with all precious jewels).

At her lavishly-decorated home in the rear of her Clinton Street headquarters in Kleindeutschland, Mandelbaum threw fabulous parties that gave her a chance to show off her illicitly earned wealth. According to Walling, "In the winter she frequently gave entertainments to thieves of both sexes and outside friends, and the receptions were conducted with as much attention to the proprieties of society as though Mrs. Mandelbaum's establishment was in Fifth Avenue instead of in a suspicious corner of the East Side."

With the skills Sophie already had as a pickpocket, she had no difficulty becoming a member of Mandelbaum's inner circle. From under the master's wing, Sophie learned how to manipulate the police and the court system. She also became adept in a variety of shoplifting techniques, including wearing skirts with hidden pockets and carrying large umbrellas into which she surreptitiously dropped pilfered items.

It was at Mandelbaum's establishment where Sophie met another poor German-Jewish immigrant named Adam Worth. Just a year or two older than Sophie, Worth also began his criminal career a child pickpocket in New York. As a young man he found his way to Mandelbaum, where, like Sophie, he learned to both appreciate and steal the finer things in life. Worth would go on to become a successful bank robber and art thief. Eventually he moved to England, where he passed himself off as a member of high society while continuing to commit crimes.[11]

This drawing from Sophie's memoir shows Mother Mandelbaum examining stolen jewels in her Clinton Street shop. Her fake chimney and hiding place for stolen items is shown on the right.

Life with Ned Lyons Begins

By the time she was 17, Sophie had blossomed into a stunning young woman with a slim figure, gray eyes and copious amounts of dark brown hair.[12] She was as intelligent as she was attractive, with a fiery spirit to match. Many men in New York's large criminal community were drawn to her, including Edward "Ned" Lyons. Sophie never discussed how she met Ned, who became her second husband, but they may have been introduced in 1865 through a mutual acquaintance, Kate Gorman. (It was rumored that Gorman had at one time been married to Ned Lyons herself, though no concrete evidence of this marriage has surfaced.[13])

Born around 1841, Gorman, also known as Red-Headed Kate, was a native Irishwoman and likely a role model for Sophie. According to the *New York Times*, Gorman had been picking pockets since she was 11 years old, and although she was often arrested, she invariably wriggled her way out of the charges against her. By 1865 she had accumulated substantial capital and owned about $35,000 worth of property in Williamsburg, Brooklyn.[14]

In February 1865, Gorman was arrested on petty larceny charges for stealing a pair of opera glasses from a woman's pocket as she left a theater on Broadway. For her resulting court appearance, Gorman employed the same attorney, S.A. Stuart, as Sophie's father had when he was tried on conspiracy charges in 1862. She ultimately had better luck than Jacob Van Elkan, because she was discharged after her arrest papers were conveniently lost.[15]

Sophie despised Ned Lyons by the time she wrote her memoir, blaming him for many of the failures in her life. "My friends and companions were always criminals, and it is not surprising that in my early womanhood I should have fallen in love with a bank burglar—Ned Lyons" was the sum total of what she had to say about how she met her second husband. Nonetheless, there's no doubt he captivated her shortly after they met, nor can it be said that she didn't love him passionately during the early years of their union. By October 1865, Sophie was pregnant, and on December 15, 1865, the couple married in New York, just 10 days before Sophie's 18th birthday.[16] Sophie and Ned welcomed their first child, George Edward Lyons, on July 18, 1866.[17]

Ned often claimed England as his birthplace, but like so many immigrants to America in the 1840s, he was actually born in Ireland. In 1849 a 10-year-old Ned Lyons immigrated to Boston from Liverpool, England, along with his widowed mother, Bridget, and his three sisters. Ireland's Great Famine was at its peak at this time, and many people joined them in fleeing the country.[18] The ship Ned and his family traveled on, the *Uriel*, carried Irish laborers, servants, and their children to America.

Not long after arriving in the New World, Ned and his mother settled in Lowell, Massachusetts, a mill town about 30 miles northwest of Boston.[19] Ned married a local girl named Mary E. Welch in 1856, when he was only 16.[20] Four years later he abandoned Mary and moved to New York City.

Like Sophie, Ned started his criminal career early. By the end of the 1850s he had already served one term in the Boston House of Correction and was moving back and forth between Boston and New York City to avoid being arrested.[21] After he relocated to New York City he lived on West 19th Street in "a neighborhood calculated to develop whatever latent powers Ned possessed," according to New York police inspector Thomas Byrnes.[22] While living there Ned claimed to be employed as a jeweler, though it's more likely he was stealing jewelry and removing gems from their settings.[23] He also took advantage of the Civil War, which provided him the opportunity to sign up for the Union Army to collect a $300 enlistment bonus, then desert and reenlist, collecting another bonus.[24]

Ned also made money by robbing banks. Before guns were widespread in America, bank robberies were accomplished through knowledge and skill, not by the threat of being shot. The complex nature of bank robberies meant that bank robbers were the elite of the criminal fraternity, and Ned had been part of several successful bank robberies before he met Sophie. His reputation grew and grew, giving him cachet in criminal circles. Through these robberies he came to be known among thieves as an able "cracksman"—a man who was reckless enough to handle the dangerous task of using explosives to blow open safes and bank-vault doors, but also smart enough to successfully get the job done.

Ned's physical presence was just as impressive as his intelligence and daring. Prison records from 1872 describe Ned as about five feet, seven and a half inches tall with a "fine physique" (muscular build), brown hair, red mustache, florid complexion, blue eyes, and multiple tattoos on his arms. He was a Roman Catholic who drank moderately, could read and write, and preferred to dress "like a ward politician of the higher class."[25] He was a physically powerful man who never backed down from a fight. One newspaper reporter describing Ned wrote, "it is said of him, with limited exaggeration, that if he should close on a man he could hug him to death."[26]

After their marriage, Ned discouraged Sophie from continuing to "work," according to Inspector Byrnes. Ned was a traditionalist who wanted his wife to stay home and tend to their growing family. Byrnes claimed that Sophie's "mania for stealing was so strong that when in Ned's company in public she plied her vocation unknown to him and would surprise him with watches, etc. which she had stolen. He expostulated, pleaded with, and threatened her, but without avail."[27]

Sophie told a different story about the early years of her married life with Ned in her memoir. She maintained that although she wanted to stay home with the kids, the plunder from her crimes provided an essential part of the family's income, and the couple's free spending led to an ongoing need for her to steal. She also claimed to have participated in some of the bank robberies Ned pulled off, however, no evidence exists to suggest she was actively involved in these capers. Pickpocketing and shoplifting were Sophie's areas of criminal expertise at the time, and it's more likely that she continued to pursue those activities.

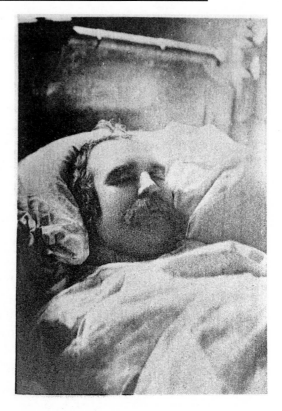

EDWARD LYONS,
ALIAS NED LYONS,
BURGLAR, SNEAK, AND PICKPOCKET.

Following this romance came motherhood and an awakening within me of at least one worthy resolve—that, whatever had been my career, I certainly would see that my children were given the benefit of a tender mother love, which I had never had, and that my little ones should be surrounded with every pure and wholesome influence. The first

Police took this unusual rogues' gallery photograph of Sophie's second husband, Ned Lyons, in 1881 while he was recovering in a Connecticut hospital after being shot. It was terrible for identification purposes, but it was the only photograph the police had of him at the time. It was published, along with Ned's biography, in Byrnes' *Professional Criminals of America.*

few years of my married life were divided between my little ones and the necessary exactions which my career imposed on me. Ned Lyons, my husband, was a member of the boldest and busiest group of bank robbers in the world. Here and there, all over the Eastern States, we went on expeditions, forcing the vaults of the biggest and richest banks in the country. We had money in plenty, but we spent money foolishly.[28]

The couple welcomed their second child, a daughter named Florence, in 1868. The following year Sophie was pregnant again.[29] With two young children and a third on the way, Ned searched his underworld contacts for a fresh bank-robbery scheme, preferably something big that would allow him and his family to live in luxury for years to come. He found it in 1869 when, with several other well-known bank robbers, including Jimmy Hope, George Bliss, and Max Shinburn, he began to plot the robbery of the Ocean Bank in lower Manhattan.

The Big Bank Job

Ocean Bank was on the first floor of a five-story brownstone building at Fulton and Greenwich streets, just north of Wall Street. The inner vault, which was made of steel encased in masonry, could be reached only by breaking through three heavy doors, each of which was equipped with a strong lock. Because the bankers assumed the vault was impenetrable, they didn't bother employing a watchman to patrol on the weekends. The bank's sole security during those hours was a handyman who came by occasionally to check the premises from the outside.[30]

The bankers clearly hadn't appreciated the ingenuity and perseverance of the clever thieves at work in those days. Two weeks before the robbery was committed, one member of the gang rented the basement rooms beneath the vault and established what appeared to be a reputable business. The robbers settled in and got to know all the routines at the bank as well as its security—or lack thereof. They also set up a partition in the "business" that allowed them to work behind it and not be seen from the street.[31]

Once the bank closed on Saturday, June 26, 1869, the thieves got to work with crowbars, drills, and picks. After the ceiling of their "business" was breached, they had access to the floor below the vault doors. By daylight on Sunday morning they had created an opening in the floor large enough for a man to fit through. From there they went inside the bank and worked on breaking though the locks to the doors protecting the inner vault. After forcing their way through those doors, they blew open the vault.[32]

When the Ocean Bank clerks arrived on Monday morning they found the safe doors open and the vault torn to pieces. Tools, mortar, bricks, and debris were scattered everywhere, along with gold coins that

THE OLD OCEAN BANK BUILDING.
Southeast corner of Fulton and Greenwich sts. In 1869 burglars rifled the bank vaults of securities and cash aggregating $1,000,000.

Ned Lyons and some of his criminal colleagues robbed the Ocean Bank in New York City in 1869. The thieves rented basement rooms (lower left), broke through the bank's floor and made off with a fortune. The building is shown in a 1905 news photograph taken before it was torn down.

had proved too heavy to haul away. Ned and company had made off with at least $500,000 in cash and securities; by some estimates the haul was closer to a million dollars.[33] (The bankers were reluctant to admit how much was stolen, but even the lower figure is the equivalent of more than $9.5 million in 2018 dollars.) A few of the bonds were recovered later, but the cash was gone forever, as were the robbers, who were never charged. The bankers were left mortified at the thieves' brazenness—and at their own foolishness in not making the premises more secure.

Ned and Sophie were jubilant over the success of the Ocean Bank robbery. If they were careful, Ned's part of the "take" meant they wouldn't have to pull another crime for years. On top of that, they now had enough money to invest in an honest business and never risk being jailed or going to prison again.

They began taking steps in the direction of the straight and narrow. First, they bought a brownstone on 110th Street in East Harlem to escape the overcrowded slums of lower Manhattan. (At the time, Harlem was a leafy suburb of Manhattan, populated mostly by better-off immigrants from Ireland and Germany.) They even put some of their stolen cash in the bank.[34]

From their origins as poor immigrants they had, through crime, enormously improved their lot in life. By 1870, Ned and Sophie were wealthy New Yorkers who could buy almost anything their hearts desired in the greatest city in America. They also had three healthy children: George, age four; Florence, age two; and baby Eugenia.[35] Life was looking good for the Lyons family, just as it so often does before things go terribly wrong.

3

Escape from Sing Sing

Hurling the key into a snowdrift, I ran to the waiting sleigh. Ned was standing beside the sleigh with a big warm fur coat outstretched in his arms. Without a word I slipped into the coat, hopped into the sleigh, and Ned gave the horses a clip with the whip and away we dashed toward Poughkeepsie. The long fur coat and stylish hat which Ned had brought made me look like anything but an escaped convict. After a good warm supper at Poughkeepsie, we took the night train for New York and reached there safely the next morning. And so we were free!

—Sophie Lyons, *Why Crime Does Not Pay*

The year 1869 came to a dramatic close when Ned got into a street fight with Jimmy Haggerty, a notoriously violent Philadelphia-based thug. The evil-tempered Haggerty, who would be killed in a saloon brawl in 1871, managed to bite off a chunk from the top of Ned's left ear.[1] Ned recovered from the injury, but the absence of part of his ear was a disaster for a professional criminal because it meant he would be far more easily recognized. Sophie suggested he grow his hair and side-whiskers longer to cover up the identifying anomaly.

Although he was still flush with cash from the Ocean Bank job, Ned couldn't turn away from robbing banks. He relished the excitement of planning a robbery and the danger involved in carrying out the plans, which made him the perfect candidate for a pitch by his pal Jimmy Hope. Hope was a native of Philadelphia and a well-established burglar prior to the Ocean Bank robbery. His latest target? The safe in the paymaster's office at the Philadelphia Naval Yard.

The plan was for Ned, Hope, and another thief to rob the safe one hot night in August 1870. That plan changed when the trio was interrupted in the process of moving the safe. The other two men had time to escape,

EDWARD LYONS.

NED LYONS, alias GEORGE JACKSON.

Train Robber and General Thief,—has been a fugitive from justice since June, '87, when he was one of a gang who robbed a R. R. train at Kent, O. He was described as follows: Age 41 to 50 years; height 5 feet 8½ inches; weight 198 pounds; complexion fair; eyes dark blue; hair brown, bald on top of head; mustache brown; left ear gone; three crosses on front and three on back of left forearm; string of beads around waist in India ink.

This rogues' gallery photograph of a middle-aged Ned (left) served as inspiration for a similar engraving (right) included in *Grannan's Pocket Guide to Noted Criminals*. Note that part of Ned's left ear is missing; he tried to hide the deformity with long sideburns. Sophie and Ned were separated by the time the photograph was taken.

but Ned was held at gunpoint, arrested, and later arraigned. Fortunately for him he wasn't recognized, despite his missing ear. Ned told the police his name was Edward Sanman, and as soon as he was released, he jumped bail and left the city.[2] Unfortunately, more bad luck followed him.

The next month Ned was arrested with the same partners in the middle of robbing Smith's Bank in Perry, New York. Unknown to the burglars, the citizens of Perry had formed a vigilance committee that patrolled the streets at night. The committee got wind of the robbery and interrupted it. Ned and his pals ran off, but the Perry men quickly surrounded the city and cut off access to the trains. Ned was cornered. Shots were exchanged, but eventually he surrendered. This time his companions were also captured.[3]

In the trio's haste to get away from the bank, they had left plenty of incriminating evidence behind. Consequently, Ned, under the alias Robert E. Hapgood, was convicted of burglary and sentenced to five years in Auburn Prison.[4] This was a disaster from Ned's perspective because Auburn, a state prison built in 1817 in the Finger Lakes Region of New York State, was regarded as tough to escape from. Auburn also had a code of silence that was strictly enforced by the guards—inmates there were housed in three-and-a-half-foot-wide individual cells and they worked and ate together without ever uttering a word to each other.

Sacrifices for Freedom

Upon learning Ned's fate, Sophie immediately began working to get her husband moved to Sing Sing in Ossining, New York, located 30 miles north of Manhattan. Sing Sing was much closer to Manhattan than Auburn Prison, and Ned had friends incarcerated there.

More important, though, was the well-known fact that some of the guards at Sing Sing were willing to take bribes in exchange for special services. Sophie had cash on hand from the bank robbery to pay bribes. At Ned's request she left the children with Becky Moore, a neighbor in Harlem who was the wife of fellow criminal Langdon W. Moore.[5] Sophie headed next to Albany, the state capital, to work on Ned's transfer to Sing Sing.

In Albany she found a mystery man to assist her in getting Ned transferred. A reporter for *The Sun* described this individual as "a very smart lawyer and politician." He was also someone who wanted not only money but sexual favors from the beguiling young woman. Desperate to get Ned moved, Sophie complied with his request, and the two began having an affair. The lawyer succeeded in getting Ned moved to Sing Sing on February 6, 1871—and then promptly demanded his $1,500 payment.[6]

Back in New York City without her husband, Sophie retrieved her children from the Moore home and resumed shoplifting. She managed to steal unnoticed for several months, until September 25, 1871, when she was caught trying to smuggle a $40 cloak from a store on Broadway and Tenth Street.[7] Two weeks later she was convicted at the Jefferson Market Police Court of grand larceny under the alias Susan Lockwood and sentenced to five years at Sing Sing.[8]

In a surprising turn of events, Sophie placed her children in the orphanage on Randall's Island—the island that was also home to the House of Refuge, where Sophie was first incarcerated—instead of leaving them with Becky Moore.[9] She then departed for the women's prison at Sing Sing, arriving on October 9, 1871.[10] (Ironically, her mother or stepmother, Mary, joined her there a few months later after she was convicted of receiving stolen property in New York.[11])

Life at Sing Sing

The female prisoners at Sing Sing were held separately from the men in an 1837 prison built on the grounds of the much larger men's prison.[12] A reporter for the *New York Times* toured both the male and female facilities at Sing Sing and wrote an article about his experience, "Our State Institutions," published on December 25, 1871. Of the 117 women in the prison at that time, the reporter selected two inmates who stood out and described them in his article. The women weren't named, but they were likely Sophie and Mary Elkin.

> In the sewing room sat a girl of unusually attractive appearance—a beautiful face, elegant figure, soft brown hair and delicate complexion. In spite of her uncouth prison dress, she looked as though she had been born and bred among the elite of society—one of nature's noblewomen. "Yes," replied the official, in answer to my whispered remarks on her personal appearance and beauty, "she is a very pretty girl. There's no doubt of that. But," he added with an emphasis, "she's a very bad one. Why sir," he continued, "that girl is a married woman and the mother of three little children. But she comes from a family of thieves. This is her second term of imprisonment here. That woman," pointing to another and older prisoner, "is her mother, also here for the second time. We've got the father and husband over in the male prison."

The reporter went on to describe in detail the horrific procedures employed in the men's prison as punishment for breaking the rules, including the "dark cell" (for solitary confinement) and various heavy iron devices that could be locked onto a prisoner's leg, neck, or head.

Both genders performed contract labor of various sorts unless they were too old or feeble to do so. The men made shoes and saddles and quarried marble at a hill near the prison. A handful of the women prisoners did cooking, cleaning, washing and ironing. Most of the women spent their days sewing summer-weight men's jackets. The prisoners, or course, were not paid for their work. Each seamstress earned the prison 22.5 cents per day. This was such a piddling amount that Sing Sing generally fell far short of its goal of having the female prisoners pay the cost of their prison housing and meals.[13]

The Couple That Escapes Prison Together...

According to Sophie, who wrote about it 40 years afterward, the escape from Sing Sing involved multiple visits from an outside co-conspirator, her friend Red Leary; forged prison passes; a duplicated stolen key; and a meeting she had outside the prison grounds with Ned, who was dressed like an Indian chief, following his own escape. Sophie had a flair for the dramatic, and her version of events was likely fictional, though Ned did secure outside help to free his wife. Of course, Sophie's narrative put herself front and center as the supposed mastermind of the plans.

A more plausible account of the escape appeared in New York's *The Sun* newspaper in July 1873, half a year after the escape. According to the article, Ned was hampered by not being able to access his money while in prison. He managed to get a message to friends on the outside asking for someone to bankroll the escape. Knowing Ned still had plenty of cash from the Ocean Bank robbery, "Big Mike" Murray, owner of a faro bank and gambling hall at 135 Eighth Street in New York City, agreed to fund the operation in exchange for a large fee.[14]

Because the plan required the help of someone inside the prison who had a job in the prison office and was trusted by the warden, Ned became friendly with an inmate named John Reilly, who worked as a clerk in the warden's office.[15] Reilly was a bright young man who'd been imprisoned at Sing Sing on a grand larceny conviction in 1869. Since then the warden had come to believe in Reilly's honesty and reliability. The imprisoned clerk was persuaded to prove the warden wrong by helping in the escape attempt in exchange for his own freedom.

Gentlemen's clothing, wigs, and fake whiskers were smuggled into the prison from the outside by a guard who had been bribed. Reilly hid them in a niche under a dark stairway near the office. He also stole some documents from the office that allowed an accomplice to send a telegram to the warden and chief clerk of the prison. The next step required patiently waiting for something to happen that could plausibly be used to lure the two men away from the prison. That something came in the form of Horace Greeley's death.

Greeley, the famed author, politician, and founder of the *New York Tribune* newspaper, died in Pleasantville, New York, on November 29, 1872. Although he'd wanted a small funeral, his wishes were ignored, and a grand affair was planned to celebrate his life on December 4, 1872, at New

This photograph (taken in the early 20th century) shows the front entrance to Sing Sing in Ossining, New York. Ned Lyons made his escape from this spot in December 1872. He returned a few weeks later and broke Sophie out of the prison. Library of Congress.

York's Church of the Divine Paternity.[16] Lo and behold, a telegram arrived at Sing Sing, allegedly from a prison supplier, offering the warden and chief clerk a good view of the funeral procession from his office. The pair jumped at the chance to watch Congressman Greeley's coffin pass by.[17]

Soon after the warden and chief clerk left the prison grounds, Jack Tierney, a well-spoken, elegantly dressed man with an extensive criminal background, arrived at Sing Sing in a coach driven by a crook dressed to look like a coachman. Tierney, who bore a strong resemblance to the novelist Charles Dickens, was allowed into the prison for a quick tour.[18] Reilly was keeping an eye out for Tierney and saw him enter Sing Sing's front doors. Because Reilly wasn't guarded while at work in the warden's office, he was able to leave and locate Ned, who was at work in one of the prison workshops.

Together, Reilly and Ned ducked into the dark stairway, threw off their prison stripes, and donned their disguises. They emerged from the shadows looking like prosperous dandies. When Tierney's tour was over, the transformed inmates joined him at the entrance, sauntered out of the prison, and jumped into the waiting coach. By the time the warden and chief clerk heard of the escape and arrived back at the prison, the three men were long gone. So was a significant amount of cash—bribes paid by Mike Murray to facilitate the escape were reported to be about $3,000.[19]

Two weeks later, Ned went back to Sing Sing to rescue the love of his life. Sophie had managed to get a job in the kitchen of the prison hospital, which allowed her to remain outside her cell later in the day than other prisoners. Disguised in his wig and whiskers and wearing gentlemen's clothing, Ned arrived at the hospital one evening, arms laden with an enormous basket of fruit for the poor, sick prisoners. He banged on the door and Sophie, who was at work with another female prisoner, opened it. She accepted the basket and asked the other woman to take it upstairs, giving her a moment alone with Ned.[20]

Sophie escorted her husband to the door where he pulled out a fur cloak from under his coat, threw it over her prison dress, and pulled her outside. It was snowing heavily, but Ned had a sleigh waiting on the road nearby to take them to a station. There they boarded a train to New York and never looked back.[21]

4

Jealousy and Betrayal

It was not altogether lack of money or the desire to live a decent life which made me plead with Ned to reform. The fact that there was a reward on both our heads and that at any minute some ambitious detective was liable to recognize us was beginning to tell on my nerves. Ned used to try to laugh my fears away by saying that I saw policemen in my sleep. Probably I did—at any rate, I know that for months, asleep or awake, I would jump at the slightest sound, thinking it was an officer come to take us back to Sing Sing. We could not live natural lives but had to be constantly dodging about, and occasionally running to cover for long intervals.
—Sophie Lyons, *Why Crime Does Not Pay*

Ned Lyons was extremely angry when he discovered that Sophie had removed their children from Becky Moore's home in Harlem and put them in an institution before she began her prison sentence at Sing Sing. Adding insult to injury was the fact that Ned's favorite child, baby Eugenia, had died in the orphanage on Randall's Island while he and Sophie were imprisoned.[1] The Lyons' marriage was beginning to crack under the weight of their legal and personal problems.

After escaping Sing Sing, Ned tracked down his remaining children, George and Florence, and reclaimed them. New York City was no longer safe for the Lyons family, so they went north to Montreal, Quebec. A move to Canada made sense because at that time the United States and its northern neighbor didn't have an extradition treaty, which meant the police wouldn't come calling for the couple.

With the promise of relative safety and the financial security of a portion of Ned's spoils from the Ocean Bank robbery, it seemed like the Lyons family could at last move forward. Then Becky Moore came calling.

Sophie suspected that Becky, whom the *New York Times* described as a "very handsome woman," had developed an interest in Ned that went beyond pure friendship.[2] Sophie had been happy to put distance between her husband and Becky and wasn't at all pleased to see her again.

Affairs of the Heart

Becky Moore was born Rebecca Sturge in Southwark, a borough of London, on May 28, 1845.[3] She journeyed from England to America with her parents and sister in 1855 and settled in New York.[4] By the time she married Langdon W. Moore, around 1869, she was the widow of a "sporting man" named Daniel "Dad" Cunningham.[5]

ORIGINAL IN ROGUES' GALLERY, BOSTON.
Obtained by fraud and falsehood, Feb: 21, 1880; since copyrighted without my knowledge or consent, and sent among the nations of the earth.

Langdon Moore and his wife, Becky, lived near Ned and Sophie in Harlem. The couple took in the Lyons children after their parents were sent to Sing Sing. Later, Becky Moore asked Ned for help getting her husband out of prison. This rogues' gallery photograph of Moore was published in his memoir. Obviously he wrote the caption.

Shortly after Ned was sent to Sing Sing, Langdon Moore was sentenced to seven years in the Maine State Prison for robbing the Lime Rock Bank in Rockland, Maine.[6] After Ned broke out of Sing Sing, Becky requested his help to get her husband out of prison. She asked Ned to contact a few of his criminal friends and raise $2,500 in cash. Once they had the money, Becky was to bribe the warden into providing her husband with a glowing record that would earn him a pardon from the governor.

Ned agreed to help and secured the cash for the bribe. With the money in hand, he and Becky traveled to Maine. The plan was for Becky to smuggle the money into the prison in her sleeve, discreetly show it to the warden's wife, and ask her "where was the best place to put it."[7]

Before Becky could get inside the prison and flash the cash, the warden intercepted a message Becky had sent to her husband confirming that she and Ned had the bribe money. Fearing other inmates might hear rumors about the bribe and use it against him, he refused to take the bait.[8] Becky and Ned had no choice but to leave Maine without securing Moore's release.

Several years later, after he was released from prison, Moore stabbed a man named Herbert Thompson to death. The reason? He suspected his wife of being unfaithful to him with Thompson, so he followed the pair to a New York hotel. He watched them as they checked into a room, then he broke in and found them engaged in an intimate act. He promptly murdered Thompson and was arrested and charged with the crime.[9] (The charges against him were eventually dropped, likely because authorities deemed the killing to have been justified due to the sexual relationship between Thompson and Moore's wife.)

Given Becky's later infidelity, Sophie probably had good reason to be suspicious of the woman's relationship with Ned. When her husband returned from the trip to Maine, Sophie accused him of having an affair with Becky.[10] Ned denied the accusation and attacked her back, saying he'd heard a rumor that she'd had a sexual relationship with the lawyer who'd helped get him transferred from Auburn to Sing Sing. Sophie denied this at first, but eventually she confessed that she *had* slept with the lawyer, but she placed the blame for the whole affair on Ned because he'd ended up in prison.

Ned was furious over Sophie's unfaithfulness, despite the fact that she'd done it to help him. He went to Albany and tracked down the lawyer, threatening him with violence unless he returned the $1,500 Sophie had paid him. Ned's reputation as a man willing and able to use aggression to get his way was well established, so the lawyer swiftly handed over the money. Ned then returned to Montreal, where he discovered that Sophie had left him and gone to New Orleans.[11]

The couple's separation was short-lived. Despite their romantic troubles, Sophie returned to Ned, and the couple remained together for several more years, during which time three more children were born. In 1874, Sophie had a second son, Victor. Charlotte, known as Lottie, came along in 1875, and Mable was born in 1876.[12] Sophie's jealousy over Ned's relationship with Becky Moore meant that she refused to ever again let another woman care for her offspring. Instead, she placed the five children in Catholic boarding schools in Canada. The Great White North, however, wouldn't remain home for Ned and Sophie.

From Bribes to Legal Fees

Ever drawn to robbing banks, on the night of December 19, 1874, Ned attempted to rob the Hochelaga Bank in Montreal. He was interrupted during the process, though, and forced to leave his burglar's tools behind. The next day he went to the bank, where he posed as a depositor and anxiously inquired whether the police had any clues as to the burglar's identity. He was told that they didn't yet, but there was a detective working on the case.[13]

Concerned that the Montreal authorities might suspect him for the attempted bank burglary, Ned and Sophie returned to America and found a place to live in Jersey City, New Jersey. Located just west of lower Manhattan, across the Hudson River, Jersey City was reputed to have corrupt police officers open to bribery. As long as Ned and Sophie paid them off, they assumed they could carry on their criminal activities without fear of being arrested.[14]

Almost two years went by without the couple experiencing any police problems. During this time, Ned and Sophie widened the scope of their operations and were working again in New York—this was a mistake. The pair had become too confident of their ability to stay out of legal trouble, and their luck ran out on October 4, 1876, when police stopped them while they were picking pockets at the Riverhead Fair in Suffolk County, Long Island. They told the officers their names were James and Sarah Richardson and offered a bribe of $1,000 cash if the officers would let them go. The officers declined the bribe and arrested them.[15] Shortly afterward, the police figured out who they really were and promptly returned them both to prison.

Ned remained locked up for the next few years at Auburn Prison, New York's most secure penal facility. For her part, Sophie understood the importance of a good lawyer—it was one of the many finer details of criminal life she'd learned from Mother Mandelbaum. Consequently she hired the best lawyer she could afford, a young man named James Ridgeway. Her investment paid off handsomely: Despite New York having passed a law in 1874 that required an escaped prisoner who'd been recaptured to complete his or her full sentence, Ridgeway argued that because Sophie's sentence had expired before the law was passed, she couldn't legally be kept in prison. The New York Supreme Court agreed with Ridgeway.[16] Sophie had barely changed into her prison garb when she got the good news that she was free.

Her next move was to take the first train bound for New York on the Hudson River Railroad. An article in the *New York Daily Herald* provides a glimpse of Sophie at this pivotal moment in her life. (Given the exceptionally flattering description of her in the article, it's reasonable to suppose she supplied the information to the reporter.)

> Although at least thirty-five years of age, she was a strikingly handsome woman. Her head was set as grandly on her shoulders as may be seen in the busts of the Greek Juno. Her whole bearing was notably easy and dignified; she would inevitably have been singled out as a person of distinction, perhaps a woman with a history worth knowing. No one who saw her [on the train] could fail to notice, either, her piercing and observant eyes sparkling from under the black line of her brow and turning to every side with restless circumspection. She took a hack and drove off hurriedly as soon as the train reached New York, and her fellow travellers may never know whom they had the honor of accompanying that day, unless this paragraph chances to meet their eye. This elegant lady was the notorious Sophia Lyons, who has the reputation of being the most dexterous and successful woman thief in this country, and she was on her way from Sing Sing prison to her old home in this city.[17]

After arriving in New York, Sophie withdrew all of her money from the bank and said goodbye to a few trusted friends. It was a bittersweet moment: Never again would Sophie Lyons reside full-time in the state where she'd spent more than two decades of her life.

Her new home base had to be a reasonably large city where she was unknown. It also had to be close to Canada so she could keep an eye on her children. The prosperous, rising city of Detroit, Michigan, was the perfect choice for Sophie's new center of operations, in part because Windsor, Ontario, was within easy reach of Detroit via the ferryboats that crossed the Detroit River.

Of course, Sophie also needed to replenish her dwindling supply of cash and had no intention of going straight in order to do so. Picking pockets and shoplifting couldn't pay for expensive lawyers or cover boarding school fees for five children, though. To expand her "business," Sophie turned to another illegitimate method of raising money that would employ her talents as an actress and a swindler. She hoped it would make her a wealthy woman too.

5

Attempted Suicide and Blackmail

This seems to be a characteristic of all women swindlers—to deceive even their closest friends and never to tell any one the whole truth about their nefarious schemes.
—Sophie Lyons, *Why Crime Does Not Pay*

Two days before Christmas 1877, a police officer watched as a woman shoplifted a pair of 90-cent slippers from a store in Detroit, Michigan. He thought it strange she made no attempt to hide the crime and, after he arrested her, he asked why she did it. She told him that the reason was simple: She wanted them. This was such an odd, unexpected response that he suspected she was high on morphine. He took her to the Wayne County Jail, where she was arraigned for larceny.[1]

The woman told police her name was Harriet Smith. Detectives obtained a warrant to search her home on 23rd Street. The woman's housekeeper let the police in (and informed them that her last name was also Smith). Inside they discovered lace, silks, shawls, and women's shoes that very likely had been stolen from department stores in Detroit.

Police suspected the name Harriet Smith was an alias, but they couldn't determine the jailed woman's real name. She wasn't in jail long before she tried to commit suicide by hanging herself from the jail bars with her handkerchief.

Officers at the jail found her limp, unresponsive body and quickly cut her down. Her first words after they revived her were "Where's my babies?" One of the officers picked her up to carry her to a room on a lower level, but she thrashed in his arms in an attempt to throw them both down the stairs. Fortunately he was able to get her under control, regain his balance, and make it to the basement room. Upon being briefly left alone again, the woman once more tried to commit suicide, this time by wrapping comforters around her head to suffocate herself.

In 1877, Sophie was placed in the jail in Detroit, Michigan. She then tried to hang herself there. Detroit Public Library.

After she was revived a second time she cried, "Oh why didn't you let me die?"[2]

A *Detroit Free Press* reporter later obtained an interview with the woman. She told him a long sob story, saying that she had been sent to live with an uncle after her father died and had attended Vassar College at her uncle's behest. While at school she became addicted to morphine. After graduation, she married a wealthy man and moved to England with him. The couple had two children and traveled all over Europe until her husband died in England. She then chose to return to the United States, leaving her money with the uncle and her children with other relatives. Somehow after that she lost both her fortune and her children and still couldn't break free of her morphine addiction. She told the reporter she was despondent, had no friends, had seen too much trouble, and didn't care what happened to her.

Several parts of the woman's story conflicted with the facts. Despite claiming that she had no money, she said her children "are and always will be well cared for." She also declared she was "not ready to die, am not good enough," even though she had tried to kill herself multiple times. She was even, supposedly, willing to go to jail for as long as the court saw fit to incarcerate her. The reporter was impressed with both the woman and her tale and convinced she was telling the truth. He described her as "well read, sings nicely and is well informed on all current matter of interest."[3] The police, however, didn't agree—they insisted that the woman hadn't had any morphine while in jail nor had she shown signs of withdrawal, so the addiction part of her tale was fiction.

She was brought into court for a hearing a few days later. Upon entering the courtroom she spotted Elbert Crofoot, an attorney who specialized in representing Detroit's saloon owners. She sprang at him, tried to strike him in the face, and then began to weep. Apparently he'd called her a few "choice epithets" when he saw her at the jail sometime earlier. The woman later said she was sorry for making such an "unwomanly exhibition" but she simply couldn't stop herself from lashing out.[4]

Detroit's Criminal Appeal

The woman who had tried to kill herself and then attacked Elbert Crofoot was Sophie Lyons, but the police didn't know that yet. Prior to her arrest in Detroit, Sophie had spent a few days in Boston. Something about her behavior there caught the attention of two sharp-eyed detectives, and they followed her to several stores. At some point she realized they were tailing her. Finally, one of the men stood right behind her at a children's clothing counter. She proceeded to steal several inexpensive items—pairs of socks and stockings—making no attempt to hide the theft. It was as if she was daring the detective to arrest her; he obliged. She was charged with shoplifting, convicted, and sentenced to a year in the Boston House of Correction.[5]

Sophie being Sophie, she immediately appealed her sentence. In court she cried and described how she'd been abused and forced to steal as a child. She also revealed that she had five children to support on her own. The district attorney was sympathetic and placed her case on file instead of sending her to prison. He told her to get out of town, and said he that if she were arrested in Boston again, she'd serve her full sentence.[6] Sophie headed to Detroit, where she'd already set up a home base at the intersection of 23rd and Fort streets, near the Detroit River in the south-eastern portion of the city.

Detroit was ideal, not only for its proximity to Canada, where So-phie's children were attending boarding school, but also for its combina-tion of shopping districts and wealthy citizens. The city had grown from a population of close to 80,000 in 1870 to more than 116,000 by 1880. Al-though Detroit was still nowhere near the size of New York, where Sophie first delved into the world of crime, it still offered plenty of opportunity for talented criminals like her.

Detroit was to be Sophie's home base, however, she didn't plan to limit her criminal activities to that city. She intended to engage in lucra-tive criminal activities in other large cities in the Midwest and on the East Coast.

Mrs. Lucas' Cincinnati Sojourn

On May 30, 1878, a well-dressed, good-looking woman in her early 30s registered at Reid's Hotel in Cincinnati, Ohio, as Mrs. S.E. Lucas.[7] She told the desk clerk that she was an actress from St. Louis, Missouri, in town for an engagement. She paid three weeks in advance for her room and board and offered a local dressmaker as a reference. The dressmaker confirmed that she knew a Mrs. Kate Lucas who was an actress in town for work. She mentioned that Mrs. Lucas had paid in advance for her dresses.

Upon settling into her room, the woman called on Cincinnati real es-tate broker W.B. Dennis. She told him she owned land near Spring Grove, a beautiful and popular local cemetery, and hoped to sell the property. She asked him to meet her at her hotel room so she could show him the deeds. Sensing a lucrative deal, Dennis was happy to oblige—he had no idea what he was getting himself into.

After he arrived at her room, she closed and locked the door behind him, then began to disrobe. She suggested he do the same and asked him to join her in bed. Dennis told police that, after he'd refused the offer, she threatened him with a revolver. Whether motivated by desire or fear, Dennis undressed. To his shock and amazement, the so-called Mrs. Lucas gathered up his clothes and tossed them out the window.

She demanded $1,000 from him and threatened to charge him with a "serious offense" if he didn't pay up.[8] Dennis agreed to pay and promptly wrote out a check. She also insisted he write a confession stating that he "had attempted an assault on Mrs. Lucas."[9] After the transaction was completed, she called a hotel employee, who brought his clothes to the room. They both redressed and, before he left, she demanded his gold watch and the cash in his wallet—Dennis quickly handed them over. To ensure she received her funds, she told him she would accompany him to the bank. He requested they stop at his office on the way. While there, Dennis managed to sneak out the back and go to the police station. He brought an officer back to his office, where the woman was arrested.

She told the police that she'd known Mr. Dennis for a year and he'd asked her to marry him many times, but she'd always refused. She said he'd tried to "take advantage of her" in her hotel room, and the money was offered as compensation for the "wrong he would have done her."[10] He was rich, she said, and could easily afford the payment. She claimed to be a widow with small children and in great need of money.

Mrs. S.E. Lucas, better known as Sophie Lyons, was running a variation on a classic blackmail swindle called the badger game. During the mid–19th century, prostitutes who robbed their clients were sometimes referred to as "badgers."[11] By the 1870s, robbery of a prostitute's client had evolved into a confidence swindle called the badger game. During the badger game, a criminal posing as a respectable woman would, "by a free exercise of her fascinating charms, lead on some rich and confiding citizen until he had placed himself in a compromising position."[12] In other words, she'd get him alone in a room with her under the pretense that she found him irresistible and couldn't wait to have sex with him. After the man removed his clothes, the woman's accomplice, posing as her husband, brother, or father (take your pick) unexpectedly returned home from an out-of-town trip. He would storm angrily into the bedroom and demand hush money to keep the man's indiscretion private. If things went as planned, the hapless victim quickly paid up and left, figuring he'd managed to avoid a close call with public humiliation.

Sophie, however, chose to dispense with the male partner and run the entire scam on her own.

A subsequent police investigation revealed that Mrs. Lucas had successfully lured a number of men to her hotel room, enticed them to disrobe, and then blackmailed them. None of these men had gone to the police, too concerned with and embarrassed about what would follow if their indiscretions became public. Only W.B. Dennis involved law enforcement.

Ultimately "Mrs. Lucas" was held on a blackmail charge and put on trial. Testifying to the strange goings-on at Reid's Hotel was Frank Aspinwall, the grandson of a jewelry-store proprietor whose shop was located nearby. Aspinwall had seen a pair of pantaloons sail out of a window at the hotel and land in the alley.[13] He retrieved the pants and left them with the hotel clerk. In the following days he recovered another pair of pants and a silk tie and turned those items in to the front desk as well. At one point, according to Aspinwall, a coat flew out of the window and became stuck on a roof. Mrs. Lucas exited the front door of the hotel and asked Aspinwall to get it for her, promising him a quarter the next day as payment. The young man thought the rain of clothing was odd, but either he didn't investigate why it was happening or he didn't want to admit he'd looked into it for fear of being accused as an accessory.

The case drew interest from men all over the city, as described by a report in the *Cincinnati Daily Star*.

> When the hour for Mrs. Lucas' trial arrived, the Court-room was jammed to its utmost. From twenty to thirty men had hold on the back of the prisoners' bench. The reporter's bench was besieged by men anxious to hear as much of the developments that were expected to be made, as this was the best place in Court for a good hearing…. All of them, lawyers, reporters, doctors, colored and white men, of every nationality, seemed anxious to get into the true inwardness of the affair.[14]

On June 22, 1878, Mrs. Lucas waived her examination by the court. Her attorney asked for her to be released on her own recognizance, saying that his client could never be convicted, but the judge didn't agree. Eventually a bail of $500 was set. Sophie paid the amount and promptly left town, eager to move on to fresh hunting grounds to play her unique and devilish version of the badger game. Meanwhile, Cincinnati police still believed her real name was Kate Lucas and were reportedly anxious to "renew their acquaintance with the fair widow."[15]

The Room 11 Affair

On July 9, 1878, a beautiful woman of wealthy and refined appearance arrived in Boston, Massachusetts. She booked one of the best rooms at the upscale Revere House in Bowdoin Square in the name Louisa Sylvan. The Revere House was considered the most prestigious hotel in a city preoccupied with social status.[16]

After settling into her rooms, Mrs. Sylvan contacted Charles E. Allen, a prominent and well-respected attorney who also happened to be a much older bachelor. Claiming to be a widow, she arranged to meet him at his office in Pemberton Square the following day for a consultation about a house she wanted to buy.[17]

The meeting went smoothly, and Sylvan requested that Allen meet her later that day to continue discussing business at her suite at Revere House. Allen was captivated by the lady's charms and, though her request was unconventional, he readily agreed to the meeting. After he entered her room, she commented on the warmth of the day and suggested they'd both be more comfortable if they removed their clothing. She then proceeded to undress. The bewildered attorney later described her charms as "irresistible" and gave in to what he realized was an evil temptation. "She was so bewitching and fascinating that I could not help it," he admitted to the police.[18]

The moment Allen's clothes were off, Sylvan grabbed them, threw them into a trunk, and locked it. After all, clothing sailing out the window of the Revere House would have attracted too much attention. To

Revere House, shown in 1885, was an upscale Boston hotel where Sophie tried to blackmail attorney Charles Allen in 1878 by enticing him into bed with her. She then locked his clothes in a trunk and left with the key. Boston Pictorial Archive, Boston Public Library.

Allen's astonishment, she demanded he write her a check for $10,000 to unlock the trunk and return his clothing to him. He initially refused, but after realizing she wasn't going to give up, he complied—then shared that he didn't have that much money in his bank account. Sylvan tore up the check and requested he write another one for $1,000 immediately and pay her more in cash the next day. Seeing no other way out of his predicament, Allen agreed to her demands. Satisfied, Sylvan redressed and left for the bank, locking the door behind her.[19]

What she didn't know was that some of Allen's checks had been stolen recently, which made the bank unusually cautious with his account. In order to cash Allen's check, the bank cashier asked the so-called Mrs. Sylvan to bring in someone who could identify her. She told him she was new in town and had no local contacts. The cashier became suspicious and called the police, who arrested her. She tried to tear up and swallow Allen's check on the way to the station, but the officers stopped her from doing so.

Once at the station, the officers inquired as to Mr. Allen's whereabouts and when Sylvan had seen him last. She said she didn't know where he was and couldn't remember when she'd last seen him. Now highly suspicious, the officers searched her and found a key from Revere House marked #11. Next they went to the hotel and used the key to unlock Room 11. Inside they discovered Allen sitting on the bed in his underwear. He told them the story of how the woman had obtained his clothing, locked it in her trunk, and then blackmailed him.[20]

In Sylvan's version of the events, she'd known Allen for quite some time and had been to his office often. But according to her, the relationship went well beyond business. She admitted that she and Mr. Allen "had had some good times together." She insisted he'd given her the money as a gift and consequently the police had no reason to get involved.

During the 19th century, a woman who had a reputation to uphold would *never* declare publicly that she'd had an affair or make even an oblique reference to having received payment for sexual services; doing so would brand her as a courtesan. When the police questioned Mrs. Sylvan, it became quite clear that despite being well spoken and having a refined appearance, she wasn't a woman of good reputation and had no fear of saying as much. She stated, without a hint of shame, that she was Allen's mistress and she'd done nothing wrong.[21]

She also insisted it was Allen's fault that his clothes got locked in the trunk. She claimed he asked her to call for a servant boy to bring drinks to the room. After he realized the boy might notice his clothing draped on a chair, he told her to put the clothes in the trunk, which locked automatically. "If Mr. Allen had not acquiesced it would have taken a bigger woman than I am to have locked up his clothes, as he still had considerable vigor in spite of his aged look," she commented, managing to tell her version of the story while also insulting her victim's appearance.[22] She even claimed she'd gone alone to the bank because he was too tired to accompany her. She said she'd gently tucked him into bed before leaving to cash his check.[23]

The police saw through her tale, charged her with blackmail, and lodged her in the Cambridge Street Jail. Her bail was set at $2,000. The amount was paid the next day by two bondsmen, freeing Sylvan, who forfeited bail and left town.[24] At the time, Boston detectives didn't realize they'd arrested—and lost—the infamous New York criminal Sophie Lyons. Instead, they put out a warrant for Louisa Sylvan after she failed to appear for her blackmail trial.[25]

Setting the Stage for Future Schemes—and Problems

Back in Detroit, the prosecution determined that the December 1877 shoplifting case against Harriet Smith was weak and dropped the charges at the end of July 1878.[26] Authorities there still didn't know her real name and had no idea they were dealing with a notorious shoplifter and pickpocket turned blackmailer. She simply became known as the "Beautiful Morphine Eater" and the "Morphine Woman," because Detroit newspaper reporters chalked up her irrational behavior to drug addiction. These inaccurate stories of Sophie's addiction to morphine wound up following her for years.

Despite an occasional arrest, Sophie frequently got away with her solo badger game. It was highly lucrative and she had no intention of quitting. After all, it was a swindle that tapped into her natural ability as an actress. It also gave her a chance to benefit from the hypocrisy hidden below the surface of polite society: Well-thought-of men were allowed to take advantage of women, behaving like rascals so long as they maintained the appearance of propriety. However, if a woman strayed from the straight and narrow and people found out, her name would be blackened forever. As a woman with a criminal past, Sophie had no respectable reputation to worry about, so why not make good money off the situation? Sophie chose her victims carefully to try to ensure that they would give in to her demands for money rather than risk their good names.

Most satisfying of all, Sophie's schemes allowed her to take revenge for a specific injury done to her in the past. Her victims may well have been proxies for the Albany lawyer who'd demanded $1,500 in payment and then forced Sophie to sleep with him to secure his help in getting Ned transferred to Sing Sing.

Sophie didn't attempt suicide again, but her erratic behavior, including incidents where she angrily and violently lashed out at others in public, continued to plague her. She also continued to have difficulty controlling her urge to steal, engaging in theft at moments when she was very likely to be caught. These episodes, which may have been early signs of mental illness, became more frequent as time went on.

In the immediate future, Sophie had more pressing problems on her plate than her mental health issues. She was wanted by the police in Boston and Cincinnati. Her husband would soon be released from Auburn, and she knew he wanted to resume their marriage. His anger over the Albany lawyer proved that Ned Lyons was a jealous man. If he found out about his wife's sexual blackmail scams, he would likely go into a rage.

Then there was the problem of Sophie and Ned's oldest child, George. The 12-year-old was a rebellious boy on the cusp of becoming a teenager. He'd recently escaped from his boarding school, and Sophie knew she didn't want him at her Detroit home, where he would see and hear things he shouldn't. She was going to have to do something drastic about George.

6

Accusations and Outrage

During this time my children were approaching an age when it would no longer do to have them in our home. Our unexplained absences, our midnight departures, our hurried return in the early morning hours with masks, burglars' tools, and satchels full of stolen valuables would arouse curiosity in their little minds. One thing I had sworn to do—to safeguard my little ones from such wretched influences as had surrounded my childhood.
—Sophie Lyons, *Why Crime Does Not Pay*

On a clear, cold morning toward the end of January 1880, a stylishly dressed woman and a boy dressed in rags walked into an old market building on Manhattan's Lower East Side. The first floor of the building, located on Grand Street, between Ludlow and Essex streets, still housed the stalls where vegetables, cheese, fish, various meats, coffee, and other small items had been sold since the 18th century. The upper two stories of the building, which were added in the mid–1850s, housed the Essex Market Police Court, the 10th Ward Station House, and a dispensary.[1]

As the pair approached the court, the woman motioned to the officer standing by the door. "Officer, I want you to arrest that boy," she cried, indicating the ragged child at her side. When the policeman asked her why, she replied, "He is my son. He is a bad boy and won't stay home." The boy protested, but the woman ignored him while an affidavit for her complaint was prepared.[2]

Gazing down at the mother and son from his seat at the bench, Justice Murray asked the woman to explain her side of the story first. After confirming the boy was her 13-year-old child, George Lyons, she said:

I found him yesterday in the street and I have learned that he has been going around in drinking saloons and singing. I have sent him to three different schools, but I could not keep him in any of them, and now I want him sent to the House of Refuge, where he will be kept out of harm's way till he becomes a man.[3]

Justice Murray then asked George for his version of events. In a clear voice and with tears running down his cheeks, he said, "That woman is the wife of Edward Lyons, the burglar. Ask the detectives who he is and who she is. She herself is a thief who has done time…"[4] He wasn't able to finish his sentence because his mother, pale with anger, sprang at him and hit him in the face. Justice Murray ordered her removed from the courtroom.

George then told the judge he recalled living on 110th Street in Harlem when he was a small boy. At one point, he and his sisters had been awakened in the middle of the night by several policemen barging into their home and arresting their parents. For reasons he didn't understand, he and his sisters were placed in the orphanage on Randall's Island. Later he was convicted of disorderly conduct and spent six months at the House of Refuge on Randall's Island.[5] He continued with the disturbing story of his life:

> One day I was sent for and taken to Detroit, where I met this woman, who said my name there was Robinson. In the house were lots of jewelry and silks and laces and clocks. My father, I learned, was then in prison. Many men came to see my mother and I often heard them talk of robberies. One of them took a fancy to me and said I would be greater than George—meaning my father. My mother took me to Montreal and put me in different schools, one after another, but I wanted to stay home. Then she said I was getting to know too much and she took me to a police station and told them to keep me there. The next day a man that I had seen at my mother's house came to the station and gave me a ticket to New York and five dollars.
>
> When I got here I went to work for Mrs. Woodward, a second hand furniture dealer in Ninth Avenue. I remained there about five months and got 25 cents a week, my board and some dirty, old clothes. Then I went away and took a bed at the Boys' Lodging House in West Thirty-fifth Street, and began peddling flowers for a florist. He made me work from 6 o'clock at night until 8 or 9 in the morning. While selling flowers in the saloon I became acquainted with Dan Kerrigan [part owner of the Star and Garter saloon]. He heard that I had a good voice and he engaged me to come and sing. A man who had seen me at Kerrigan's told me he would give me a home.
>
> I met my mother on Ninth Avenue yesterday for the first time in many months. She told me to come home with her and she would buy me a new suit of clothes. I went with her to a house where there was a strange man. I told her last night all I had done. Today she told me that she was going away.[6]

George also insisted that his mother "had two husbands" and that she was a thief. He claimed he had personally seen her stealing while they were in Montreal.[7]

Next, Justice Murray had the woman brought back into the courtroom to tell her side of the story. In whispered tones she admitted that she was Sophie Lyons and that Ned Lyons, who was still in prison, was her husband. She talked about their escape from Sing Sing and how they'd hidden for a time in Canada before being rearrested. She also described how she'd been abused as a child and forced to steal by her mother. She offered no explanation—and apparently wasn't asked—why she had her young son sent, on his own, from Detroit to New York City with $5 (worth about $130 in 2018 dollars) in his pocket.

The judge had George held overnight in the cells while he decided what to do with him. George protested, screamed, and pleaded not to go, but he was sent anyway. In an act chillingly similar to the one his mother had tried in the Detroit jail, George attempted to hang himself by tying his handkerchief around his throat and then attaching the other end to the bars of his cell. Also like Sophie, he was discovered in time and revived.[8]

The next day Justice Murray had the boy brought back into court and asked him to demonstrate his singing ability. George sang "Ave Maria" in Latin, and the judge, impressed with the boy's voice, said he believed George's story and had decided to send him to a local Catholic church. George would stay under the care of the priest there for the time being while Sophie returned home.

Introducing "the Other Man"

Six months later, when the 1880 federal census was taken in Sophie's Detroit neighborhood in June, she was listed as Sophia English, a resident at 51 23rd Street.[9] Also listed at that address were her husband, George English, and their five children: George, Florence, Victoria, Lottie, and Mable. (Sophie's son Victor was incorrectly identified as a female, but the children's ages were all correct.) George English, the head of the household, was described on the census as a 45-year-old "Broker (money)" who was born in Michigan. All the children were recorded as being the offspring of George English, with the exception of the youngest child, Mable, but that may have been an oversight on the part of the census taker.

Who was George English? The name George English may have been an alias used by Ned Lyons. His son George told Justice Murray that other criminals referred to his father as "George." Ned completed his latest sentence and had been released from Auburn Prison during the summer of 1880, though the exact date of his release can't be verified. It's also possible George English was the man's real name and he was in fact a known "confidence operator" who worked primarily in New York.[10] However, English was never reported to have worked or lived in Detroit, at least not under that name, nor was he ever associated with Sophie. The third possibility is that George English was an alias used by a man named Hamilton "Ham" Brock, a Vermont native born in 1839. Because Brock was regularly involved in horse racing, both as a trainer and later as an owner of a betting parlor, he was often described in the news as a "sporting man."[11] But Ned Lyons saw him as something else entirely: his wife, Sophie's, lover.

By 1878 Brock resided in Boston, where he worked as the proprietor of an event venue called Revere Hall.[12]

On January 22, 1878, Brock was shot with a horse pistol. The bullet entered his left breast and exited near his shoulder. Brock claimed a shooter was a man whom he didn't know who'd approached him in the street and shot him for no reason. Witnesses to the event claimed Brock was drunk and had accidently shot himself while hanging out at a brothel with friends.[13]

HAMILTON BROCK.

Ned Lyons was jealous of Hamilton Brock because he believed Brock was Sophie's lover and accomplice. In 1880 he tried to shoot Brock but missed, so Brock shot him instead. This drawing of Brock is from an 1894 newspaper.

However he got his wounds, Brock was taken to Revere House in Bowdoin Square to recover. The upscale hotel was located close to his workplace, Revere Hall, and it was the same hotel where Sophie tried to blackmail attorney Charles Allen on July 9, 1878. There is no record of how Brock and Sophie became acquainted, but it's possible they met and began their affair while both were residents at the Revere House.

Sophie was arrested in Boston for attempted extortion of Allen that July, but in August she skipped bail and left the city.[14] In November Brock absconded from Boston with $18,000 in stolen bonds.

The following April he was arrested in Montreal, Canada. It was reported that he agreed to give the bonds back and return to Boston in exchange for not being prosecuted.[15] It can't be proven, but it's possible he and Sophie were together in Montreal—a city where she had lived and where she was connected to the criminal fraternity. With Sophie's help Brock may have been trying to dispose of the stolen bonds.

Brock did not keep up his end of the bargain with law enforcement. He neither returned to Boston nor handed over the bonds, and in October 1879 he was arrested in Chicago. Taking a leaf from Sophie's book, his lawyer successfully demanded a writ of habeas corpus from the court in Chicago. Brock was bailed out and he skipped town.[16] Possibly he spent time at Sophie's Detroit abode (giving her son, George, the idea that his mother "had two husbands").

Ned Lyons was released from prison during the summer of 1880. Someone (the likely suspects being his son, George, or even Sophie herself) spilled the beans to him about the relationship between Brock and Sophie. The knowledge that his wife had been involved with another man made the hot-headed Ned furious and he went on the warpath.

A Face-Off at the Star and Garter

By the fall of 1880 Brock surfaced in New York City, where he was running the Star and Garter saloon at the corner of Sixth Avenue and 30th Street. (Dan Kerrigan, one of the saloon's owners and a friend of young George Lyons, had died in January 1880.) Thanks to the rival gangs roaming the streets of lower Manhattan at the time, saloons required a secret entry password to keep gang fighting off of their premises. In the early morning hours of October 24, Ned showed up at the Star and Garter with his friend Tom McCormack. The pair had been drinking, but they were still in control of themselves. Ned gave the correct password, "I am Stetson from Boston," and entered the saloon with McCormack by his side.[17]

The pair found Brock seated at a table just inside the door and positioned themselves on either side of him. An argument ensued, with Ned claiming he could "lick" Brock, aiming a revolver at his stomach and threatening to blow a hole through him. Brock pleaded with Ned not to shoot and tried to grab the revolver away from him. The men struggled, and Ned pulled the trigger. Miraculously, the gun's hammer jammed on

Brock's coat sleeve, giving him the opportunity to get the gun away from Ned and throw it on the floor. After others in the saloon separated the two, Brock ran down into the basement, and Ned picked up his pistol off the floor before leaving with McCormack.[18]

Brock then went out to the street, located a policeman, and told the officer that Ned Lyons had tried to shoot him. Brock gave a description of Ned to the officer and shared his fear that he would return and try to attack him again. The policeman agreed to stay in the area and keep an eye out. Appeased, Brock returned to the saloon.

Shortly after 6 a.m., Ned banged on the side door of the Star and Garter and shouted out the password. Evidently one of the employees hadn't been told not to admit him (or was open to a bribe), because soon Ned approached Brock, who was standing behind the bar, and announced that he was going to kill him. Ned fired a shot at Brock that missed, buying him time to duck behind the bar before Ned could shoot again. Brock then stood back up with his own pistol in his hand and fired three shots at Ned, two of which hit him.[19]

One bullet entered Ned's right breast; the other passed through his cheek and into his mouth. Ned ran out of the saloon screaming that he'd been shot. He was taken to New York Hospital on West 15th Street, where his injuries were deemed life threatening. While there he told authorities his name was George E. Lenning.[20]

Meanwhile, the police located Brock hiding on the third floor of the building that housed the Star and Garter and took him to the Jefferson Market Police Court. Although the judge said he believed the shooting was largely justifiable because Ned had been the first to shoot, he still charged Brock with felonious assault. The charge didn't hinder Brock for long, however—he was soon released on $1,000 bond.[21]

Two days later, a reporter from *The Sun* got hold of a letter Ned sent to a friend from prison that explained why he'd tried to shoot Brock. He'd become convinced that Brock was romantically involved with Sophie and had persuaded her to leave the children in various boarding schools and join him in Boston while he (Ned) was in prison. Ned explained his feelings toward Sophie and Brock in the letter.

> I ought to have nothing but contempt for this creature they call my wife, but knowing how she has been used by Brock, I feel some pity with it. This dog Brock put up the job at the Revere House. Under the guise of my friend he betrayed her, and got her to leave home and her children, taking with her the means I left for their comfort.[22]

Evidently Ned didn't realize that Sophie had pulled similar blackmail scams in Cincinnati on her own before the attempt in Boston. Possibly he couldn't come to grips with how his home life had fallen apart during his years in prison, and he needed someone other than Sophie to blame. Or it may have been Sophie who placed the blame on Brock in an effort to shield herself from Ned's rage. Whether Brock deserved that blame is questionable: Although he worked very close to the Revere House when Sophie tried to blackmail Charles Allen, Brock was never arrested for any crime related to the notorious "Room 11 affair."

"Louisa Sylvan" Goes to Trial in Boston

While Ned was recuperating in a hospital bed in New York, the Boston police finally figured out that the woman in the Room 11 case—the one who'd previously been known as Louisa Sylvan—was actually Sophie Lyons. Soon afterward, Sophie was located in Detroit, taken to Boston, and put in jail.[23] When she was informed that her husband had been shot and might die "she affected to be deeply grieved," according to a report in *The Sun*.[24]

During the October 1880 trial for the extortion of Charles Allen, Sophie's cousin Samuel (referred to as her brother) testified that she had been at his home in New York on the relevant dates.[25] The prosecution, however, saw through the testimony, pointing out that Sophie hadn't seen Samuel in 24 years, so why would she suddenly pay him a visit?

The prosecution had a more difficult time proving Sophie Lyons was the woman who'd lured Allen to the hotel. There had been a substantial amount of confusion over the true identity of Louisa Sylvan. A woman named Myra DeWolf, who apparently resembled Sophie, was arrested in August 1878 as Sylvan. She was later let go when she was able to show she had been elsewhere on the day of the crime.[26]

To capitalize on the confusion, Sophie's lawyer called various people as witnesses who identified DeWolf as Sophie, demonstrating the uncertainty over the blackmailer's identity. An embarrassed Allen testified that even he couldn't be sure the defendant was the woman he'd gotten into bed with in Room 11.[27]

As was her custom, Sophie wore a veil to hide her face when she was in court. It seems bizarre that Sophie was allowed to keep her veil on during the trial, but the concession wasn't without precedent. In 1854 a woman who went by the name Henrietta Robinson (though everyone agreed this wasn't her real name) was tried for the arsenic murders of two of her neighbors in Troy, New York. "She entered the courtroom well attired, but so closely veiled that no one was able to catch a glimpse of her features" was how the scene was later described.[28] She kept her veil on throughout her trial, despite the fact that the judge repeatedly asked her to remove it so the jury could see her face during witness testimony. She did remove it briefly in order for witnesses to identify her, but immediately after showing her face she replaced the veil. Consequently, she became known as "the Veiled Murderess." She was ultimately convicted of the murders and sentenced to be hanged, though her sentence was later commuted to life in prison.[29]

By 1870, Robinson had spent many years in Sing Sing.[30] Sophie joined her there, from October 1871 until December 1872, and may have met Robinson before the latter was moved to the State Asylum at Auburn. At the very least, Sophie would have heard Robinson's story while she was at Sing Sing and taken away from that tale a lesson on the usefulness of wearing a veil to hide one's identity—even in a courtroom.

Ultimately the prosecution failed to prove beyond a doubt that Sophie Lyons was the woman who'd lured the attorney to the Revere House, locked up his clothing, and blackmailed him; her trial ended in a hung jury.[31]

This undated rogues' gallery photograph of Sophie shows the kind of hat, veil and shawl she liked to wear in order to disguise herself. National Portrait Gallery, Smithsonian Institution; gift of Pinkerton's, Inc.

The Aftermath

Charles Allen's reputation was ruined thanks to the notoriety of the "Room 11 affair." He wanted to forget the whole episode and never hear the name Sophie Lyons again. For her part, Sophie was held briefly in a Boston jail for a retrial of the Allen case, but the second trial never materialized. Sophie wasn't thrilled with having been held in jail, tried and forced to pay the associated hefty lawyer's fees; she would never set foot in Boston again.

Meanwhile, Hamilton Brock realized he was out of his league when dealing with the likes of professional criminals such as Sophie and Ned Lyons. He left New York City and returned home to Vermont, where he married Kate Gilman in 1882.[32] He continued his involvement with horse training and apparently lived an honest life until his death from kidney disease in 1897. There was no mention in his obituary of his criminal past. Instead he was described as "a true and loyal friend whose word was as good as a bond."[33]

Ned astonished his doctors—and disappointed the police—when he recovered from his bullet wounds in New York. Sophie kept the children and his last name, but she'd had enough of his jealousy and violence. As far as she was concerned, her marriage to him was over. She returned to Detroit without him.

7

Arrest After Arrest

By this time the fear of the disgrace which threatened him and his family had made him a nervous wreck. He begged so piteously for me to help him save his good name that my womanly sympathies got the better of me and I finally consented.
—Sophie Lyons, *Why Crime Does Not Pay*

Around 11 a.m. on March 18, 1881, a veiled woman dressed in black entered the Bank Chambers building in downtown Detroit. She made her way to the offices of the Detroit City Railway Company and inquired after its president, George Hendrie. She was told that Hendrie was engaged and would be free shortly, so she took a seat outside of his office to wait.[1]

After Hendrie's colleagues left his office, the veiled woman entered. She demanded Hendrie make reparations to her. "Reparations for what?" Hendrie asked. "You know very well what I mean," she replied. Hendrie told her he had no idea what she meant. Upon hearing his comment, she pulled a revolver out from under her cloak, aimed at him from across his desk, and fired. The bullet missed and lodged in the wall behind Hendrie.[2]

The mystery woman wasn't the only one who'd been waiting to speak to Hendrie. A man named John Smith, who'd been hoping to ask Hendrie about a teamster's job, heard the woman exclaim, "I've been a bitch for you, George Hendrie!" followed by the report of a gun. Smith became alarmed and ran into the office, where he and Hendrie disarmed the woman. Smith held her arms while Hendrie called for the help of his colleague, Sidney Miller. After Miller arrived, Hendrie left the office and summoned the police.[3]

Officer Patrick Haley arrived on the scene and arrested the woman, who refused to make any statement about the shooting but did ask for her revolver back. (It wasn't returned to her.) Thanks to the notoriety of the Charles Allen extortion case tried in Boston just a few months earlier, the Detroit superintendent of police, Andrew Rogers, realized the female shooter was Sophie Lyons.[4]

But who was George Hendrie? And what was his connection to the criminal Sophie Lyons?

Revenge for Mistreatment— or So the Scandal Goes

George Hendrie, a wealthy Detroit industrialist, was one of Sophie's blackmail targets in 1881. After he refused to comply with her demands, she went to his office and tried to shoot him. *Compendium of History and Biography of the City of Detroit and Wayne County, Michigan* (1909).

Hendrie was born in Glasgow, Scotland, in 1834.[5] After graduating from a Scottish high school, he immigrated to Hamilton, a city in Ontario, Canada. There he started a cartage (hauling) business with his brother, William. In 1859, Hendrie relocated to Detroit, where he began another cartage firm and secured contracts for the business with two railroads: the Great Western Railway and the Detroit & Milwaukee Railroad.[6]

Six years later he married Sarah Sibley Trowbridge, the daughter of a wealthy Detroit banker.[7] His businesses thrived, and Hendrie purchased the Detroit City Railway in 1876. He made improvements to the company's lines and increased the total mileage the railway operated to around six and a half miles.[8] By 1880, Hendrie and his wife had three children, and he was considered a wealthy man—a perfect mark for Sophie.[9]

After her attempted shooting of Hendrie, rumors began circulating in the newspapers, even as far away as Boston. Papers there reported that Sophie had borne Hendrie's illegitimate child a few months earlier. Although evidence of Sophie having given birth around that time can't be found, it's possible the "reparations" she demanded from him involved a child he'd fathered with her that she'd been forced to give up.[10]

Assuming Sophie delivered a child at full term in late January 1881, she would have gotten pregnant in late April or early May 1880. This means she would have been about six months pregnant during her Boston trial for the blackmail of Charles Allen in late October 1880. Yet the Boston newsmen, who were happy to report every salacious detail of that case, failed to mention anything about Sophie looking pregnant in the courtroom (though it's possible she was able to disguise the pregnancy using a cloak or cape).

On March 19, 1881, the day after the shooting incident, Hendrie refused to come to court to make a complaint against Sophie, a married woman with a bad reputation who had spent time in prison. Even though Ned Lyons wasn't released from Auburn until the summer of 1880, if Sophie had gotten pregnant that spring, the alleged baby would have been assumed to be Ned's. (Sophie's paramour at the time, Hamilton Brock, was another father candidate.) Hendrie was no fool, though. If he and Sophie did indeed have an affair, especially one that produced a child, he knew his best bet was to deny any relationship with her, or that he even knew her. And that's precisely what he did.

Officer Haley, however, wasn't content to let the matter rest. After all, it wouldn't do for the Detroit police to allow people to go around threatening respectable citizens with pistols. Haley and John Smith, the witness who helped him arrest Sophie, eventually agreed to lodge the complaint that Hendrie refused to.[11] Ultimately, the charge brought against Sophie was that she "feloniously, wickedly and with malice aforethought did make an assault with intent to kill and murder George Hendrie." She pleaded not guilty.[12]

Hendrie's wife, who had been out east when the shooting occurred, returned to Detroit in early April. Possibly Hendrie had hoped the case would be wrapped up by then, but unluckily for him, it wasn't. At Sophie's bond hearing on April 15, Hendrie testified that he didn't know Sophie Lyons and had no idea why she'd want to kill him. He also said under oath that some unnamed person had made an engagement for him to meet with her that was "unauthorized by me." He claimed that he was "solicited to make an engagement" with her, which he declined to do.[13] Basically, Hendrie tried to cover all the bases by denying any relationship with Sophie in his testimony.

Another witness at the hearing, Thomas Manning, testified that he was on Griswold Street near the Detroit Post Office the day before the shooting. At that time he saw a woman he identified as Sophie walk toward Hendrie. As she passed by him she said, "I will give you twenty-four hours to see me; and if you don't I will make it hot for you."[14] Manning testified that several people had heard what the woman said to Hendrie and laughed. He asked Hendrie what she meant, and he replied that he didn't know.

Given that Sophie's past blackmail efforts were directed at men she knew and had successfully lured to her, it's likely Sophie and Hendrie did have a sexual relationship of some kind. The details are what's confusing. Did he offer her financial support in exchange for sex? Did she then try, unsuccessfully, to blackmail him? Only Hendrie and Sophie would know for sure.

Regardless, Sophie's bond was set at $5,000, and she was sent to the Wayne County Jail to await trial. The case was heard in the Recorder's Court on May 14. Specifics of that hearing weren't released, because Sophie's attorneys made a motion to quash the results, but records do show that the charge against Sophie wound up being dropped and she was set free.[15] However, just 10 days later she was arrested as a "suspicious person" and examined by several doctors specializing in mental illness in an effort to determine her mental state.[16] They were unable to agree on whether she was insane, so she was released the next day.[17] Sophie then sued Superintendent Rogers and several other members of the Detroit Police Department for $10,000 in damages for their wrongful conduct.[18]

Despite the scandal, which apparently came close to breaking up his marriage, Hendrie and his wife stayed together and had four more children between 1882 and 1893.[19]

Ned Lyons Burns Another of His Nine Lives

Meanwhile, there was more trouble brewing back east for Ned Lyons. During the early hours of July 31, 1881, a man was arrested for the attempted burglary of the J.B. Johnson store in South Windham, Connecticut. Johnson had been tipped off about the burglary (supposedly by Hamilton Brock) and had stationed three night watchmen at his store. One of them interrupted a trio of burglars as they prepared to blow open the store's safe and proceeded to scuffle with them.

Two of the thieves managed to escape, but the watchman was able to shoot the remaining burglar in his abdomen and neck. The wounded thief was taken to the hospital with serious injuries that were thought to be fatal. Detectives interviewed him, but he refused to identify himself or make any statement. Not to be circumvented, the detectives sent a description of the man to newspapers around the country in an effort to identify him.

> A wounded burglar in custody who refused to give his name. He is about 40 years of age; is stout and well built, and will weigh about 180 pounds. He is five feet and eight inches in height; has sandy hair, short side whiskers, a thick, short sandy mustache, blue eyes, high forehead and a genial and prepossessing countenance. Was dressed in dark clothes. Distinguishing marks about his face are a scar on his nose, another on his neck and his left ear gone except the lobe. When captured he had a large stock of fine burglars tools with him.[20]

The description was effective. The New York City Police Department quickly identified the burglar as Ned Lyons, and the missing portion of his ear was almost certainly what gave him away.

Ned eventually made another miraculous recovery, though a bullet remained embedded in his back. According to New York police inspector Thomas Byrnes, Ned pleaded guilty to the Johnson store burglary in September 1881 and was sentenced to three years in the Connecticut State Prison.

Wild Times in Jackson

While her husband hovered between life and death in a Connecticut hospital, Sophie traveled not east to see him but west, to Jackson, Michigan. Known as the crossroads of Michigan, Jackson was the seat of Jackson County, located just 35 miles south of Lansing, the state capital.

During the summer of 1881, Sophie sat on the horse block outside the Jackson home of Almon Patterson, a married man in his late 60s, and publicly demanded "hush money" from him. Patterson had made a fortune as a druggist and taken up real-estate investing after retiring from the drug business.

Though it was barely mentioned in the press at the time, Sophie, using the alias Kate Loranger, had played her badger game with Patterson in March 1880 while his wife was out of town. She'd arrived in Jackson claiming, as usual, to be a wealthy woman seeking to buy real estate and snared Patterson in her web, but he refused to pay up.[21] Sophie had become quite angry at this and smashed up some of the furniture and paintings in his house with an ax. Afterward she was charged with attempted blackmail and destruction of property, but because Patterson likely wasn't eager to experience the bad publicity a trial would bring, she was quickly acquitted of the charges.[22]

Because Sophie was distracted by various court hearings and trials related to her extortion efforts in Cincinnati and Boston, along with the attempted murder of George Hendrie in Detroit, it took more than a year for her to return to work on Patterson. But on August 1, 1881, she was back in Jackson, claiming he'd wronged her and owed her money. She made it hard to ignore her because she brought her two younger children, Lottie and Mable, with her.

While Patterson stayed hidden in his house, his wife, Lydia, emerged and told Sophie to get off their horse block. Sophie, who had taken a short break from yelling and was doing needlework at the time, moved to the ground and continued to work on her craft project.

Jackson wasn't a big city like Boston or Detroit, so no one knew quite how to react to the spectacle unfolding on Main Street. Was it a joke, or was the lady serious? Most people politely tried to ignore Sophie. Daniel Hibbard wasn't one of them.

Hibbard was a rugged pioneer of Jackson County who had built up substantial business interests over the course of 45 years and was now one of the wealthiest men in town. All that money couldn't buy him likability, though; his violent temper made him extremely unpopular. Why he decided to intervene isn't known, but he approached Sophie "with abuse and throwing water upon her and her two children from a garden hydrant."[23]

Two men who happened to be passing by tried to stop Hibbard. He responded by intentionally hitting one of them with the nozzle of the water hose. Hibbard then left and returned with a gun and threatened Sophie with it. Undeterred, she managed to grab the gun from him. By this time a crowd had gathered, and they urged her to shoot him, which she did, though the bullet missed his head. Hibbard proceeded to jump into his buggy and drive off. The police arrested Sophie and took her and her traumatized daughters to headquarters, whereupon the authorities returned the children to their home in Detroit.[24]

Due to the sensational nature of the Hendrie shooting mere months earlier, a sharp-eyed reporter for the *Boston Globe* correctly put two and two together when reading an article about the Jackson incident. He realized that the woman's scam sounded like the work of Sophie Lyons. Soon afterward, the *Globe* published a story about Sophie's blackmail adventures in Jackson.[25]

On October 10, 1881, Sophie, under her real name, was bound for trial in Jackson for "murderously assaulting" Hibbard, but she was bailed out of jail and didn't appear for her hearing in November.[26] Instead, she sent word through her attorney that she was too sick to leave her bed, causing the case to be postponed.[27]

As for Hibbard, his bad temper kept him embroiled in scandal. The very next year he tried to shoot his son-in-law, Edwin Smith, over business losses.[28]

Whether Sophie ever got any money out of Patterson remains an open question. Records do show that in 1892, Lydia Patterson sued her husband for divorce after 40 years of marriage, citing infidelity, cruelty, and indecency—with Sophie Lyons listed as the co-respondent in the suit.[29]

Like Mother and Father, Like Son

Ned and Sophie weren't the only members of the Lyons family to face charges in 1881. Sophie's worries about her oldest son, George, falling into bad company came to pass when he was arrested with two other teenage boys in New York on August 29. George and his pals were charged with entering several homes in Manhattan by way of their coal chutes and burglarizing them.[30]

George, who was described in the news as the head of a gang of sneak thieves, was convicted of burglary. In court he acted the tough guy and told the judge he was 17 (though in reality he'd just turned 15). If he'd been truthful about his age he'd have been sent to the House of Refuge and he likely wouldn't have stayed there long.

However, George insisted he wanted to be sent to the state prison rather than Elmira Reformatory, a penal institution for offenders aged 17 to 30 that offered academic classes and vocational training but had indeterminate sentencing. In other words, a prisoner was held at Elmira until the warden decided he had reformed and could be released. "You'd better have me hung, judge," commented George after being sentenced to Elmira anyway.[31]

　　With her husband and son in prison and she herself facing a charge of assault in Jackson, it would have made sense for Sophie to stay on the right side of the law and out of prison for the sake of her four other children. But anyone who expected Sophie to do what was sensible didn't know her very well.

8

A Spy in the House

I reached my hand into his pocket, got a grip on the wallet,
and was about to give the quick snap of the wrist and jostle,
which is part of the pickpocket's technique, when I felt a heavy
hand on my shoulder.
  —Sophie Lyons, *Why Crime Does Not Pay*

During the summer of 1881, a woman named Theresa Lewis showed up at Sophie Lyons' Detroit home and asked whether she had a room to rent to a poor widow.[1] Sophie might have refused, but this particular woman had paid her a kindness during a trying time in her life. The out-of-character choice proved a problematic one.

Weeks earlier, Sophie had been held in jail while doctors hired by the Detroit Police Department examined her to determine whether she was insane.[2] Lewis happened to have visited the jail during the investigation and offered to sit and read the Bible with Sophie. Although Sophie didn't normally rent out rooms (or read the Bible), she decided to let Lewis move in, charging her $4 a month rent and proposing that Lewis could pay the rent amount by doing sewing for Sophie. The woman agreed to the arrangement and moved in. Afterward, Sophie shared stories with Lewis about her criminal background, claiming that she'd reformed for the sake of her children and was now on an honest path in life.[3]

For her part, Lewis was born in 1841, the daughter of a respected Detroit physician named James Curran White and his wife, Therese Beaubien. She married George Lewis in Louisville, Kentucky, in 1866, but he died just seven years later, leaving her with a young son to support.[4]

With her father also deceased, Lewis returned to Detroit and moved in with her sister and brother-in-law, Thomas and Isabelle Kearney.[5] The Kearneys lived in a house on 24th Street, not far from Sophie's home on 23rd Street. The new living situation wasn't a pleasant one, however, because Lewis and Thomas Kearney didn't get along. After a short time, Kearney asked his sister-in-law to move out of his house. She landed on Sophie's doorstep as a result.

The Trial That Captivated Detroit

Lewis' room was in the front of Sophie's home, which meant anyone who needed to get to the back portion had to pass through it. Consequently, over the next few months, Lewis observed a great deal of what she considered to be unusual activity. Sophie was often out of town, and her housekeeper, Sarah Brew, picked up packages at the post office that were addressed to Sarah English or Sarah Smith. Lewis realized that the packages, mailed from various cities in Michigan, Ohio, and Indiana, contained expensive jewelry and watches. In addition to the mysterious mail, men often showed up at odd hours and asked to speak with Sophie. Suspicious, Lewis began taking notes of everything she saw and heard.[6]

After she'd accumulated a fair amount of information, Lewis went to the police station and secured a meeting with Superintendent Andrew Rogers. She told him she had important intelligence related to criminal activity taking place at the home of Sophie Lyons. She also proposed that she could spy on Sophie and bring Rogers evidence of her activities—for a fee. Rogers, who'd known Lewis and her family for years, was sick of dealing with Sophie and her criminal exploits. Though it was an unconventional ar-

Andrew Rogers was chief of the Detroit Police Department when Sophie first moved to the city in the late 1870s. He was forced to resign after she accused him of taking bribes but was later rehired. Detroit Historical Society.

rangement, he agreed to the plan, assigning patrolman Jesse Williams to be Lewis' departmental contact and confirming she would be paid for her work.[7]

During September and October 1881, Lewis gathered evidence, including the discarded wrappings from packages Brew had picked up at the post office, and gave it all to Williams. The Detroit police examined the wrappings, then returned the material to Lewis with instructions to surreptitiously return it where she found it in Sophie's house.

It didn't take long for an experienced operator like Sophie to figure out she had a snitch in her midst. She threw Lewis out, but she didn't stop there. Sophie took an approach to the situation that, if it worked, would allow her to kill two birds—Lewis and Rogers—with one stone.

In mid–November, Sophie lodged a complaint with the police that her ex-tenant, Theresa Lewis, had stolen several hundred dollars' worth of jewelry, furs, and other expensive items from her home. The police searched Lewis' trunks at the Kearney home and found a diamond earring, a fur cloak, and a variety of other items Sophie claimed had been stolen. Lewis was arrested, and Rogers ordered that no one be allowed to speak to Lewis without him present.[8]

The case that captivated Detroit residents opened on December 2, 1881, with Sophie taking the stand as the first witness against Lewis.[9] She explained how she'd met Lewis and then stated confidently that the hat Lewis had on in court was hers and that Lewis had stolen it. She admitted she'd sent hundreds of packages to her housekeeper but insisted she hadn't sent any that contained stolen jewelry or watches. An article that appeared in the *Detroit Free Press* the next day reported some of Sophie's testimony word for word, along with breaks for laughter.

> All the property identified is my property. The opera glass in court is mine. I bought it ten years ago; I swear they are mine. Mrs. Lewis had no glass when she came to my house. I do not identify the watch in court. I lost one, however, while Mrs. Lewis was at my house. I told her of it, but did not accuse her as she was always praying. (Laughter.) She prayed every night, and she persuaded me to do so, but then (shaking her head) I—I—(the remainder of the sentence was lost in laughter). I did not see Mrs. Lewis take a thing. I found my fur coat in Mrs. Lewis' sister's house. It was in a trunk.[10]

Two witnesses testified that Lewis had asked them to loan her $10 in temporary exchange for the diamond earring that Sophie claimed belonged to her. Both refused to loan her any money. Thomas Kearney swore that his sister-in-law had left several trunks at his house. He also stated that he'd asked her to leave his house at least 50 times and that he wasn't on good terms with her, but he admitted that she'd never stolen anything from him.[11]

Evidently Sophie had been allowed by the Kearneys to search Lewis' trunks, which gave her the opportunity to plant some of the items she later claimed Lewis had stolen. Sophie's housekeeper, Sarah Brew, identified the items in evidence that were supposedly stolen by Lewis and said they belonged to her employer.

Superintendent Rogers refused to admit he'd agreed to pay Lewis to gather information about Sophie's activities, but he did inform the court that he'd met with her and told her he "would be very glad to learn any information relative to stolen property."[12] He swore that he hadn't authorized Lewis to steal anything from Sophie's house, but he did admit she'd brought four watches to the police station that she claimed had been in a package picked up at the post office by Brew, along with the packaging. After Lewis returned the watches to Sophie's house, the police found them in local pawnshops. Rogers insisted he'd never seen the other items Sophie claimed Lewis had stolen from her home and Lewis had told him the diamond earring was a gift from her late husband.[13]

Before Lewis took the stand, she and Sophie had a chance meeting outside the courtroom. Sophie, her face covered in the usual veil, came up to Lewis and "laughed in her face and made sneering remarks." Lewis told the crowd that Sophie had "threatened to shoot me and I will report this to the judge."[14] The women then entered a courtroom that was filled to capacity with spectators eager to see more fireworks erupt between them.

The court warned Lewis "not to drag the name of any reputable citizen into the matter as far as it related to Mrs. Lyons' doings."[15] This was evidently done in an effort to keep George Hendrie's name out of the trial. Given that the attempted shooting of Hendrie by Sophie had been resolved just mere months earlier, Hendrie wanted no additional publicity about that event to appear in the press.

Lewis testified that when President James Garfield's funeral procession went through Cleveland, Ohio, in September 1881, Sophie had gone to see her brother, Mollie Matches.[16] This was actually the nickname for John Larney, a former childhood pickpocket in New York City who earned his moniker by disguising himself as a match girl when he stole. Larney was indeed living in Cleveland, and although he and Sophie weren't biologically related, they probably had known each other since their youth.[17]

JOHN LARNEY, alias MOLLIE MATCHES, alias
THOMAS DOLAN, alias GEO. KING.

BANK SNEAK.—White ; nationality Irish ; age 43 years ; height 5 feet 7 inches ; weight 160 pounds ; build stout ; complexion florid ; eyes blue ; hair brown ; beard full and brown ; part of anchor on forearm ; small mark on back of same arm.

JOHN LARNEY.

As he appeared in the Ohio Penitentiary after his hair had been clipped and beard shaved. Was released from the Pen. at Columbus, O., March 14, 1892, after serving a term of four years, for a crime committed in Ashtabula Co. During his stay in the Pen. he made considerable money selling nicknacks made by the prisoners, such as canes, toothpicks and other articles, which he purchased of the makers and sold to visitors. He had a stand at the door leading into the prison from the guard room.

John Larney was better known as Mollie Matches because he pretended to be a matchgirl while working as a child pickpocket in New York. Sophie and Larney later worked together as pickpockets in Ohio in 1881. These engravings were made from photographs of Larney for *Grannan's Pocket Guide to Noted Criminals*.

Lewis also swore that one of the many packages picked up at the post office by Brew was a parcel mailed from Cleveland containing four gold watches. It had been sent to Detroit while Sophie was in Ohio for Garfield's funeral. Lewis described examining the packages' contents and making lists of the identification numbers on the watches for the police. This was how detectives were able to identify the watches when they were later located in pawnshops.

According to Lewis, Robert McKinney, who regularly attended the trial with Sophie, fenced the items Sophie had stolen. According to the *Detroit Free Press*, the 42-year-old McKinney had established a "Tweed-like" ring of criminal operations in Bay City, Michigan, during the Civil War.[18] By 1881 he'd relocated to Detroit and was fencing stolen goods. He also often accompanied Sophie when she left town.[19]

McKinney, however, wasn't Sophie's only criminal friend, as Lewis saw it. She also associated with Edward "Big Ed" Rice and Emanuel

"Minnie" Marks. These men were sneak thieves (robbers who employed distraction and subterfuge rather than explosives or violence) who had stolen $2,080 from the First National Bank in Detroit on June 22, 1881.[20] The day before, Rice and Marks had come to Sophie's house and asked for her help in their scheme.[21] Lewis said she overheard Sophie tell Rice that she was being too closely watched by the police to get involved, but she apparently did something to assist in the crime anyway, because Lewis saw Rice hand Sophie a package of money at the home after the robbery had been committed.[22]

Many Detroit citizens stepped forward and testified as to Lewis' honesty and good character.[23] At least partially as a result, she was found innocent of stealing items from Sophie's home.[24] Superintendent Rogers, however, fared far worse after his latest run-in with Sophie.

Rogers was well regarded in Detroit and had been a city police officer since 1865, but some of Lewis' testimony showed him in a bad light. She claimed that after Rice and Marks left the house, Sophie exclaimed, "Now I have the Chief of Police in my hands. He gets from $250 to $500 on every robbery committed in Detroit."[25] The prosecuting attorney came to Rogers' defense, stating that the only issue was "Did Mrs. Lewis steal the goods? Insinuations have been made by every thief whom Mr. Rogers has sent to prison against his integrity."[26] Nonetheless the damage to Rogers' reputation was done. He resigned from the force before the Lewis trial was even over, telling a *Detroit Free Press* reporter on his way out that "it has always been my aim to serve the public faithfully." (The powers-that-be must have agreed, because Rogers was later rehired.[27])

Turned Tables in Ann Arbor

One of the packages Lewis had shown to the Detroit police came from Ann Arbor, 45 miles west of Detroit. It contained a gold chain and a watch with a number engraved on the back. The police recorded the watch's number and later discovered it matched the number on a watch that had been reported stolen at the county fair in Ann Arbor on October 6, 1881.[28]

Ann Arbor, home to the University of Michigan, was a small city with a population of just over 8,000 people in 1880. The Washtenaw County Fair, held in 1881 on parkland south of the university, gave farmers a place to display their harvest bounty and compete for cash prizes. "There were ninety entries of poultry, about sixty of sheep, 165 of fruit and sixty-five of grain and seeds," reported the *Detroit Free Press*. Oxen, swine, horses, "fat cattle," and steer were also on display, along with flowers, butter, cheeses, and sweetmeats. There was a hot air "balloon ascension," and purses of between $40 and $150 were offered in a variety of horse races. There was even a competition for the prettiest baby.[29] It was the kind of event that offered myriad opportunities for pickpockets.

Cold, rainy weather dogged the fair during its first two days, but on the third day the sun shone and the crowds swelled. Harriet Cornwell, the elderly wife of a wealthy paper-mill owner, attended the fair that Thursday. She was in the Floral Hall when a lady wearing a broad-brimmed hat with a veil stopped and asked her whether she'd dropped her handkerchief. Cornwell wasn't sure but after checking realized she had. The woman kindly offered to find it for her. Cornwell wasn't in good health, and she gladly accepted the offer. The woman asked bystanders to move back so she could locate the hanky. After she found it, she handed it to Cornwell. She then left so quickly that she seemed to have vanished into thin air—Cornwell didn't even get a chance to thank the veiled stranger for her kindness.[30]

It wasn't until later that Cornwell noticed her gold watch and chain were missing. She thought the items might have been stolen at the fair, so she filed a police report. She did not, however, associate the loss with the woman who'd retrieved her handkerchief. That woman was none other than Sophie Lyons.

Sophie was charged with "larceny from the person" for the theft of Cornwell's valuables after the Detroit police notified the police in Ann Arbor that they'd found the watch and chain in a Detroit pawnshop, where it had been pawned by Sophie's fence, Robert McKinney. She was jailed in Ann Arbor, and her trial began at the Washtenaw County Court House in December 1881, shortly after the Lyons-Lewis case finished in Detroit.[31]

In order to obtain a conviction, the prosecutors had to prove that it was Sophie who had stolen Cornwell's watch and chain. Cornwell herself was too ill to attend the trial, so the prosecutors had to verify, using other witnesses, that Sophie had been seen at the fair in Ann Arbor on the day the items were stolen. Some witnesses were certain they'd seen her in Ann Arbor. Others weren't so sure, perhaps because she wore a wig and veil during the trial. Meanwhile, Sophie's attorney, Colonel John Atkinson, found several witnesses who knew her and could testify with confidence that she'd been in Detroit the day the watch and chain were stolen.[32]

According to the prosecutor, when the judge ordered Sophie to show her face to a witness, she "sprang like a panther, tore her wrappings from her head and face and rushed to the witness, thrusting her face close up" to the witness' face. She kept her back to the courtroom and immediately replaced her hat and veil after the witness got a look at her.[33]

This anecdote is but one example of Sophie's volatility in court. At times she cried, asking who would care for her children if she went to prison. Other times she threatened violence against the prosecution's witnesses. She had a sharp tongue and appeared to enjoy using it.[34] One of her favorite recent targets was about to give her even more reason to do so.

Theresa Lewis—the same woman whom Sophie had tried to frame in court weeks before—was now an important prosecutorial witness for the trial in Ann Arbor. Just like Lewis' trial in Detroit, Sophie's trial drew large crowds to the courthouse. Sophie's anger seemed to have reached a fevered pitch in Ann Arbor, and many people hoped to hear Sophie fling insults at Lewis.

When the judge asked the two women to stand next to each other so their heights could be compared, Sophie hurled herself at Lewis and sent her flying across the courtroom. Another day, while the two waited at the station in Detroit for the train to Ann Arbor, Sophie approached Lewis and insisted that the gloves she had on were hers and that Lewis had stolen them. A fight ensued, complete with face scratching and hair pulling. It ended only after the watchman at the depot was finally able to separate the women.[35]

The prosecution prevailed in Ann Arbor. In March 1882, Sophie was convicted of stealing Cornwell's watch and chain and sent to the Detroit House of Correction—only to be released seven months later, thanks to the work of Colonel Atkinson, who'd convinced the Michigan Supreme Court to reverse her conviction. The prosecutor refused to give up, though, and tried her again in Ann Arbor.

Apparently confident she'd be acquitted, Sophie brought her young son, Victor, to the courtroom to hear the jury's verdict. By a vote of eight for guilty and four for acquittal, she was convicted again in February 1883. After the verdict was announced, Sophie melodramatically cried out, "I am not guilty! There is no justice for me in Ann Arbor! My

Sophie was twice incarcerated at the Detroit House of Correction in the early 1880s after being convicted of grand larceny in Ann Arbor, Michigan. Look closely to see the bars on the windows. Library of Congress.

child, you have no mother."[36] Again she was sent to the Detroit House of Correction.[37]

A reporter was allowed to interview Sophie at the prison in May 1883. Now 35, she had recently recovered from a serious illness and undergone a marked change in appearance.

> She is no longer the attractive and rather pretty looking woman she was when walking about the streets of Detroit some months ago. Her complexion is very sallow, her once shapely and well cared for hands have lost their symmetry and look rough and course. A coquettish sparkle of the eyes and a girlish arching of the neck and shrug of the shoulder when greatly pleased at some remark, only remain to remind one of the woman who has occupied a considerable share of the public attention.[38]

When Theresa Lewis' name came up in the conversation, Sophie's response shocked the reporter.

> Every sentence she uttered against her [Lewis] was wormwood and gall. Every muscle of her face and body suddenly grew rigid, her hands became firmly clenched and her frame fairly trembled with suppressed passion and hate. There was not much in the catalogue of ingratitude or of offenses even of a more serious nature that she did not charge upon Mrs. Lewis.[39]

At the mention of her partner, Robert McKinney, Sophie simply sighed and looked down. McKinney had been convicted of receiving stolen property the previous November and was serving his sentence in the state prison in Jackson.[40]

According to Emma Betzing, a matron at the Detroit House of Correction, Sophie was subject to violent fits of temper while she was incarcerated. When she was under the spell of one of these fits, she refused to come out of her cell, sometimes going without food for three or four days at a time. When she was in a better state of mind, she still bickered with the matrons and requested special favors. At one point she turned on all the taps in the bathroom, causing it to flood, and insisted she was confused about how to turn them off.[41]

Atkinson again appealed Sophie's conviction, and once again he was successful: The Michigan Supreme Court overturned Sophie's second conviction in July 1883. With her money nearly exhausted on lawyers' fees and her health poor after two incarcerations, Sophie begged the judge to drop the charges, but he refused—he ordered a third trial of Sophie Lyons in Ann Arbor. It didn't seem to matter to the authorities how much public money was spent to prosecute a relatively minor crime. "It would not be a bad reputation for Washtenaw County that it was a hard one for criminals," reported the *Ann Arbor Courier*.

Sophie's third trial in Ann Arbor was held in March 1884. Three trials on the same charge was a record for her, though it wasn't one she'd ever brag about. Fortunately for her, the third time was the charm. With Colonel Atkinson at the helm of her defense once more, she was finally found not guilty.[42]

The whole ordeal had been incredibly costly, but Sophie did finally escape conviction for the theft of Cornwell's watch and chain. Yet her legal troubles weren't over. She was immediately returned to Detroit, where she was arraigned on charges related to the pickpocketing of four watches in Cleveland during the Garfield funeral. After being bailed out, she attacked her mortal enemy, Theresa Lewis, on the street, an act that landed her right back in jail for assault.[43]

The Ann Arbor trials and incarcerations had taken their toll on Sophie Lyons, both financially and physically. They also harmed her children, who'd played no part in any illegal activities yet ended up paying the highest price of all for their mother's crimes.

9

Lost Children

At last I resolved to write to the institutions where my boy and girl were located and explain that I was unavoidably detained and out of funds, but promising to generously repay them for continuing to care for my children. But I was too late. The newspapers had printed an account of my arrest, and when it reached the ears of the convent and college authorities where my boy and girl were stopping it filled them with indignation to think that a professional thief had the audacity to place her children under their care. So they immediately took steps to get rid of the innocent youngsters, in spite of the fact that I had paid far in advance for their board and tuition.
—Sophie Lyons, *Why Crime Does Not Pay*

While Sophie faced trials in Ann Arbor, her four younger children attended Catholic boarding schools in Canada—far away from the possibility of discovering their mother's criminal activities, or so Sophie thought. Florence, Lottie, and Mable were enrolled at St. Mary's Academy in Windsor. Victor was likely enrolled at Assumption College School, a boys' school associated with St. Mary's that was also located in Windsor. Sophie made occasional visits across the river to see the children, telling them she was an actress and her busy career often took her away from Detroit.[1]

On January 3, 1882, a nun from St. Mary's, Sister Lucile, registered the death of Mable Lyons. The six-year-old had succumbed to scarlet fever on December 30, 1881, after battling it for nearly two weeks. Lucile chose not to the give the registrar the full name of Mable's parent, listing her as "child of _____ Lyons."[2] The St. Mary's nuns had recently read about Sophie's trial in Ann Arbor and hoped to prevent the name of their academy from being associated with such a "notorious woman criminal," as Sophie was described in the press.

Although Sophie never commented on the passing of her youngest daughter, Mable's death may have been partly responsible for her public displays of anger in Ann Arbor. Her outbursts were usually directed at Theresa Lewis, the person she saw as a snake in the grass that spied on her and informed to the police, leading to her arrest and trial. There's no reason to think the outcome of Mable's illness would have been different if Sophie had been free at the time, nonetheless every time she saw Lewis her anger boiled over into a rage.

Florence and Lottie remained at St. Mary's after Mable died—until Sophie was convicted and sent to the Detroit House of Correction, at which point she stopped paying the children's tuition. Her case had received widespread publicity in the press and the parents of other students at the school complained about their children fraternizing with the offspring of a convicted criminal. Florence and Lottie were kicked out of St. Mary's and sent to a Roman Catholic orphan asylum operated by the Sisters of St. Joseph in London, Ontario, about 120 miles northeast of Windsor and Detroit.[3]

Lottie Lyons' Near Escape

Eight-year-old Lottie didn't remain at the orphanage for long. The Doyle family of Essex Centre in Ontario soon adopted the beautiful little girl. When Sophie was released from the Detroit House of Correction in October 1882 and discovered her daughter had been given away to someone else, she was understandably furious. She showed up at John Doyle's house and demanded Lottie be returned to her.

Doyle refused, so Sophie took a leaf out of her blackmail playbook and sat outside the house until he came out and demanded to know why she was still there. She insisted she needed to see Lottie and threatened to hire lawyers and bring a lawsuit against him if she didn't get her daughter back. Doyle fought right back. "Now be reasonable, Mrs. Lyons," he said. "Your little girl is happy here, and she does not like you because you are a bad woman."[4]

Eventually Doyle realized Sophie wasn't going anywhere. He had no choice but to send the child out to see her mother. Sophie asked Lottie if she wanted to give her mother a kiss. "No," she said. "I do not like you, because you are a thief. You are not my mother at all."[5] Without further argument, Sophie bundled Lottie into Doyle's buggy, which was sitting outside the house, and drove off to Windsor with her daughter. Once there, she and Lottie boarded a ferry to Detroit.

Victor Lyons' "Rescue"

Turning her attention next to nine-year-old Victor, Sophie discovered that he was still at his school but was being treated very badly. She arrived and found him dirty and dressed in ragged clothes. When she

The Home for the Friendless was a shelter for homeless women and children in Detroit. Sophie's son Victor lived here in the early 1880s while Sophie was imprisoned at the Detroit House of Correction. Detroit Public Library.

asked the headmaster for an explanation, he said, "You have an amazing assurance to place your good-for-nothing brat among honest children. How dare you give us an assumed name and impose on us in this manner? Get your brat out of here at once, for if honest parents knew your character they would take their children out of school without delay."[6]

Victor was in the courtroom at his mother's second trial in Ann Arbor. After she was convicted he was so upset he began to sob.[7] When she was sent to the Detroit House of Correction for the second time, Victor ended up at the Home for the Friendless, a charitable facility in Detroit for homeless women and children that had been established by the Ladies' Christian Union in 1860.[8]

The ladies running the Home for the Friendless in 1883 were careful about who they accepted, requiring references for admission and turning away "children of depraved habits."[9] However, they sometimes took in the children of inmates at the Detroit House of Correction. Victor Lyons was judged acceptable and admitted to the institution, which was located in a menacing-looking Victorian structure on Warren and Woodward avenues. (The building resembled the Elmira Reformatory, where elder brother George was then living, but on a smaller scale.) According to a history of the place, it was "maintained rather as a preventive of vice than as a reformatory institution," but it nonetheless had the aura of a prison.[10]

Florence Lyons' Fate

Florence was 14 when her mother's legal dilemmas caused her life to change in drastic ways. Separated from her sister by Lottie's adoption, Florence remained at the Canadian orphanage until she turned 15 and was old enough to leave on her own.

Sophie, who wasn't incarcerated at the time, asked Florence to meet her at the Finney Hotel in Detroit. There, she told her oldest daughter that she'd rented some rooms in a boarding house on Fourth Street, near Michigan Avenue, and invited her to move in. Having nowhere else to go, Florence agreed. Not long afterward, Sophie decided to pick a fight. She asked Florence to sweep the rooms while she went on a daylong excursion to Toledo, Ohio, 60 miles southwest of Detroit. Florence tried to sweep the floors, but the landlady stopped her and told her she wasn't allowed to. Later that evening, Sophie returned and became enraged when she saw that the floors were still dirty. She ordered Florence out of the house, backing up her threat with a revolver. Florence begged to stay, at least until morning, but Sophie refused. At just 15 years old, Florence was out on the street.[11]

She wandered around until she found herself in downtown Detroit's Grand Circus Park, a large semicircular urban park that connected the city's theatre and financial districts. There she happened to meet a former schoolmate from St. Mary's, Bertha Robinson, who lived on Adams Street, just east of the park, with her family. Robinson took Florence home, and her mother allowed Florence to move in and work as the family's servant to pay for her room and board.[12]

After Sophie discovered this arrangement, she became violently angry and confronted Mrs. Robinson. An argument ensued, and Florence was forced to leave the Robinsons' home. Fortunately for her, Father Ernest Van Dyke, a priest at Detroit's St. Aloysius Catholic Church who was well liked in the community, intervened on Florence's behalf.[13] With his help she found employment at the House of Good Shepherd, a Catholic charity home for young girls. Florence was given a job there as a domestic in exchange for room and board.[14]

(Somewhat) Paying for Pickpocketing

At this point, Sophie had been in and out of the Detroit House of Correction after being twice convicted of larceny in Ann Arbor. A third trial finally declared her innocent, but her legal troubles were far from over.

Richly attired and wearing a heavy veil, Sophie appeared in the Detroit Police Court in April 1884 for a hearing on the charge that she'd stolen watches while in Cleveland during President Garfield's funeral. As he had in Ann Arbor, Colonel John Atkinson once again represented Sophie.[15]

Mary Sullivan, the ex-wife of Sophie's partner, John "Mollie Matches" Larney, testified that she recognized Sophie when she saw her in Cleveland, even though Sophie had worn a disguise. Sullivan, who'd resumed using her maiden name, claimed that Larney and Sophie worked together as pickpockets in Cleveland and around the country.[16]

One would have expected Larney to testify in his own defense, but he was in prison for an unrelated crime and therefore unavailable. Theresa Lewis, however, did take the stand and told her tale of spying on the inhabitants of Sophie's house and having seen the stolen watches arrive in the mail.[17] The judge determined there was enough evidence to go to trial, and Sophie was arraigned in the Recorder's Court two weeks later. After pleading not guilty, she was granted bail—and then went on the lecture circuit.[18]

Sophie appeared onstage at White's Grand Theater in Detroit wearing what looked like her blue-and-white gingham House of Correction uniform covered by a non-prison-issue black satin apron. The lecture was titled "Her Own Life," and admission was "50, 35, and 25 cts." Sophie spoke for an hour to an audience made up primarily of women. A *Detroit Free Press* reporter observed the presentation.

> Mrs. Lyons talked in a distinct but very much affected manner, endeavoring to point out the evils in the management of most prisons, and numerous causes of crime, which she interspersed with narratives of her own experience in prisons and among prisoners.[19]

The reporter went on to admit that Sophie made some sensible suggestions, including a recommendation that the city fathers hire a paid chaplain for the House of Correction and that a committee of three good men and three good women be appointed to help prisoners adjust to life after release. Unfortunately, by gliding across the stage while speaking in a low, trilling voice, she also came off as amusing. That part of the performance gave the reporter the impression Sophie was trying to portray the ghost in *Hamlet*, which certainly wasn't her intention.[20] Sophie wound up giving several "Her Own Life" lectures, but they weren't well attended, and she soon moved on from her stage work.

Meanwhile, Colonel Atkinson requested and received multiple postponements of the Cleveland pickpocketing trial. This was a smart approach because Lewis, the main witness against his client, was suffering from cancer. Lewis claimed her cancer was the result of the attacks she'd endured from Sophie, all the way up until the disease took her life in May 1886.[21]

The Cleveland pickpocketing case never did go to trial, but that didn't mean things were turning around for Sophie. If anything, they'd gotten worse. Although the year 1886 saw the death of Sophie's mortal enemy, Theresa Lewis, it also marked the death of her oldest child.

George Lyons' Sad End

George Lyons had been living at the Elmira Reformatory in Elmira, New York, since September 22, 1881, when he was found guilty of
grand larceny in New York City. His prison-intake record noted that he'd
had very limited education and "lived by dishonesty" as the leader of a
gang of young criminals. His mental condition was described as "bright
but thoroughly criminal," and his moral condition was listed as "none."
His rearing was "bad," and both of his parents were criminals with long
records.[22]

In 1882, George was interviewed by members of the New York State
Assembly as part of an investigation into possible abuses at the facility.
Although George hadn't been at Elmira long, he had quite the list of griev-
ances, most of which involved the prison warden, Superintendent Zebulon Brockway, who alone got to decide when a prisoner was "reformed"
and ready to be released back into society.[23] When asked about Brock-

Zebulon Brockway (left) was warden at the Elmira Reformatory when Sophie's
eldest son, George Lyons, was sent there in 1881. George later accused Brockway
of using cruel punishment against prison inmates, and authorities in New York
eventually demanded Brockway's resignation from the facility. *Hand Book of the
New York State Reformatory at Elmira* (Elmira, 1906).

way's general manner, George said, "One minute he would laugh at you, and one minute he would kill you; very treacherous."[24]

George had much to say about the Elmira guards as well, none of which was good. He described how he was made to work in the Elmira foundry and said the work was too physically demanding for a person of his size.[25] He claimed he was required to carry a 60-pound ladle full of molten iron but was unable to do so without slopping it on his feet and burning them. When this happened, he was sent to solitary confinement, shackled to the wall, and fed only bread and dirty water for an indefinite period. George went on to complain that the slop buckets reeked because they were not emptied for days at a time and rarely cleaned. He also alleged that one of the guards and Superintendent Brockway had brutally assaulted him.

The 55-year-old warden was a controversial figure in prison administration. He was an advocate of prison reform—including the development of the precursor to the modern parole system—who had briefly run the Detroit House of Correction before taking control of Elmira Reformatory, where he planned to put his ideas into action.[26] Academic classes along with military and vocational training were offered at Elmira, and the institution employed an accountability system in which prisoners were assigned grades one, two, or three, with one being the best, depending on how well they performed their tasks. However, Brockway also had a dark side, at times using techniques that bordered on torture in order to keep uncooperative prisoners under control.

George Lyons absolutely despised Brockway's indeterminate sentencing and grade system and told the State Assembly he would fare better in a "regular" prison. He demanded to be transferred to Auburn Prison, but the legislators neither granted his wish nor relieved Brockway of office. In fact, the warden remained in charge at Elmira until 1900, when his resignation was finally demanded due to concerns about his approach to discipline.[27]

Two years after he testified, Sophie visited George at Elmira. The boy was still determined to get out of the reformatory and insisted his mother get him released. When she told him she didn't have the power to do it, George became abusive toward her, shouting, "God pity me if I ever see you alive again."[28]

His angry words proved prophetic. In December 1885 he was transferred to Auburn Prison.[29] Two months later, on February 2, 1886, George died of typhoid fever.[30] If he'd lived to September of that year, he would finally have completed his five-year sentence and been released.

Neither Sophie nor Ned had the funds to pay for a cemetery plot and burial for their oldest child. Ned was back in state prison for a burglary he'd pulled in Palmer, Massachusetts, and Sophie had just paid a small fortune in attorney fees for her many court hearings, trials, and appeals in Michigan.[31] An Auburn Prison inmate named Jim Brady, who'd befriended George before he died and knew his father, generously offered to pay for the young man's burial expenses so he wouldn't end up in a prison grave. Sophie gratefully accepted Brady's offer, and so George Lyons was buried in Saint Joseph's Cemetery, seven miles south of the prison.[32]

10

In the Rogues' Gallery

A stone once outside its setting usually bears no "earmarks" by which it can be identified. Nothing is so easily hidden nor so imperishable as a diamond, and, as everyone knows, they have an unfailing market.
—Sophie Lyons, *Why Crime Does Not Pay*

By mid–1886, Sophie's personal life was in shambles. Her oldest son was dead, and she was estranged from her oldest daughter. Though she hadn't seen Ned for years and was anxious to be free of him, she no longer had the money to file for divorce. As she'd often done in times of crisis, Sophie did what came naturally: She stole something.

The Crime That Led to the Camera

Sophie set her sights on her long-ago home of New York City. Ostensibly on a visit to Brooklyn to get reacquainted with her sister, Mary; her brother-in-law, William Rohrs; and their four young daughters, Sophie had another, more illegal motive.[1]

On June 2, 1886, the store detective at Koch & Sons on Sixth Avenue stopped a tastefully dressed woman in black attire who appeared quite well off. He told her he'd seen her hide something under her wrap and that he intended to take her upstairs to be searched. As he marched her toward the elevator, she said, "Young man, do you know who I am? You are making a terrible mistake, and you shall suffer for this insult."[2]

When the pair arrived at the elevator, a bolt of silk slipped out from under her cloak. The detective promptly took her to the nearest police station, where she was charged with larceny and transferred to the city jail near lower Manhattan's Five Points slum, a place better known as The Tombs.

The Tombs, shown in 1896, is the colloquial name for the New York Halls of Justice and House of Detention. It was built in 1838 to house the city's courts, police, and detention facilities. This building was torn down and replaced in 1902. Library of Congress.

The woman told authorities she was a 29-year-old dressmaker from Harlem named Kate Wilson, but her deception was short lived.[3] When she appeared in court for trial the following week, a police officer recognized her and spread word of her arrest. New York police inspector Thomas Byrnes and his detectives were positively giddy to learn about the apprehension of notorious thief Sophie Lyons within their territory. Byrnes had even more reason to be joyful: Sophie's arrest provided him with a recent photo of her for his book, *Professional Criminals of America*. For years to come the engravings and drawings published of Sophie would be based on that photo. In it she gazed directly at the camera with a shrewd look in her gray eyes, a smile on her lips, and a bizarre hat on her head. Naturally, the hat had a veil, but it was drawn up to clearly reveal her face.

The photo was part of the New York City Rogues' Gallery, which got its start in 1857 after police began having photos taken of arrested persons and hanging them up inside the central station in lower Manhattan so the public could be wary of these individuals and help keep an eye out for them. According to a *New York Times* article about the gallery published on December 5, 1857, "The culprits of New York, pickpockets, burglars, shoplifters, forgers, and the whole genus of swindlers, owe no debt of gratitude to Monsieur Daguerre." This was a reference to Louis Daguerre, the Frenchman who invented photography in 1839. The piece went on to note how "science is certainly on the side of morality, honesty, and the great family of virtues." In addition to the photo, police did their best to keep a written

record of the person's criminal history, along with their "true name" and all the aliases the individual was known to use. By 1860 most large American police departments had a rogues' gallery.[4]

After she was found guilty of shoplifting the silk, Sophie was sentenced to six months at the penitentiary on Blackwell's Island.[5] She used her connections to pull strings and wound up getting an early release. Her next stop was Philadelphia, where in late October 1886 she was again arrested for shoplifting. The difference here was that she was in the company of a woman going by the name Kate Goodheart, who was also reported to be an experienced thief.[6] (The woman may in fact have been Sophie's old pal Kate Gorman.)

This 1886 image from the New York City Rogues' Gallery is the most well-known photograph of Sophie. It accompanied her biography in New York police inspector Thomas Byrnes' book *Professional Criminals of America.*

Getting arrested was nothing new for Sophie, but she was about to experience a different level of notoriety and recognition thanks to Inspector Byrnes and his soon-to-be-published book. *Professional Criminals of America* was essentially a traveling rogues' gallery. It gave policemen, reporters, and anyone else interested in crime and criminals the opportunity to familiarize themselves with the photos and biographies of the "professionals" Byrnes thought were the most prolific and dangerous in the business. He hoped the book would help officers identify and arrest the pros if they came to their locales. Of course, it also increased his public profile and earned him substantial recognition as a crime fighter—this pleased the ambitious and egotistical Byrnes.

Sophie's St. Louis Sojourn

Byrnes' book paid off for the St. Louis Police Department as early as late February 1887. Two men and a woman had been arrested on suspicion of jewelry theft. The trio had been reported to the police for "calling around at jewelry stores, pricing articles and exhibiting fine diamonds for resetting." Detectives kept an eye out and arrested them the following day near Barr's, a large downtown department store.[7]

On the way to the Four Courts building, where the police department and jail were located, the officers stopped one of the men as he attempted to get rid of his "drop bag," a professional shoplifting tool that made it easier to surreptitiously brush items from store counters into a discreetly hidden repository. This particular drop bag contained laces, handkerchiefs, and gloves. Also found on the trio were four rings from which the gems had been removed.[8]

The thieves told St. Louis police their names were George Moore, Frank Smith, and Rose Devine and everything on them had been purchased legally. Meanwhile, the owners of a local jewelry store from which a $300 pair of diamond earrings had gone missing identified the three as recently having visited their shop, though no evidence indicated the trio had stolen the earrings.[9] Nonetheless, St. Louis police decided to photograph them for the local rogues' gallery.

Unsurprisingly, all three resisted having their likenesses captured, but eventually the police managed to get their photos. They then compared the images to the photos in Byrnes' book. They were pleasantly surprised to discover two of the three individuals inside: Rose Devine was actually Sophie Lyons, and Frank Smith was an alias for Billy Burke.[10] St. Louis authorities held the threesome in jail while they tried to figure out the other man's real name. They also sent wires to other police departments to try to determine whether the criminals were wanted elsewhere.

The Other Billy the Kid

William James "Billy" Burke was born in Massachusetts on March 18, 1858, to Irish immigrant parents.[11] He was a middle child in a family of seven boys and one girl. By the time he was 12 the Burkes had relocated to Chicago.

By 1880 Burke's mother had been widowed and was working as a saloonkeeper in Chicago.[12] All of the children still lived at home with her, and the oldest son, Edwin, helped run the saloon while two of the younger brothers, Charles and Frederick, held positions in the telegraph office. (Burke's brothers' jobs later proved useful to him when he needed access to messages sent by private detectives, such as the Pinkertons.) Billy Burke told the 1880 census taker that he was a "commercial traveler," but by then he was actually making most of his money as a pickpocket and sneak thief.[13] Another brother, John "Fat Man" Burke, claimed he was a plumber but, like Billy, he also worked as a professional criminal.[14]

Although Sophie's fourth husband, Billy Burke, was only 22 when this rogues' gallery photograph was taken in 1880, he was already an accomplished thief. The photograph was published alongside his biography in Thomas Byrnes's *Professional Criminals of America*.

Known in the underworld as Billy the Kid—possibly as a nod to infamous western outlaw William Bonney (real name Henry McCarty), who was well known by that moniker and of a similar age—Burke was a short man with dark brown hair, large gray eyes, small ears, and a ruddy complexion. His round, open face appeared honest, but looks can be deceiving: In fact he was not the least bit trustworthy.

According to Inspector Byrnes, Burke also had India ink tattoos on both hands: a cross near his left thumb and a dot between his right thumb and forefinger. These were likely marks signifying his membership in a criminal gang. Byrnes also noted that by the time Burke was 28 years old he had served three terms in prison.

Burke reportedly worked with "Big Ed" Rice and "Minnie" Marks, the two men Theresa Lewis claimed she'd seen at Sophie's Detroit home shortly before the 1881 robbery of First National Bank. It was rumored that Burke was involved in that robbery, though he was never charged.[15] Regardless, Sophie may have met Burke around this time.

The St. Louis incident in 1887 hadn't found Burke out of jail for long. In the early 1880s he'd been charged with bank robbery in Cohoes, New York, and was suspected of being involved in another bank robbery in Baltimore, Maryland. He was caught and temporarily managed to avoid punishment on the Cohoes charge by jumping bail. After he was rearrested, he escaped from jail. In March 1882 he was arrested again while attempting to rob a bank in Minneapolis, Minnesota, and returned to New York to

FRANK SMITH, alias "BILLY THE KID."

SHOPLIFTER AND BANK SNEAK.—Age 26 years; height 5 ft. 6 in.; weight 150 lbs.; build stout; complexion florid; eyes gray; hair dark brown; features good; red scar in crotch of left hand; American born. Is a partner of the noted Sophie Lyons, and is credited with being the nerviest bank sneak in the country. Has been arrested 100 times. Has done several terms in different penitentiaries.

Billy Burke wore more facial hair as he aged, a characteristic visible in this engraving created for *Grannan's Pocket Guide to Noted Criminals*.

face prosecution for the Cohoes robbery. He was convicted and sentenced to five years in the Penitentiary.[16]

The India ink tattoos Byrnes noted in his book as identifying marks on Burke's hands had been burned off by the time of the St. Louis arrest, which shows how concerned he was about being identified by the book. Only two scars on his hands remained where the tattoos had been.

The (Possible) Reappearance of Sophie's First Husband

The St. Louis police were unable to identify or even find out much about George Moore. Sophie, Burke, and Moore pleaded guilty to vagrancy and associating with thieves. Each paid a $500 fine and was told to leave the city by 8:00 p.m. or face arrest again. On their way out of the courtroom they mischievously thanked the city attorney for his "kindness" in letting them go.[17]

Next on their list of places to rob, or so the St. Louis authorities predicted, was Louisville, Kentucky. The Louisville newspaper published a report on the trio that included physical descriptions and drawings based on their mug shots. Moore was described as follows:

> Aged twenty-eight, five feet and a quarter inches in height, one hundred and forty-five pounds and well built, hazel eyes, black hair and dark complexion, describes George Moore, alias Miller, another noted diamond sneak thief, as generally known as his confederate and pal Smith [referring to Burke].

The article went on to say that Moore liked to dress at the height of fashion and had a penchant for diamonds. It warned that he should be regarded as a "desperate criminal, and would not hesitate at taking life at any time to accomplish his purpose."[18] The use of violence was odd because it normally didn't tally with being a sneak thief.

So who exactly was George Moore? One possibility is that he was actually Morry Harris, Sophie's first husband. The crude drawing of Moore in the Louisville newspaper was actually based on an engraving titled "Moore, alias Levy—Husband of Sophie Lyons" from *Grannan's Pocket Guide of Noted Criminals*. (That drawing, in turn, was likely based on Moore's St. Louis mug shot, a photo that no longer exists.)

Joseph Grannan was Cincinnati's former chief of detectives who, after retiring from the police force, opened his own detective agency. Possibly inspired by Byrnes, Grannan published his pocket guide beginning in the late 1880s. He continued to update it every few years until the early 20th century. Making the book small for a police officer or private detective to carry with him while he was out on the prowl in search of bad guys was a clever idea. It would have made the book more popular than Byrnes' large, heavy tome, which was more suited for use in a police station. Grannan also included beautiful engravings based on mug shots, along with physical descriptions and short criminal bios.[19]

Harris had been known to use the alias Wolf Levy. He was even committed to Sing Sing under that name for attempted burglary in 1898.[20] He may also have used the name Moore as an alias because it was a kind of variation on his given first name. However, Harris was born in the early 1840s and thus quite a bit older than Moore was reported to be in 1887. Of course, lying about one's age to the police was pretty much standard practice for professional criminals.

Whatever name Harris used, it was never clear whether he and Sophie had gotten a divorce, despite her long marriage to second husband Ned Lyons. Whether Sophie took up with her first husband again for the purposes of larceny, and maybe even a rekindling of their early love, will remain an open question. The length of that association appears brief, though. George Moore, whoever he was, was out of the picture after the three colleagues left St. Louis.

Preparing for a Future of Her Own

Perhaps hooking up with an old flame, even briefly, lit a fire under Sophie. When she got back to Detroit, she had cash in her pockets. She hired an attorney. He filed for her divorce from Ned Lyons in the Wayne County Circuit Court on March 30, 1887. According to the lawsuit: "She alleges that during the past eight years Lyons has not provided her with a suitable maintenance, and that during the same period she has been obliged to support herself with the proceeds of her personal labor. She further charges him with desertion."[21]

Refilling her depleted coffers with the "proceeds of her personal labor" had turned out to be more dangerous than Sophie expected, thanks to detectives Byrnes and Grannan and their infernal books. Not to mention the fact that every police department now seemed to have a camera.

Even with a veil concealing her features it was hard to remain anonymous. There was no doubt in her mind that St. Louis authorities were passing her picture around to police departments in other Midwestern cities and that a crude rendition of her likeness would continue to appear in the press.

The time had come for Sophie to go beyond the United States and Canada in search of fresh hunting grounds for crime, but she wouldn't set off alone. She'd embark on this new journey with a man she'd met long ago but hadn't seen in years, due to the long prison term he'd served. They were similar in so many ways—maybe too similar for the partnership to be an enduring one.

11

Queen Meets King

The maids were honest girls and we could not do any business through them, but we followed the party from place to place expecting that some time the girl would forget to take proper care of her satchels, and then our opportunity to steal them would arrive. A few days after Mrs. Lorillard had settled at this hotel she attended some reception in Paris and, of course, her jewelry bags had to be taken from the hotel safe, where they had been placed for safety.
—Sophie Lyons, *Why Crime Does Not Pay*

Back in June 1869, a group of thieves that included Ned Lyons and Jimmy Hope successfully robbed the Ocean Bank in lower Manhattan. The caper was one of the biggest bank heists of the decade. It also happened to be one of the relatively earlier bank robberies that showed the signatures of Jim Brady: intelligent preparation, patience, and attention to detail.

Brady likely met Sophie during the planning stages of the Ocean Bank job. Their next meeting wasn't to be until almost 20 years later. By that point, Brady had become known as the King of the Bank Burglars, and Sophie was considered the Queen of the Underworld. Sophie was also in Brady's debt after he paid for the burial of her eldest son, George, in 1886. Eager to show him her gratitude, Sophie contacted Brady and they agreed to meet once he was released from prison. Sparks flew for the royal couple of crime, though not for long.

Introducing Big Jim Brady

James "Big Jim" Brady was born around 1847 to Irish immigrant parents living in upstate New York.[1] (Note: This James Brady is not the man who eventually became known as Diamond Jim Brady.) When Brady was roughly 17 years old, his father died of disease at a Washington, D.C., hospital while serving in the Civil War.[2] This left the Brady family without a breadwinner and it left Jim an angry young man. He decided life on the wrong side of the law was preferable to earning an honest wage. Shortly after his father's death, he was arrested for highway robbery in the village of Cohoes, New York.[3]

Brady towered over most other men and excelled at preventing police photographers from getting a picture of anything but the top of his "hairless scalp." He didn't manage to avoid written descriptions, however. A vaguely homoerotic one of him appeared in the *Detroit Free Press* in 1890: "He is rated by Inspector Byrnes as second to but few in his line, [and] is really a fine looking man, having the general makeup of a middle aged banker."[4]

Brady loved to use disguises and his natural talents as an actor in his crimes. Suave and sophisticated, he had an uncanny ability to trick people into thinking he was a gentleman. Yet he was also reckless in the face of danger, a trait that landed him in jail and prison more than a few times.

A Professional Thief and Escape Artist

In February 1871 a man dressed as a policeman walked into the Kensington Bank in Philadelphia and told officials there that local law enforcement had uncovered a plot to rob the bank that night. He said he wanted to return after the bank closed and bring more officers with him to assist the night watchmen in catching the thieves. Convinced by the man's story, the bankers told their watchmen to let him in later and cooperate with him.

When the man arrived with two other "policemen," the night watchmen followed orders and let the trio into the bank. Soon afterward both watchmen were overpowered, bound, and gagged. The robbers broke open two of the bank's three safes and made off with about $75,000 in cash and valuables.[5] New York City police inspector Thomas Byrnes and Robert Pinkerton, head of the Pinkerton Detective Agency in New York, believed that the use of disguises and the daring, in-your-face nature of the plot bore the hallmarks of Brady's work, though they weren't able to catch him and convict him of the crime.[6]

Brady's luck ran out later that year after an attempted jewelry theft went awry and landed him in Auburn Prison. Of course, he soon began working on an escape plot with several other convicts. According to Byrnes the plan involved "digging through four feet of solid masonry into an unused water-wheel pit, which adjoined the high stone wall on the outside."[7] It was successful and Brady was on the loose again.

Two years later, a conviction for the burglary of some optical equipment landed Brady back in Auburn, but he soon escaped a second time. A few months afterward, Brady was in New York trying to get rid of some stolen bonds. The trip resulted in a mad chase in which Brady jumped out of a second-story window and was shot in the leg by the officer pursuing him, who then arrested him. Convicted and sent to Sing Sing this time, Brady broke out yet again—it seemed there was no prison in the state of New York that could hold Big Jim for long.[8]

A couple months after escaping Sing Sing, Brady and three accomplices, including Ned Lyons' old accomplice, Jimmy Hope, attempted to rob the First National Bank in Wilmington, Delaware.[9] During the robbery the men took the bank's cashier and his family, who lived nearby, as hostages. Fortunately the family's servants escaped and raised the alarm. All four robbers were captured and convicted, and each was sentenced to 10 years in prison. The thieves were also fined $2,000 and given 50 lashes on the back. Each man took his lashes and went to jail. Each one also escaped after recovering from the flogging.[10]

Brady remained at large until August 1, 1877, when he tried to steal some clothing "under the eyes of the clerk" at a store on Broadway and was arrested. "I will go with you, sir, and you will discover your mistake," he informed the arresting officer.[11] The situation—an experienced criminal shoplifting under a store clerk's nose—was eerily similar to the crime Sophie had been arrested for in Detroit in 1877. But unlike Sophie, Brady didn't go quietly to the jail. He turned and shot at the officer, and the bullet grazed the man's cheek. He then made a mad dash for freedom through the streets of lower Manhattan with several policemen on his heels. During the pursuit, Brady shot and wounded a bystander. He was finally captured, handcuffed, and removed to The Tombs in lower Manhattan.

Realizing a conviction was likely because there had been so many witnesses to the crime, Brady shaved off his beard and managed to find a colleague who was willing to smuggle clothing into the jail for him. He exchanged his fashionable attire for workingman's apparel prior to his arraignment. The disguise was clever, but by then officials had realized they had the notorious Big Jim Brady in custody. Under the alias Oscar D. Peterson, Brady was convicted and sentenced to 11 years at Clinton Prison in Dannemora, New York.[12] He was later transferred to Auburn, where authorities watched him like a hawk—this time there would be no escape from the inescapable prison for Big Jim.

The Royal Couple's Romantic European Crime Spree

On August 11, 1888, Brady was released from prison after serving his full term. Prison had hardened his resolve to lead a life of crime, and when asked for his religion he told an official at Auburn that he was a "Materialist."[13] After reconnecting over her son George's death, he joined Sophie in Europe. Sightseeing—and larceny—were at the top of their list of planned activities.

Sophie and Brady, both talented actors who were adept at the use of disguises, deceived and flattered their way into high society in order to steal jewelry and other valuables. In her memoir, Sophie described the devious method by which she and a partner robbed a wealthy woman they'd met in Paris. Though she was careful not to mention her partner's name, it was probably Brady.

> The maid came out of the apartment with the two bags, and I met her in the hall and began to ask her some trivial question. She stopped to talk with me and laid down the bags. While I kept her engaged in conversation a comrade of mine crept up, substituted another bag for one of the jewelry receptacles and skipped off. I continued to talk a little longer and then the girl and I parted, she going downstairs to the safe with the two bags, not suspecting that I had deliberately held her in conversation while my friend had taken one of the precious bags.
>
> My associate went to another hotel and concealed the jewelry, while I stayed there in my room, not wishing to attract attention by leaving at such a critical time, for, after the robbery was discovered, if it had been found that I had left at the same time it would have been natural for suspicion to be directed at me.[14]

With his long prison stint fresh in his mind, Brady was careful not to be arrested in Europe; Sophie was less so. When a gendarme saw her picking pockets near the Arc de Triomphe in July 1888, Sophie claimed to be Madame DeVarney, a wealthy American lady with no criminal record. She spoke no French but had letters, written in English, which attested to her good reputation. Nonetheless, she was arrested and sent to the notorious prison for women, Saint-Lazare.

Sophie lost no time in getting the word of the arrest of "Madame DeVarney" to the press. American newspapers reported on the shockingly "unfair" confinement of an innocent American lady in a stinking Paris jail. After a week or two of cooling her heels in the medieval prison located in a former hospital for leprosy patients, she was released. Months later the Paris authorities discovered, to their great embarrassment, that they'd had a notorious American criminal in their clutches. Of course, by then Sophie was long gone.[15]

Robert Pinkerton sent a letter to John Shore, superintendent of criminal investigation at Scotland Yard, warning him that two noted and dangerous criminals, Sophie Lyons and Jim Brady, had joined forces and were probably working in London.[16]

According to Pinkerton, Sophie, posing as a wealthy woman unable to leave her carriage, would arrive at a bank and request the cashier come out and speak with her about a matter of great importance. When the cashier left his office, Brady would go into the bank and steal whatever cash was left unattended.

Sophie included a description in her book of how she prepared for her role in the audacious plot.

> First I bought a silver gray wig to cover my chestnut hair. It was a beautiful specimen of the wig-maker's art and cost me sixty-five dollars.
> Then I made up my plump, rosy cheeks to look as pale and wrinkled as an invalid woman's should at the age of seventy and dressed myself in the gloomiest, most expensive widow's weeds I could find.
> A pair of hideous blue goggles and two crutches completed my disguise. The glasses were to hide my bright eyes, whose habit of roaming incessantly from side to side I had an idea often made people suspicious of me; and the crutches were to bear out my story of the paralyzed limbs which made my leaving my carriage except when absolutely necessary out of the question.[17]

Pinkerton told Shore that any bank robberies carried out this way "were almost certainly the work of Sophie Lyons." Unfortunately, Pinkerton's helpful letter arrived too late: Sophie and Brady had already returned to the United States, lured by the potential prospects of a major event happening in Detroit.

A Fair Arrest

The Detroit International Exposition and Fair, inspired by the Philadelphia Centennial Exposition of 1876, opened on September 17, 1889.[18]

This engraving made for *Harper's Weekly* shows an aerial view of the Detroit International Fair and Exposition, which Sophie and her third husband, Jim Brady, worked as pickpockets in 1889. Detroit Historical Society.

Though it ran for just 10 days, it attracted huge crowds—just as Sophie and Brady had expected.

Flush with cash from their European adventures, the couple registered at the Russell House, a leading Detroit hotel, as "George Woods and wife from Chicago." Next the pair headed toward the outskirts of the city to "enjoy" a day at the fair. Yet before they could make it out of downtown, two policemen recognized a heavily veiled Sophie and arrested the pair. The horse-drawn "Black Maria" (patrol wagon) was summoned, and the duo was hauled off to jail. There George Woods was identified as Jim Brady, and Sophie's identity was confirmed.

The police searched Brady's valise and found in it a set of burglar's tools that included good-quality files, a small vise, calipers, candles, and a folding steel rule. On his person Brady had a full set of clothes made of coarse material, which he evidently intended to change into as a disguise before appearing in court.[19]

The police chief had ordered that "all suspicious characters should be arrested and locked up on suspicion until the fair was over," but the circuit court judge released both Brady and Sophie. Without evidence that either party had actually committed a crime, the arrest was in fact illegal.[20]

Brady's Lasting Influence on Sophie

Eager to be where law enforcement wouldn't recognize their faces, the couple fled Detroit for England. While there, a little surprise came along, even though Sophie had just turned 43 and Brady was also in his 40s: Their daughter, Sophia, was born in London on January 28, 1891.

A vicar named Thomas Turner baptized the child of "James Brady, a cotton broker, and Sophia Brady, his wife" on March 3 in the London parish of St. Savior.[21] The couple's residence was listed as 13 Langham Place, which was in the parish of Marylebone in London's West End. (Sophie's decree of divorce from Ned wasn't granted until January 4, 1892, so her marriage to Brady was technically a bigamous one.)

When the 1891 census was taken in England a month later, Sophia Brady, a "lodger" whose occupation was "wife," and her 15-year-old daughter, "scholar" Lotta Belmont, were listed as boarders at 13 Langham Place.[22] Neither Jim Brady nor the infant was counted. Although Sophie used Brady's surname throughout the 1890s, the queen and king had apparently parted company by the time their daughter was born.

Lotta Belmont was Charlotte "Lottie" Lyons, Sophie's daughter with, presumably, Ned Lyons. In 1891, Lottie was in England preparing herself for a career on the stage as an actress and singer. In the late 1890s she would experience brief success as a performer under the stage name Lotta Belmont. The name change was at least partly an effort to disassociate from her notorious parents, but it may also have been inspired by yet another professional criminal, one possibly closer to her mother's heart.

Frederick Bennett or Benner, who was sentenced to Sing Sing under his alias Frank Belmont, was a "New York burglar and pickpocket, having served time in Philadelphia and New York penitentiaries for both offenses."[23] Inspector Byrnes, who included Benner in both editions of his book, went on to note that "he is well known in both cities and considered a clever man." Florence Lyons' copy of *Professional Criminals of America* includes this handwritten notation below Bennett's photo: "cut his throat in court of sessions Jan'y 13/88." In an act of either theater or desperation, Bennett did indeed try to cut his own throat with a razor in the prisoner's

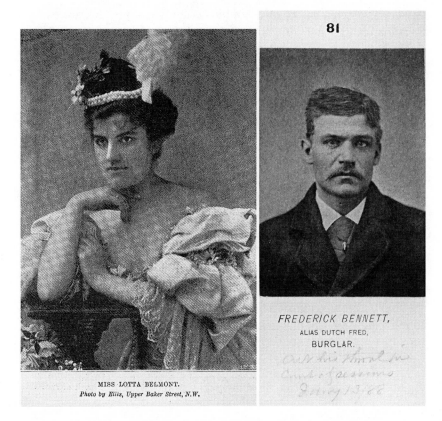

81

FREDERICK BENNETT,
ALIAS DUTCH FRED,
BURGLAR.

MISS LOTTA BELMONT.
Photo by Ellis, Upper Baker Street, N.W.

Charlotte "Lottie" Lyons, Sophie's third daughter, pursued a stage career in London, which is where this professional portrait was taken around 1898. She performed under the stage name Lotta Belmont. Frank Bennett, who went by the alias Frank Belmont, was a New York City-based criminal. Notes about Bennett's attempted suicide in 1888 were added into Florence's copy of the book by hand. Perhaps it was because he was her sister Lottie's real father? He does bear a strong resemblance to Lottie.

pen of a New York courtroom after he was convicted on charges of assault and robbery.[24] He recovered from the injury and was sentenced to a long term (his second) in Sing Sing.[25]

Why the interest in Bennett if he wasn't somehow connected to Sophie and her family? Could it be that while Sophie lived in Canada in the mid–1870s, after her escape from Sing Sing, she made a trip to New York and had a brief fling with the handsome Bennett? Or perhaps he visited Montreal, a well-known hangout for professional thieves at the time. According to Byrnes, Bennett was born in 1853, making him five to six years younger than Sophie. Sophie certainly enjoyed the company of clever, handsome men, and she particularly loved being in the company of younger men as she approached middle age. Did Lottie (or Sophie) pick the surname Belmont for her stage name as a nod to her real father? Answering these questions is impossible, but one thing is certain: Based on their photos, Bennett and Lottie bore a strong resemblance to one another.

Although Sophie and Brady had enjoyed an extremely profitable partnership in Europe, the arrival of little Sophia meant the Queen of the Burglars now had another child to support and educate. Some of her earlier crimes, particularly picking pockets and engaging in sexual blackmail, were a younger woman's games, and she was now middle-aged. Consequently, she left baby Sophia in the care of a nurse in France, with instructions that the child be placed in a French Catholic school when she was a little older.[26] (For her part, Lottie moved to Berlin, Germany, where she continued her musical studies.)[27]

Sophie, pondering new illicit schemes to earn money, returned to Detroit. She kept Big Jim Brady's surname, but after leaving her with a child, he vanished from her life.

12

Take the Money and Run

It was in Mount Sterling, Kentucky, that all this happened. I was there on a perfectly legitimate errand and had no idea that any of my criminal friends were in the vicinity. There was a circus in town that day and the long main street was crowded with sightseers. I had been watching the parade with the rest and was on my way back to the hotel for dinner when I heard some one call my name.
—Sophie Lyons, *Why Crime Does Not Pay*

On a beautiful Friday in May 1892, the citizens of Mt. Sterling, Kentucky, a town 35 miles east of Lexington, gathered along the main drag to watch members of Robinson's Circus proceed down the street. When the parade reached the Trader's Deposit Bank, a woman standing on the sidewalk in front of the bank's large window waved a white handkerchief she held behind her back. A man inside the bank took note of the signal.

As the bank's employees moved to the window to catch a glimpse of the passing parade, the man ducked behind the cashier's desk and swiftly grabbed $4,600 in cash that was sitting atop it. He shoved the bills under his coat and headed to the front door. The sudden movement caught the attention of one of the tellers, who went after the man. The teller grabbed the thief, who dropped the money on the sidewalk just outside the bank door. The teller kept hold of the man while other bank employees summoned the police.[1] No one inside the bank noticed the man's female accomplice. By the time law enforcement arrived, she'd already melted into the shadows of the sunlit day.

The man told police his name was Frank Owings. Another man, who gave his name as W.D. Schley, was found loitering in the bank's vicinity. Schley was arrested on suspicion of being involved in the robbery plot.

A woman calling herself Fanny Owings, who claimed to be Owings' wife, paid a visit to the jail to bring her husband "fruits and dainties,"

SOPHIA LYONS.

Sophie often kept her hair unfashionably short so she could more easily wear a wig as part of a disguise. The 1887 carte de visite rogues' gallery photograph of Sophie and engraving from *Grannan's Pocket Guide to Noted Criminals* (right) show the hairstyle she typically wore. Detectives may have been carrying one of these images when Sophie was arrested in Kentucky. National Portrait Gallery, Smithsonian Institution; gift of Pinkerton's, Inc.

along with fresh clothing. A Louisville newspaper provided a description of her: "The so-called Mrs. Owings is an accomplished woman, speaks several languages fluently and is a smooth person in every way. When brought into the presence of the detectives she attempted to conceal her features so as to prevent recognition."[2]

Unbeknownst to Fanny, detectives from Cincinnati had arrived in Kentucky to assist the local police in identifying the crooks. They quickly figured out that Mr. and Mrs. Owings were really Sophie Lyons and her sneak thief pal Billy Burke. Authorities found $50 in cash and about $2,000 worth of loose diamonds on Sophie, though they couldn't determine whether the gems were stolen.[3] Nonetheless, Sophie was taken into custody as Burke's accomplice. Schley, whose real identity remained unknown, was released for lack of evidence that he'd played a part in the incident.

After spending a month in the small-town jail, Sophie was able to put up her $2,500 bail and was released. At $5,000, Burke's bail was high enough that neither of them was able to raise the cash. Sophie returned for their trial, no doubt because Burke was still in jail. During the trial she was acquitted, but eyewitnesses testified against Burke, and he was found guilty. After being sentenced to three years in prison, Burke lashed out at Sophie, cursing her for her "unfaithfulness."[4] The comment might indicate Sophie was having a relationship with Schley or another man who helped pay her bail but wasn't willing to extend his assistance to Burke. It's clear that Burke felt Sophie had abandoned him.

SOPHIE LYONS, alias ROSE DEVINE.

PROFESSIONAL SHOPLIFTER.—Age 35 years; height 5 ft. 1 in.; weight 140 lbs.; build medium ; complexion dark ; eyes blue ; hair black ; features good ; born in United States ; has a habit of puckering her mouth ; Irish features ; speaks German ; two solid gold teeth in lower jaw ; has done time in the Ohio Pen. Is a partner of Billy Burk.

Another engraving of Sophie from *Grannan's Pocket Guide to Noted Criminals*. The drawing was based on a rogues' gallery photograph that was likely taken in St. Louis, Missouri. The information about Sophie having done time in the Ohio State Penitentiary is incorrect.

Tales of an Attempted London Bank Robbery

Back in March 1890, Burke, under the alias Frank Lackrose, had been arrested in London with two colleagues, William Smith, 39, and Charles Robinson, 41. The three men, who were all described as "professional American criminals," had tried to steal a bag containing £5,000 in coins and notes from the counter of Coutts' Bank by distracting the clerk who'd put the bag on the counter. Burke had lifted the bag from the counter while Smith asked the clerk a question and Robinson acted as a lookout.

The clerk, however, turned his head in time to see Burke pick up the bag, so the expert sneak thief immediately put it back down and apologized, saying he thought it was his bag.[5] The trio left the bank shortly thereafter, but their suspicious behavior was reported to police, who traced them to other banks. Lackrose was arrested along with Smith (whose real name was William Mulcahy) and Robinson. All three were found guilty at the Old Bailey on April 27, 1890, and sentenced to 18 months hard labor. Burke served his term at HM Prison Wormsworth Scrubs in Hammersmith, London.[6]

While she was in Europe in 1888, Sophie informed to the police on a criminal named Eddie Guerin, a friend of Burke's from Chicago. Along with Flash Billy (Guerin's name for Burke) and a man nicknamed Dago Frank, Guerin had pulled a sneak robbery of the Crédit Lyonnais in Lyon, France. According to Guerin's account of the crime in his 1928 memoir, *CRIME: The Autobiography of a Crook*, Sophie claimed she'd come up with the idea for the robbery and was due a cut of the proceeds. She became angry when Guerin refused to share any of the money with her because she'd taken no risks. In retaliation, Sophie threatened to tell the police who'd pulled the heist.[7]

Eddie Guerin, a professional criminal from Chicago, was a friend of Sophie's husband, Billy Burke. Guerin hated Sophie because she turned him in to the French police. He was convicted and sentenced to Devil's Island penal colony, from which he subsequently escaped. Library of Congress.

After Guerin continued to ignore her, she followed through on her threat, giving his and Frank's names to both the Paris police and Scotland Yard. She withheld Burke's name because, according to Guerin, she was smitten with him. Guerin ended up convicted of the crime and was sent to Devil's Island, a penal colony in French Guiana from which he later escaped.[8] Unsurprisingly he bore a grudge against Sophie for the rest of his life.

Burke hadn't been out of the English prison for long when he returned to America and teamed up with his pal, Sophie, to rob the bank in Mt. Sterling. In her memoir, Sophie gave an outlandish, clearly fabricated story about the heist. She claimed she just happened to be there on "honest business" when a bank sneak named Johnny Meany recognized her on the street and told her that a friend needed her help. He claimed that he and Tom Bigelow had taken advantage of the distraction of the circus parade to try to rob the bank. Meany said he'd been able to escape, but Bigelow had been caught, and the locals were about to "lynch the Yankee robber." After delivering this message to Sophie, Meany conveniently disappeared.

Sophie claimed she then arrived at a terrifying scene in which one end of a rope was around Bigelow's neck and the other end was being attached to a tree by some locals. Sophie sprang into action, screaming, "That man is my sweetheart! Don't lynch him—oh, please don't lynch him." She got to him and hung onto him, telling the crowd if they were going to lynch her man they'd have to lynch her too. According to her tale, the sheriff intervened, thanks to her efforts, and the locals cooled off. Instead of being lynched, both of them were hauled to jail. (She didn't explain why they also took her to jail.)

Besides the fact that Sophie's story doesn't match news reports of the crime, Tom Bigelow, a professional criminal from Sophie's New York City days, died in New Orleans in November 1886—nearly a full six years before the events in Mt. Sterling.[9] So although Sophie was many years too late to save her friend's life, the attempted lynching tale made a good story and was also designed to cast the citizens of Mt. Sterling as Southerners in search of a good lynching.

A Newly Single Mom

After a four-year wait, in 1892, Judge Gartner of the Wayne County Circuit Court approved Sophie's divorce from Ned Lyons on the grounds of desertion. During the hearing, Sophie told the judge that she wanted the divorce because Ned had often been abusive, swearing at her and knocking her down. She claimed he'd even threatened her with a revolver and told her he'd give her no financial support unless "she did some of the hustling herself."[10] (Naturally she made no reference to her bigamous marriage to Jim Brady.)

During the hearing, Sophie claimed that she and Ned had only four children. She also incorrectly listed their ages: Florence, 17; Charlotte, 15; George E., 13; and Victor, 12. The truth was that she'd had at least six children during the period she and Ned lived together (though possibly not all were fathered by him) and three of them, including George, were deceased by then. The Lyons children still among the living in 1892 were Florence, 24; Victor, 17; and Charlotte (Lottie), 16. Sophia Brady wasn't Ned's child, and Sophie didn't mention her.

This pattern of lying about her children continued well into the future. Whenever newspaper reporters interviewed her about her life, Sophie gave incorrect information about the names and ages of her children. It's likely she did this because she wanted to keep people from finding the kids and revealing aspects of her criminal past to them.

Immigrant Smuggling and Marriage Scams

Soon after she returned from Kentucky, Sophie became involved in two illicit operations in Detroit. The first was helping to smuggle illegal Chinese immigrants into the city from across the river in Windsor.

The Chinese Exclusion Act, passed in 1882, was a federal law that prohibited the immigration to the United States of skilled and unskilled laborers from China. An unintended effect of the law, which was strengthened and tightened several times in the 1880s, was that it created a market for human trafficking in locations close to American borders and on the coasts. Sophie's participation in the operation, which certainly would have involved payment to her, reportedly originated from a meeting she'd had with "a prominent Chinaman of Chicago."[11] The man was not named, however, he was likely a member of a criminal tong (gang) based in Chicago's Chinatown.

Sophie was evidently desperate enough for cash to get involved in the operation, but given how well known she was to the local police, she was a poor choice to work as a smuggler. After being recognized while boarding a streetcar with a Chinese man in April 1893, Sophie was arrested. No charges were made against her.[12]

She embarked on a new illicit scheme in the fall of 1893, when she began placing ads in newspapers throughout America announcing a "marriage bureau" she'd opened in Detroit. The ads claimed that a young lady had been left a fortune by her father on the condition that she marry a "rural young man."[13] Men interested in being considered as a potential husband for the "young lady" were told to send a letter with their details and contact information. The marriage bureau, like many that popped up during that era when there were more single men than women in rural America, was a scam.

Although she operated the fake marriage bureau out of her home on 23rd Street, Sophie was aware that using the U.S. Postal System to commit mail fraud was a federal crime, so she directed responses to a post office box she'd opened in Windsor. Any man who wrote back was sent a flyer with a somewhat different story than the one in the newspaper, designed to appeal to men of various ages.

This flyer described "the many rich widows and other young women who are pining for the right young man." According to the *Detroit Free Press*, the flyer went on to note: "A second letter follows, which contains three photos, one of which is labeled 'rich widow' who is none other than Sophie herself. There is also a clipping, purporting to be from a newspaper, telling of her elegant apartments and the magnitude of the business."[14] If the man wanted to be considered as a husband for the "rich widow" or "lovely young women," he was told he needed to send $5 to become a member of the bureau. Letters and cash flowed in from all across America from gullible, desperate men taken in by the scam.

Little did these men know they were being sent bogus letters by young women whom Sophie had hired to work for her as "typewriters" (typists). At least one woman who answered Sophie's ad for employment showed up at the house to apply, recognized Sophie, and immediately headed for the door. She went to the police and reported probable illegal activity going on at the house. The police then began to watch Sophie's home and eventually realized she was running a scam operation via the mail. However, because the mail was delivered to Canada, she wasn't actually breaking any U.S. laws. When questioned, Sophie laughed and said she was a law-abiding citizen who had as much right to conduct a matrimonial bureau as anyone else.[15] Detroit authorities hoped alerting the British government would put a stop to Sophie's Canadian operation, but evidently it continued for a while.

One Last Go for Old Times' Sake

In November 1894, Sophie made one last attempt at sexual blackmail, though this time everyone's clothing stayed on. A wholesale merchant from New York had come to Detroit on business and was introduced to Sophie by a business colleague (or perhaps a business enemy). She was described to him as a "cultured" widow and a person of irreproachable character.

After they met, Sophie told the old man she planned to visit New York soon. He was, of course, completely unaware of her history as a blackmailer. Impressed by her intelligence, education, and refinement, he told her he wanted to introduce her to his 25-year-old unmarried daughter.

Sophie arrived in New York, and the merchant's daughter visited her at her hotel, the luxurious Gilsey House, a Second Empire–style building at Broadway and West 29th Street. Just as she'd reeled in the father, Sophie charmed the daughter and struck up a friendship with her. She even became a regular visitor at the pair's home.

One evening while she was visiting, a neighbor called and asked the daughter to join a card game happening next door. Sophie encouraged her to go, saying she was happy to spend time alone with her father. Shortly after the daughter left, Sophie turned to the man and told him to take his hands off of her. Because his hands weren't on her, he was puzzled and wondered whether she had suddenly gone insane. She then informed him that she would tell the servants he'd tried to molest her and threatened to make the allegation of sexual assault public if he didn't immediately write her a check.

Realizing she was serious, the old man agreed and wrote out a check for $20,000 on the condition that she say nothing to his daughter. Sophie agreed, took the check, and left the house. However, before she was able to cash it, she was recognized by a New York detective and arrested. The police contacted the man in order to begin legal proceedings, but he refused to take Sophie to trial due to the notoriety that would inevitably follow.[16] Yet as is wont to happen, the story was leaked to the national newspapers—though without the details of the man's identity.

Embarking on the Road to Reform

Despite her attempt at blackmail, Sophie apparently had reform on her mind as well in November 1894. It was then that she sent a letter to a New York newspaper, complaining about articles that had appeared in various newspapers recounting her criminal career.[17] In the letter, which was published by newspapers nationwide, Sophie made the argument that there were many people engaged in honest professions who had criminal backgrounds. This proved, in her opinion, that criminals were capable of reform. Though she didn't state it outright, the inference was that she had reformed and was leading an honest life.

Sophie also wanted it known that she was legally divorced from Ned Lyons, "the bank burglar," as she called him. She said that she hadn't lived with him for 17 years. By late 1894, Ned had been released from prison in Ohio and was part of a New Jersey gang that sold worthless counterfeit

Ned Lyons.   Sophie Lyons.
[A Notorious Pair of Pennyweightors.]

These drawings of Ned and Sophie Lyons were made for an 1894 newspaper article about their criminal exploits. The press still associated Sophie with Ned even though they were divorced. The item at the top is a dark lantern, a piece of equipment burglars used at night because its sliding shutter could be moved to quickly hide candlelight.

money in an elaborate swindle called a green-goods scam.[18] Sophie understood that if her name continued to be associated with Ned's, it would be hard for her to ever live down her past. Ironically, her letter only rekindled interest in their criminal backgrounds: During the early months of 1895, several articles were published recapping Sophie's life of crime.

Perhaps when Sophie wrote that letter she was also thinking about someone else's reform. Billy Burke would be released from the Kentucky prison the following year. No longer "Billy the Kid," Burke would be 37 years old when he got out, but he was still in his prime. He was smart, appreciated fine clothes, always dressed tastefully, and thoroughly understood how to create the illusion that he was a member of respectable society.

In many ways, Sophie and Burke were like yin and yang: He was sociable, calm, and friendly, whereas Sophie was given to fits of anger and temperamental outbursts. She had forgiven him for his unusual (for him) outburst against her three years prior, when he cursed her at the finish of their Mt. Sterling trial. After all, she understood his anger was due to the fact that he was miserable at the prospect of serving *another* term in prison after having been released from prison in London just a year earlier.

Sophie truly cared for Burke and hoped to keep him close to her. In the future she would devote much of her time, energy, and money to trying to keep him out of prison. But even for someone as clever and devious as Sophie, that often proved to be a losing battle.

13

The Heredity Theory

He took me into a large building which I heard was the police station. He asked a man to let him see some pictures, and when he got the pictures he showed me one of them which he said was you; and he said you were a thief and the police had to keep your picture so they could find you when you stole things.
—Sophie Lyons, *Why Crime Does Not Pay*

News about Sophie Lyons tended to travel quickly. For example, a Louisville newspaper reported in January 1895—just two months after Sophie publicly stated her opinion that criminals were capable of reform—that she had been arrested in St. Louis after detectives recognized her and tailed her to her hotel. A court hearing resulted in no charges against her, but she was told to get out of the city by the end of the day.[1] By that May she was back in New York City, where she was arrested for shoplifting at the R.H. Macy & Co. store on Sixth Avenue.[2]

Word of Sophie's latest entanglements with the law may well have inspired one of her children to take drastic measures.

Setting Sail from the Past

On July 10, 1895, a young man enlisted in the U.S. Navy at League Island in Philadelphia. He told his enlistment officer that his name was Carleton C. Mason; that he was born on May 1, 1872; and that he lived in New York. He was just over five feet, eight inches tall with blue eyes, brown hair, and a fair complexion.[3] He likely didn't realize his father, Ned Lyons, had been arrested in the same location 25 years earlier for trying to rob the safe in the Navy paymaster's office.

When Carleton was actually born—April 4, 1874—his parents named him Victor Emanuel Lyons. As a child of the infamous Ned and Sophie Lyons, he was often abandoned and had to work to support himself from an early age. His mother didn't want him to know she made her living as a professional criminal, so she tried to keep him separated from his siblings, particularly his older sister, Florence, because she feared Florence might divulge family secrets to him.

Victor was deeply ashamed of the surname Lyons and wanted to live down the scandals associated with it. William Somerville, a Detroit police officer who befriended Sophie and her children, took Victor in after he left the Home for the Friendless.[4] While living with the Somerville family, Victor was able to attend the local public school, where he may have been bullied about his family's criminal history. As a teenager, he legally changed his name to Carleton Mason to avoid being associated with his mother and father.[5] He never used the name Victor Lyons again.

Although we can't know for sure that news of his mother's most recent arrests led Carleton to join the military in mid–1895, the timing is certainly interesting. What is clear is that he enlisted for three years as a fireman (similar to an electrician) aboard the USS *New Orleans*. As soon as he set foot on that ship, he was able, at least for a few years, to leave Sophie and her legal problems behind. That was probably easy to do considering the *New Orleans* was involved in several engagements with the enemy in Santiago, Cuba, during the Spanish-American War. Carleton survived the war and reenlisted for another three years.

SOPHIE LYONS'S SON,
Who is a Member of the Olympia's Crew.

Victor Lyons changed his name to Carleton Mason to avoid being associated with his parents. After a difficult childhood, he joined the Navy, serving in the Spanish-American War. This drawing of him accompanied an 1899 *Detroit News* article.

Protecting Burke from a Pittsburgh Prison

Meanwhile, Sophie continued to come to Billy Burke's aid when he fell into police clutches, even though this caused her name to continue to be associated with his.

On December 7, 1895, Burke and Henry "The Swindler" Schindler stole $450 from the counting room of the *Commercial Gazette* newspaper in Pittsburgh, Pennsylvania, before fleeing to Detroit.[6] As soon as Sophie heard about the crime and Burke's involvement in it, she hired two attorneys. They used obscure legal arguments to try to keep Burke and his pal from being extradited back to Pittsburgh, where they faced almost certain conviction.[7] These efforts failed, however, and Burke and Schindler were sent back.

At the Pittsburgh jail, Burke tried Jim Brady's technique of arriving dressed like a gentleman, then shaving his mustache and donning workingman's clothes in order to confuse prosecution witnesses.[8] Unfortunately for Burke, the disguise attempt didn't work. He and Schindler were convicted and sentenced to two and a half years in Pittsburgh's Western Penitentiary.[9]

Raised Suspicions and a Nature-versus-Nurture Debate

While Burke was incarcerated, police and private detectives in large cities continued to target Sophie, often arresting her for flimsy reasons.

On June 21, 1896, detective Mary Plunkett recognized her inside a Sixth Avenue dry-goods store in New York, despite the heavy black veil covering her face. (Big-city stores had recently put aside their sexism and begun hiring women to catch shoplifters, who were themselves usually women.) Plunkett followed Sophie out of the store and shouted, "This woman is the notorious pickpocket, Sophie Lyons, and the police want her."[10] Plunkett tried to stop her and physically struggled with her, but Sophie managed to get away and board a streetcar. Plunkett followed her onto the streetcar and continued to denounce Sophie as a thief until the conductor stopped the car and called for two policemen, who arrested Sophie. Plunkett claimed a customer's pocket was picked a week earlier in her store, and she suspected Sophie as the perpetrator.

Sophie was arraigned as a "suspicious person" at her old haunt, the Jefferson Market Police Court in Greenwich Village, but was discharged when Plunkett didn't show up for the hearing. On her way out of the courtroom, she commented: "It's not a very good way to encourage reform by dragging a woman with a past through the street and pointing her out to onlookers as a notorious thief. I don't want to pose as a martyr, but I do think my arrest was an outrage." She then lifted her veil to show her face to a *Sun* reporter, telling him, "I look like a scarecrow today but I was once considered pretty."[11] Sophie was almost 50 years old. There was no denying that she'd aged substantially since 1886, when the New York City police had last photographed her.

As was often the case, Sophie's tongue was her own worst enemy. Before leaving the courtroom, she informed the reporter that her grandfather was "a cracksman to whom Scotland Yard doffed its cap." Such remarks led authorities to doubt her claims of reform and continue to watch her closely. They also caused journalists to write stories proclaiming Sophie was "a thief by heredity."

She retaliated against this accusation by writing a letter that was published in *The World* newspaper on June 28, 1896. In it she discussed her life growing up in a family of criminals.

I have read the arguments of a number of writers who seek to prove that crime is a hereditary instinct. I cannot, will not, believe it. The mere thought almost drives me crazy. Under different conditions I know I should have been different. Under the present conditions I know that my children are pure, high minded and noble as any human beings possibly can be. The heredity theory is false.[12]

Sophie was in her late 40s and beginning to show her age when this rogues' gallery photograph was taken. National Portrait Gallery, Smithsonian Institution; gift of Pinkerton's, Inc.

In the letter she publicly forgave her father for the unspecified abuses he committed against her. She said she'd recently visited his grave and laid flowers there. "I kissed the ground, not because it was sacred, but because it was the grave of my father. I forgive him now all the injury he ever did to me."[13]

Parental Fates

After getting out of prison, Sophie's father, Jacob, relocated to Catskill, New York, where he ran a grocery store.[14] Around 1883 he moved to Kingston, New York, and operated a "variety store," according to city directories. He may have steered clear of criminal wrongdoing during his later life, but given his history it's possible he ran a fencing operation out of one or both stores.

In 1890, Jacob applied for a disability pension, claiming he suffered from rheumatism, dyspepsia, and diseases of the lungs, liver, and kidneys as a result of his brief military service during the Civil War. Jacob told the doctor examining him as part of the pension-qualification process that he was having trouble urinating and that he'd suffered from gonorrhea as a young man. The doctor described him as "feeble" and determined that Jacob's medical problems, which included senility, were primarily the result of "vicious habits" and old age. Jacob's pension request was approved to the tune of $6 per month. That amount was later increased to $12 a month.[15]

Five years after applying for his military pension, Jacob died in Kingston and was buried in Wiltwyck Cemetery.[16] A Civil War tombstone marks his grave, a memorial to his three months in the New Jersey Infantry.

After Jacob's death, Maria, the woman he'd been living with in Kingston, applied to receive a widow's pension based on his service. Her claim stated that she and Jacob, both widowers, wed in New York in August 1879. Without proof of Maria's marriage to Jacob, the federal government refused to grant her a widow's pension. (It's possible Maria never submitted proof because she was illiterate and didn't understand this requirement: She signed her pension application with an X rather than her signature.) Although we can't be sure they were ever officially married, Jacob and Maria may well have lived together. Regardless, Maria resided in Kingston until February 4, 1899, when she herself passed away.[17] Her household goods were posthumously auctioned off to pay back her many debts.[18]

Based on the information in the pension application, Mary Elkins, the woman who taught Sophie to be a thief, had died by 1879, though her exact date of death is unknown. She may have died at Sing Sing, where she'd been sent to serve a four-year prison term in November 1876. Sophie reminisced acrimoniously about Mary in 1896, stating:

> [I] never knew a mother's caress, never knew what it was to be folded in loving embrace to a mother's breast. Even now I have on my arms scars made [of] a red-hot poker with which my mother sometimes punished me. Never once did I receive a word of encouragement. Every day I was cursed.

Sophie claimed that her early harsh experiences in her family had made her a kinder mother to her own children. She insisted that she never resented "the torture" she was subjected to, and it never occurred to her to run away. When she was arrested during her childhood, her main worry was, supposedly, "Who will be bringing money home to mamma now?" But almost 40 years later the memories of those childhood experiences were still fresh in her mind. "The recollection of my sufferings, my yearnings for sympathy and loving words is [*sic*] as strong to-day as when I was a child."

Daughter Disparities

Saying one thing and doing the opposite was a regular pattern for Sophie. Despite announcing in *The World* that a "great mistake in the rearing of children is to make one the favorite," Sophie's three daughters received very unequal treatment from their mother.

Florence maintained an on-again, off-again relationship with her mother while living in Detroit in the 1890s. Sophie disapproved of Florence working as a nanny or maid for wealthy families because she viewed this menial work as beneath her daughter's talents, training, and ability, yet she wasn't willing to provide financial assistance to ease her burden.[19] In addition to dealing with Sophie's scorn and lack of support, Florence was forced to look for work under an alias, Florence Edwards, so her employers wouldn't realize she was the daughter of the notorious Sophie Lyons.[20] Those who did discover the truth about her parentage usually fired her on the spot.[21]

Despite their differences, Sophie occasionally requested Florence's help, such as when she sent a letter to Pinkerton Detective Agency operative Seymour Beutler following a run-in with him in New Jersey. Beutler was the agency's "camera eye," a detective with an unusually good visual memory who was adept at identifying an individual based on his or her mugshot, even when the person was in disguise.[22] In the snarky 1897 letter, Sophie thanked Beutler for the very courteous "manner in which you insisted upon my leaving New Jersey" and invited him to "make my little house your home" the next time he was in Detroit.[23] Not wanting the Pinkertons to have a sample of her handwriting, she had Florence write the letter for her.

Meanwhile, Lottie was living in Europe and studying to become a professional singer and actress, presumably on her mother's dime.[24] In 1897 she made her first stage appearance at the Prince of Wales Theatre in London under the name Lotta Belmont.[25] Her career went well, and she continued to win small roles for the next several years. Sophie frequently mentioned Lottie in interviews, describing her as an "opera singer."

The same year Lottie made her debut, Sophie took what she claimed was a pleasure trip to London and France. In reality, she was visiting her daughters. In London she took immense pride in seeing Lottie perform, and in Paris she removed her young-

Sophia Brady, later renamed Madeline Belmont, was Sophie's daughter with her third husband, Jim Brady. This drawing made from a photograph that appeared in an 1898 newspaper article shows her as a young child, possibly during her early years living in a French convent. No photographs of Madeline have survived.

est child, six-year-old Sophia Brady, from a French convent school.[26] Sophie soon began referring to Sophia as Madeline Belmont, likely as a way of hiding her identity. In April 1897 the pair sailed back to America on a ship called the *Umbra*. Madeline, who didn't remember her mother, was quite seasick. The confused little girl complained in French, "I don't belong here. I want to go in the garden."[27]

A stop in New York on the way to Detroit led to Sophie's arrest at Trinity Church in Manhattan. Sophie had walked by the church during the funeral of a wealthy citizen and popped her head in for a look at the expensively dressed crowd. She didn't get beyond the door before local law enforcement recognized her and took her to jail. When asked what she meant by going into the church, she replied that she had serious thoughts of reforming—the police were unconvinced. "We can't let you into Trinity with the swells," replied one officer before letting her go.[28]

A (Somewhat) Unexpected Reunion

Might Sophie have intended to pick some wealthy pockets at the church? Perhaps, especially considering the financial difficulties she experienced in the late 1890s. She turned to Billy Burke for aid, even though he'd avoided reuniting with her after being released from Pittsburgh's Western Penitentiary in May 1898.[29]

The month after his release, Sophie wrote to John Ryan, a crooked pal of Burke's, stating that she was seriously ill and in desperate need of cash. She pleaded with him to get a message to Burke: "Ask him to remember the many thousand dollars of my money I sent to him to secure his release in the 20 years of my acquaintance with him, with the exception of one present, $20.00 would cover all I ever received from him." Nor had Sophie forgotten that Burke cursed her in public before he was taken off to prison in Kentucky. "No suffering, no hardship I did not endure for him. A public sneer he made of me, I endured all.... Speak to him before 'tis too late," she begged.[30]

Shortly after Burke was released from prison in Pittsburgh, he paid a visit to William Pinkerton at his office in Chicago. Twelve years Burke's senior, Pinkerton was the eldest son of Allan Pinkerton, the famed detective who founded his eponymous agency in 1850.[31] Pinkerton, who took the reigns of the agency's Chicago office after his father's death in 1884, was said to possess an "instinctive altruism" that allowed him to view crim-

William Pinkerton, head of the Chicago office of the Pinkerton National Detective Agency, shown seated at his desk in 1904. Pinkerton was on friendly terms with Sophie's husband, Billy Burke, and met with Burke at his office. A photograph of Pinkerton's father, Allan Pinkerton, who founded the agency in 1855, hangs on the wall to the right of the chandelier. Library of Congress.

inals as human beings and even to admire the most daring and clever among them.[32] Despite being on opposite sides of the law, the two men were on friendly terms. Checking in with area detectives when he arrived in Detroit or Chicago, the two cities he visited regularly, after serving time in prison was a habit of Burke's. Pinkerton cultivated a relationship with Burke and credited him with helping the agency by sharing information about stolen items over the years of their acquaintance.

The Pinkerton Agency was under contract with certain banks and jewelers throughout the United States to track the whereabouts of professional criminals. Pinkerton suggested to Kidstone, the agency's codename for Burke, that he "go straight." Burke replied that he couldn't because he owed a lot of money to many people and could never earn enough honestly to pay it all back. However, he did promise Pinkerton that he wouldn't rob any of the banks or jewelry companies protected by the agency.

Pinkerton noted in his report on the meeting that Burke "looks considerably thinner than he did years ago. But his memory is clear and his eyes are as bright as a man who never did a days [*sic*] time in prison in his life." He warned that Burke's brother worked in the Western Union office and any messages the agency sent by telegram about Burke or other sneak thieves had to be written in code to avoid the brother sharing the information with Burke. Pinkerton offered Burke $50 to help him get back on his feet, which Burke declined. Instead he took $20, which he promised to repay with the first money he got. Pinkerton predicted, correctly, as it turned out, that Burke would eventually find his way back to Sophie in Detroit.[33]

In July 1899, James McDonnell, chief of detectives for the Detroit police, had Burke arrested. Then he called a meeting and "introduced" Burke to the cashiers and tellers from every bank in the city, telling them: "Burke is a love of Sophie Lyons or her husband, I don't know which. Sophie calls him her lover and I guess that's what he is. Certainly, as long as he remains in this city we will be troubled with such men as Burke."

McDonnell announced that anytime Burke was seen on the street, he'd be arrested. Burke's attorney objected to this plan, saying it was clearly unconstitutional, but McDonnell insisted that this was the policy regarding Burke and nothing would change it.[34]

With a cloud of police surveillance and harassment hanging over their heads, Sophie and Burke took refuge at her cottage on 23rd Street to plan their next move.

14

Transitions

I discarded all my old gowns and had to get additional trunks to hold the new ones. Soon I had accumulated three or four times as much jewelry as I could wear at one time. With the prudence for which I was always famous, I put the surplus rings and brooches in a safe deposit box.
      —Sophie Lyons, *Why Crime Does Not Pay*

At the dawn of the 20th century, Detroit was the 13th largest city in America and still growing rapidly.[1] Electric lights illuminated public buildings, major streets were paved with asphalt, and electric trolleys traversed them. Culturally speaking, Detroit was home to two colleges, an art museum, a public library, and a professional baseball team. It was also on the verge of becoming the manufacturing center for gas-powered automobiles, a new industry that would transform it into America's economic powerhouse. Amid all this change, Sophie Lyons was a constant.

Sophie had lived in Detroit for nearly a quarter of a century. She had owned her house at 23rd and Fort streets for many years and been a witness to the city's development, which included a growing real-estate market. Although Sophie's neighborhood was too far from downtown Detroit to be considered a fashionable place to live, housing construction in the area was increasing, and middle-class residents were moving in. Sophie realized her best bet at benefiting financially from Detroit's growth was to get into real estate.

Apparently Sophie Lyons, the notorious criminal, was contemplating trading in her life of crime for the honest vocations of landlord and real-estate broker. However, purchasing real estate required capital, something Sophie was short on at the time, so she wasn't ready to give up her criminal career just yet.

A Profitable European Crime Spree

In the late summer of 1899, Sophie and her younger lover, Billy Burke, knew they couldn't pull any jobs on their home turf due to the heavy surveillance, so they packed their bags and headed to England and mainland Europe, where they remained for the next year and a half.

The crimes the duo committed overseas during that trip are somewhat shrouded in mystery. Given their proclivities they probably passed themselves off as society people; gained the trust of their intended victims; then stole money and jewelry through a combination of con artistry, Sophie's forte, and sneak thievery, something Burke excelled at. Most of their victims may never have realized who robbed them.

They didn't stay out of trouble, though. The Pinkerton Detective Agency recorded Burke as having been arrested for loitering in a Liver-

WILLIAM BURKE.

280   NOTED CRIMINALS.

FRANK SMITH, alias "BILLY THE KID."

SHOPLIFTER AND BANK SNEAK.—Age 26 years; height, 5 feet 6 inches; weight, 150 pounds; build, stout; complexion, florid; eyes, gray; hair, dark brown; features, good; red scar in crotch of left hand; American born. Is a partner of the noted Sophia Lyons, and is credited with being the nerviest bank sneak in the country. He has been arrested 100 times. Has done time in several different penitentiaries. See other cut of him on page 39.

Billy Burke was known for his love of stylish clothing, attire evident in the rogues' gallery photograph printed in the book *Our Rival the Rascal* (left) and in the engraving based on it that appeared in *Grannan's Pocket Guide to Noted Criminals* (right). Nice clothes and good grooming helped Burke trick people into trusting him.

pool bank in September 1900 and for committing grand larceny in Budapest, Hungary, in October.[2] According to the *Detroit Free Press*, Sophie had been imprisoned in Paris in November 1900. In March 1901 the paper noted that German police had requested the couple's criminal records from American authorities, but it's unlikely they were convicted of anything because they soon returned stateside.

By June 1901, Sophie was back in Detroit with "seven trunks full of grand Parisian gowns and a jewel box choked with diamond rings, brooches and other gems of value."[3] She claimed she had reformed and was now worth $100,000 but she didn't explain where she got her newfound wealth. She told the press she'd had an audience with the pope in Rome in which he'd blessed her and she'd kissed the hems of his robes. "I feel a much better woman now, and the police won't have any trouble with me for awhile anyway," she ironically commented to a reporter.[4]

Despite her boasting she continued to watch her money like a hawk. She wrote a letter to the government pension office in 1902 to inquire about her father's uncollected pension following his death in 1895.[5] It couldn't have amounted to more than $24 or $36, but she insisted that, as his daughter, she had a right to his unclaimed money. The government apparently disagreed and denied her claim.

In July 1901, Sophie paid $10,000 cash for a three-story brick mansion close to her 23rd Street home with plans to lavishly remodel it as her personal residence.[6] She also bought another house in the neighborhood, located at 926 Fort Street, and rented it to a doctor named Thomas Kenning. A dispute quickly arose between them after Sophie claimed that, as part of the rental agreement, she was supposed to have a room for herself in the house. Kenning said he wouldn't allow her in the house under any circumstances because of her nefarious reputation—though renting from a criminal apparently didn't phase him. Kenning won the lawsuit.[7]

Catching Up with the Lyons Children at the Turn of the Century

Florence Lyons, who was in her early 30s, unmarried, and still going by Florence Edwards, also lived in Detroit in the early 1900s.[8] She had been estranged from her mother for several years. In addition to lavish gowns and expensive jewelry, Sophie had brought ten-year-old Madeline back to Detroit from Europe in 1901. Sophie made up with Florence and asked her to return home and help care for her half sister. Florence agreed to the plan so she could get to know Madeline, but things didn't go smoothly.

In testimony she gave under oath years later, Florence recalled this tumultuous period, saying that her mother instructed her to draw a cold bath for Madeline each morning. Florence, who had experience with childcare because she'd worked as a nanny, thought this was cruel, if not downright dangerous, and refused to do it.[9] Sophie became extremely angry with her for defying instructions and blew up, throwing Florence's trunk out on the sidewalk and ordering her to leave the house.[10] There was likely more to the story, though.

The *Cincinnati Enquirer* reported that an unnamed person had informed Madeline of the truth about her mother's criminal past.[11] It would make sense that the unnamed person was Florence. She had seen the emotional upheavals experienced by her younger siblings, Carleton (Victor) and Lottie, when, as children, they learned about Sophie's profession from people outside the family. She likely wanted to break the news to Madeline herself rather than let her hear it from a stranger, but the plan backfired in a major way, causing a rift between Florence and Sophie that lasted for many years.

For her part, Madeline was an extremely bright child. "She's not very pretty. That's her father's fault; but she's sharp, I tell you," Sophie commented to a reporter.[12] Because Sophie didn't want Madeline to hear any other rumors about her criminal past, and since she now had the funds, she enrolled her youngest daughter in a Catholic boarding school in Montreal. Madeline stayed there for a year and a half. Sophie then took her back to Europe, in 1903, and enrolled her in another convent school in Paris.[13,14]

Meanwhile, Carleton moved to Massachusetts after his honorable discharge from the Navy. In 1901 he joined the Masonic Lodge in Charlestown, north of Boston, where he worked for two years as an electrical wireman.[15] According to city directories, he then moved to nearby Malden, Massachusetts, where he ran a billiard and pool hall for the next few years.

What about Lottie, known professionally as Lotta Belmont? Sophie claimed that her daughter was at work as a concert singer in Naples, Italy, between 1899 and 1901.[16] While it's possible that statement was true, there's nothing in the press to back it up. The final press mention of Lottie performing was in November 1898, when she was one of a handful of "well-known Artistes" appearing at a benefit bazaar for British seamen at Grosvenor House in London.[17] A photograph of Lottie, in fancy dress clothing that may have been a costume, appeared in a July 1899 edition of *The Sketch: A Journal of Art and Actuality*, a London-based illustrated weekly focused on arts and high society. Unfortunately no article accompanied the photo, which might have been placed as an ad for the photographer.

Lottie was enumerated on the UK census in March 1901. At that time she lived in a student boarding house on Oakley Street in the Chelsea district of London. Her profession was recorded as "Stage/Art," and several of her seven housemates also had jobs in the theater or in the arts.[18] If her stage career continued after that date, the press no longer took any notice of it.

Burke's Legal Troubles in Detroit

After Sophie dropped off Madeline in Paris, she decided to do some more traveling, journeying to Monte Carlo, Egypt, and the Holy Land. All the while she managed to stay out of police clutches.[19] Burke, who was with Sophie for part of this time, wasn't as lucky: In July 1903 he was arrested for grand larceny in Paris but ultimately wasn't convicted.[20]

In May 1904, Sophie and Burke returned to Detroit from their latest overseas adventures. Police immediately pounced on Burke, arrested him, and told him to leave Detroit on the orders of police superintendent John J. Downey.[21] Burke told the curious press: "I am a property holder here and you have no right to order me out of the city. I want to live here." He also said he was working as a real-estate agent and then cheekily offered to sell the arresting officer a house. According to the *Detroit Free Press*, Burke spoke with a cockney accent upon his return and appeared every bit the dapper little Englishman, complete with full beard. He had also aged considerably since he was last seen in the city.[22]

After Burke was freed from custody, he and Sophie obtained a court order that required Superintendent Downey to show a valid reason for having Burke arrested. The judge refused to hear the order but did tell Downey to stop having his men arrest Burke without cause.

The following month, Burke was arrested for allegedly trying to lure a respectable girl into a house of prostitution. Sophie insisted it was a "put up job," and she was probably correct. She and her ex-policeman pal, William Somerville, paid Burke's $2,000 bail, and he was released. As they left the courtroom, Sophie loudly proclaimed that she was going to clean up the dives in Detroit in order to "show up" the police.[23] The charge against Burke was later dropped.

Accident or Arson?

On the night of April 8, 1905, a fire broke out at Sophie's home. Fortunately, everyone inside was able to escape without injury. The home of one of her neighbors, Juliette Remiatte, was also partially burned.[24] By Sophie's estimate, her house had sustained $2,000 worth of damages (more than $56,000 in 2018 dollars). Sophie also claimed someone had broken into the damaged house after the fire and robbed her of clothing and hats worth $635 (almost $18,000 in 2018 dollars).[25] Her assertions, particularly regarding her personal items, may have been an effort to inflate her losses for insurance purposes.

It's also possible that Sophie herself was responsible for setting the fire. She had a long, contentious relationship with Remiatte's aunt and uncle, Carlos and Juliette Libert. The Liberts were a brother and sister who had lived on 23rd Street for many years. Sophie had once offered them a very low price for their house, but they refused to sell, so she in turn made their lives miserable. She even went so far as to insert a classified newspaper ad offering their home for sale: "A four-room house, with gas and water, beautiful fruit trees, lot 30 by 150 feet."[26] Her asking price for the Liberts' property was $800. Sophie denied that she'd placed the ad, but admitted she couldn't stand the Liberts and accused them of not paying their property taxes.[27]

Marie Petier, Juliette Libert's companion, later testified that Sophie paid neighborhood boys to throw rocks at the Libert home and yell obscenities at them. Petier also said that when the Liberts refused to remove a wooden porch at the rear of their house, Sophie climbed over a fence between her house and the Libert property and chopped down the porch. She described how the Liberts suspected Sophie of setting fire to her own home several times, along with setting fires that had broken out in their home over the years. In addition, Petier stated that Sophie could be "peaceful and friendly" one minute, then suddenly her personality would change and she'd become "angry and violent." Other area residents testified that Sophie's rapid personality shifts, along with the vendettas she carried against neighbors, including the Liberts, caused many in the community to fear and shun her.[28]

As the year 1905 drew to a close, Sophie and Burke headed back to Europe for some rest and relaxation. As it turned out, Sophie needed this vacation because the next few years would prove tumultuous ones for her, both personally and professionally.

15

Speaking Through the Press

The stealings of a clever "sneak" often run as high as $100,000 in a single year. But what benefit does he get out of this easily acquired wealth! It invariably goes as easily as it comes, and, after a few months, he is as badly in need of money as he was before. I can count on the fingers of one hand the "sneaks" who are getting any real happiness out of life—and they are all men and women who, like myself, have seen the error of their ways and reformed.
—Sophie Lyons, *Why Crime Does Not Pay*

On a warm day in August 1908, Bertha O'Brien, a reporter for the *Detroit Free Press*, was granted an interview with Sophie Lyons. The two women sat together under the trees outside of Sophie's house at Fort and 23rd streets.

Sophie "wore a skirt of brown Panama cloth with low heeled brown shoes, a simple white shirt waist and a short black silk coat with a large lace collar. Long white cotton gloves were drawn up to her elbows. Her hair, half grey, was 'done' in a soft pompadour." According to O'Brien, Sophie had a timeless quality because she "couldn't afford to grow old." Her face, which was "becomingly plump," was attractive, and her voice had "unusual modulations that are not unmusical."

O'Brien, who found Sophie to be a fascinating interview subject, didn't ask questions so much as listen while she opined about life, love, and her criminal past. Completely charmed, the reporter described Sophie as a "genius in her special sphere."[1]

A Ruse to Reach Burke

Much of the interview revolved around Billy Burke, who had been in prison since the previous October. He had tried to sneak off with $5,000 from a U.S. Treasury office in Philadelphia while a buddy, Charles Watkins, distracted the clerks. The pair was spotted during the robbery and fled without the cash, but police officers chased them. Although he'd been wiry and quick on his feet in his youth, Burke was now 50 years old and had a game leg, a lingering injury from a fall during a bank robbery in Toledo, Ohio. He'd also gained a lot of weight over the years. Needless to say, both men were quickly captured.

Because Burke hadn't done much criminal work in Philadelphia, the police didn't recognize him at first, and Watkins had only a minor record as a pickpocket. They gave the police aliases, hoping to be released swiftly. However, the authorities in Philadelphia identified Burke by a rogues' gallery photo received from the New York City Police Department.[2] More and more law-enforcement officials were relying on mug shots, along with a new identification technology called fingerprints, to recognize individuals they'd arrested. Burke learned this the hard way.

When Sophie heard about Burke's arrest, she was furious: "And he only got $5,000 and then was pinched? And me in debt for $31,000 now and him getting pinched for $5,000! I'll trounce the stuffing out of him when I get him."[3]

She probably assumed he would manage to avoid a conviction—just not with any help from her. This time Sophie didn't hire an expensive attorney to keep Burke out of prison. Nor did she rush to Philadelphia to console him.

Burke was ultimately found guilty of the attempted robbery and received a two-part punishment: a $500 fine and a three-and-a-half-year sentence at the Eastern State Penitentiary.[4] Built in 1829, Eastern State was one of the oldest prisons in the United States. A castle-like fortress located east of the Schuylkill River, in the heart of Philadelphia, Eastern State was originally considered revolutionary because its layout lacked any communal spaces and kept inmates in solitary confinement. The design was meant to assist inmates' rehabilitation by allowing each prisoner time to reflect on his crime and, presumably, see the error of his ways.

Prisoners spent 23 hours a day in their cells. Each prisoner took meals in his cell and was allowed a single hour each day for exercise in an individual area enclosed by a high wall so he couldn't see the other prisoners. On the positive side, Eastern State was the first prison to have faucets with running water set above flush toilets in each cell, plus hot water that ran through pipes and kept cells heated, to some extent, in the winter.

Nonetheless, the enforced isolation took a heavy toll on the psyches of many Eastern State inmates. For a man as sociable as Burke, enduring a sentence there was likely especially difficult.

By the time Sophie spoke with O'Brien, her attitude toward Burke had changed.

> Billy Burke is my husband, my lover, my pal. He's a great man. None of your little weaklings afraid of his own shadow. He's the kind of man who does things and stirs up people. Most men never do anything—they just talk and blab a lot. Billy Burke does things. He went down to Philadelphia and put his hand down into the treasury for $100,000. He failed. Well if I had been with him he wouldn't have failed. I don't fail. He won't next time, either. Next time I'll be with him and we'll accomplish what we set out to do. Mark my words we will. They needn't pity me for being his wife. Nothing enrages me so much. I'm proud of him and I love him. Don't let them make excuses for him.
>
> Billy Burke has no faults. He is perfect. Why we've known each other for 27 years and we've been pals all that time. Why shouldn't I love him and be loyal to him. True, he loves pretty women and every new one he sees, he's after. But what of that? Isn't that perfectly natural? And I love him for it. But do you know what the test of a man's heart is? Why his pocket book.[5]

Given that Burke had spent his entire adult life as a criminal, much of it in prison, Sophie's observations about his supposed greatness were peculiar. Even more astonishing was her public admission that Burke fooled around with other women and that she was not simply okay with the situation but she even loved him for his infidelities. Never before had Sophie Lyons shown *any* inclination to be generous with someone who took what she felt to be hers or who crossed her in any way. Perhaps she realized she had to tolerate his cheating so he'd return to her after he was released from prison, but to say she loved the idea of him being with other women was far-fetched.

Although Sophie generally loved the limelight and often courted news reporters for interviews, the timing of her open-ended interview with O'Brien may have been more of a way to get a message to Burke in prison, letting him know that she regretted the angry words she'd said about him shortly after his arrest and that she desperately wanted him back. She went on to describe to O'Brien the many gifts of jewelry and fine clothing Burke had given her, which she interpreted as a testimonial of his great love for her. What Sophie actually exposed by sharing that she equated the extent of his love to the monetary value of his gifts was a bleak, insecure side of her personality.

Surprising Revelations

One of the most surprising aspects of the interview was the revelation that Sophie didn't consider her days as a criminal to be behind her, despite the fact that she'd been trying for several years to give Detroiters the impression she was earning her living as a landlord and generally leading an honest life. Apparently after Burke was out of prison, Sophie saw them on the road together, pulling more cons and sneaks.

She told O'Brien she would turn 60 later in 1908, though she'd understated her age by a year (which was minor compared to her usual standards). She also overstated the age difference between herself and Burke as 18 years (it was actually 11).

Additionally, Sophie disclosed that she was writing a book. "Not a cheap trashy book, but a book people won't be ashamed to have on their drawing room tables." Despite dropping this news, she refused to reveal what the book was about.

The interview ended with O'Brien asking, "Who would have dreamed to see her that this was Sophie Lyons of world-wide and dubious celebrity?" Who indeed?

Mother versus Daughter

Six months after her conversation with Bertha O'Brien was published, Sophie and her eldest daughter, Florence, were in the middle of a highly public argument that the Detroit newspapers reported about with relish.[6] It all started when 40-year-old Florence, described by the paper as "a pretty brunette slightly above medium height," and her four-year-old daughter, Esther, found themselves in dire straits.

In September 1903, Florence married Joseph Bauer, a man 14 years her junior who turned out to be an abusive alcoholic. Despite their only daughter being born in September 1904, Bauer was unable to hold down a job. The final straw for the marriage came when Florence's brother, Carleton, paid a visit to Detroit. Carleton had decided to move from Massachusetts to Seattle, Washington, where he planned to seek work as an electrician. He stopped in Detroit to see his mother and sister on his journey west. Bauer, who knew nothing of Florence's family background, thought Carleton was an old flame of his wife's and accused them of being lovers. Florence broke down and told him the truth: Carleton was her brother, and he'd originally been named Victor Lyons. She was also forced to admit that her parents were the notorious criminals Ned and Sophie Lyons.

The truth about her family made Bauer even angrier than when he thought his wife was simply cheating on him. He attacked Florence, breaking her right arm and leaving her face bruised and bloody.[7] Sophie insisted that her daughter had let "a man decorate her face and break her arm." She also told the press that Florence had married Bauer without her knowledge or consent.[8] Apparently Sophie felt that because 35-year-old Florence hadn't asked her permission to marry, her daughter had gotten no less than what she deserved from her husband.

In July 1907, Florence moved out with her daughter and filed for divorce from Bauer.[9] To further distance herself from him, she changed the spelling of her and Esther's surname to "Bower." With her injured arm Florence struggled to find work, and when she did find a job, sometimes her employer would discover she was the daughter of Sophie Lyons and she'd be fired.[10] A local florist eventually took pity on her and allowed her and Esther to stay in his barn. The barn was

Daughter of Florence Lyons Bauer, and alleged grandchild of Sophie Lyons. It was to support this little one that the mother turned a hand organ in the streets of Detroit.

Sophie had only one grandchild: Esther Bauer, Florence's daughter. This photograph from a 1908 *Detroit News* article shows Esther as a little girl, prior to when the spelling of her surname was changed to Bower.

tolerable in the summer, but as the Michigan winter drew near Florence knew she had to find better lodgings.

The only source of parental support Florence had left was her mother. Ned Lyons had been kicked out of Toronto, Ontario, in February 1906, after he tried to pull a green goods scam and got caught.[11] The then-67-year-old was described in the press as being broke and "a physical wreck."[12] But asking her father for help wasn't an option. Later that same year the once-famous bank robber died in obscurity in the charity ward of a New York City hospital. Apparently none of his family mourned his passing, because his body went uncollected and he was buried in a potter's field.[13]

One day in November 1908, Sophie, dressed in silks and diamonds, passed by Florence, who was playing a hand organ near the public library in downtown Detroit while wearing clothes befitting a beggar.[14] Instead of embracing her daughter, who had clearly fallen on extremely hard times, Sophie turned to her companion, pointed to Florence, and said, "That woman is a fake."

Florence begged for her mother's forgiveness, but Sophie wasn't in the mood to be merciful or even logical.[15] "If that perfumed vagrant can prove that she is my child after my death, she is entitled to the sum of $5.75 under my will—$5 allowed by law, and 75 cents my free legacy," Sophie commented to a reporter at the *Detroit Free Press*.[16]

The Detroit News reported that Sophie was willing to acknowledge Florence as her daughter but she deeply regretted having spent money on her education. Sophie extended this sentiment to Lottie and Madeline too. "I should have had my daughters taught to wash dishes, sew and do housework, instead of sending them to the best schools and convents in this country and Europe," she remarked to the reporter.[17] This was a major turn-around from the past, when Sophie proudly discussed her younger daughters' academic and artistic accomplishments.

Much of Sophie's anger at Florence still stemmed from the fact that she told her siblings about their mother's criminal past.[18] In Sophie's mind this was an unforgivable sin.

Florence wrote several times to her mother, but her letters were returned unopened. She tried to visit Sophie's home more than once, but Sophie turned her away. On one of those visits, Sophie stuck her head out of the window and shouted at Florence, who was a practicing Catholic, "Go string your rosary."[19]

Before he was sent to prison in Philadelphia, even Billy Burke tried to intervene on Florence's behalf. He implored Sophie to see reason and help her daughter, if for no other reason than to ease the suffering of her innocent grandchild—Sophie ignored him.[20]

In desperation, Florence wrote to her mother one final time, begging for forgiveness and reconciliation.

> In my hour of poverty, suffering and sorrow I have asked you to speak one kind word to me, and when I went to see you, you told me to go away and I went, did I not, Mother? Dear, you have never cared for me. My life you blighted when I was only a child. My road was rocky and hard to bear. In silence and in humble resignation I bore it. I bowed my head to it all. You despise me. Why? Because I am poor and ragged, but beneath these rags beats a human heart, which you have broken with untold unkindness.
>
> Money, houses, diamonds, don't make happiness mother. Health, contentment, is God's greatest blessing. Mother I am a hard working woman and have always led a good life. You have no reason to be ashamed of me.[21]

Sophie's reply was harsh and uncompromising.

> This is a very different letter from the one you wrote me when you were at the House of Good Shepherd. Have you forgotten the time you told your little sister her mother was a thief, you good-for-nothing hypocrite. The drunken teamster and [his] offspring shall never be recognized.[22]

In a postscript to the letter, Sophie suggested Florence share it with the press, which she did. Yet as the argument between the two women continued unresolved, the public's interest waned, and the once-intriguing saga faded from the news.

Fallout from the Feud

Sophie remained estranged from the only blood relations she had in Detroit: her daughter and granddaughter. She claimed she was planning to write her memoirs and insisted she wasn't lonely. She consoled herself with her books and the companionship of her dog, Tinker Burke, a Saint Bernard she'd brought home from Berne, Switzerland. She claimed that her love for her dog proved she wasn't "brutal."[23] (Ironically, the dog later attacked Sophie and had to be put down.[24])

Another interesting detail to arise from the mother-daughter feud was an admission from Sophie that she wasn't *actually* married to Burke because he already had a wife: "She [Florence] once told me that she wouldn't marry another woman's husband. Well the only marriage I recognize is the bond of love and affection. They are the only ties that the divorce court cannot sever. Billy has given me $100,000 worth of diamonds and he's got a mortgage on me."[25] Multiple sources do seem to back this up. New York police inspector Thomas Byrnes described Burke as "married" in the biography he wrote of the thief for his 1886 book. Additionally, when Burke was an inmate at Wormwood Scrubs in London, he was listed on the 1891 English census as a married man.[26] Unfortunately the name of Burke's first wife remains a mystery.

Before the animosity between mother and daughter faded from the public eye, the *Detroit Free Press* noted that Florence was the daughter who most resembled her mother. Florence even ended one of her letters to Sophie with a desperate plea: "Do not cast me aside. Some day maybe you will have to call me back. With love. From your devoted child, Florence Bower."[27]

In the end Florence's words would turn out to be prophetic.

16

Marriage and Memoirs

Loyalty to his comrades is another trait found in almost every professional criminal. "Honor among thieves" is a phrase commonly used, but few realize upon what a strong foundation it rests. I know of innumerable instances where criminals risked their own liberty and even their lives in order to assist a comrade in danger.
—Sophie Lyons, *Why Crime Does Not Pay*

On a freezing day near the end of February 1910, a reporter from the *Detroit Free Press* made his way past piles of snow on the sidewalk and approached the house at 42 23rd Street. He knocked at the door and waited. A short, portly, middle-aged man opened the door. The reporter asked to speak to the owner of the home, Sophie Lyons. The man told the reporter that Mrs. Lyons was unavailable. The reporter asked the man whether the rumor that Billy Burke was out of prison and back in Detroit was true. The man stated flatly that the rumor wasn't true and that Burke was definitely still in prison.

The way the resulting newspaper story was reported made it clear that the man who answered the door was presumed to be Billy Burke, though during the face-to-face interaction both sides played their own games of pretend: Burke pretended not to be himself, and the reporter tactfully pretended not to recognize him.[1]

Old Habits and New Changes

Burke had recently been released from the Eastern State Penitentiary in Philadelphia. After he arrived in Detroit, he paid a visit to a local police station to chat with a detective. In this case, he told the detective he was very glad to be out of Eastern State, where he'd been put to work in a chair factory. Burke said he much preferred his freedom in Detroit to making chairs for the state of Pennsylvania. He also claimed his arrest in Philadelphia was a "fluke" that shouldn't have happened.

After years living together as husband and wife, Burke and Sophie made a trip to Windsor and finally—officially—tied the knot just days after he got back. Burke was listed on the marriage record, which was dated February 12, 1910, as a 54-year-old Roman Catholic who worked as a real-estate agent and whose usual residence was Toledo, Ohio. Sophie was listed as a "Jewess," age 55, who also resided in Toledo. She said her mother's name was Rachel Levay and her father's was Jacob Von Elkan.[2] In reality, Burke was 51, and Sophie was 62.

Sophie's Controversial Investments

Sophie had not sat idle while Burke was in prison. Rather, she'd spent her time buying more real estate in Detroit. By 1908 she estimated that she owned $80,000 worth of property in the vicinity of Fort and 23rd streets.[3] She supposedly spent much of her time renovating her properties, but she also devoted at least some of her energy to riling up her neighbors.

Against the objections of the neighborhood's white residents, Sophie announced her plan to lease her 22nd Street property to Mary E. McCoy, a formerly enslaved woman who'd been born in an Underground Railroad station in 1846. She was the wife

Mary McCoy was an African American philanthropist in Detroit. She opened a shelter for black orphans in a house Sophie rented to her in 1909. Sophie's white neighbors objected to the rental, but a judge ruled that it was legal.

of the renowned African American engineer and inventor Elijah J. McCoy, and she'd earned a reputation in Detroit as a compassionate philanthropist and a staunch advocate for the rights of African American women and children in Jim Crow–era Detroit.[4] McCoy planned to use the house as a shelter for African American women and children.

Many of the white neighbors objected to having a "negro charity" in the area and took Sophie to court over it. They cloaked their racist objections to the lease with arguments that the house was too small, that it would bring too many children to the neighborhood, and that property values would fall. The judge who heard the case was more candid. He agreed that "the coming of negro residents might cause depreciation in the value of property," but he ruled that there was no law against it. Sophie won the battle.[5]

The McCoy Home for Colored Children opened on the property in 1909, and by 1910 it had 24 residents.[6] The establishment provided shelter to homeless black women and children, some of them orphans, and gave residents with small children the ability to work while their children were safely cared for at the home. McCoy, who served as the home's first matron, was beloved by the city's black community, even after her tragic death in a car accident in 1923.

Sophie's motivation in leasing the house to McCoy's charity may have been partly inspired by goodwill (though she was collecting rent on the property), but she also voiced her own racist sentiments and basked in the anger of her white neighbors. She claimed they were jealous of the fact that most of the houses she owned were rented.[7] She also told one of the neighbors who took her to court that after the orphanage opened there would be "20–30 pickaninnies" (a racial slur for a black child) sitting on the fence laughing at him.[8]

A Pinkerton Visit and Swedish Adventures

Burke didn't hang around Detroit enjoying wedded bliss for long. By December 1910 he was in Chicago, where he dropped by the offices of the Pinkerton Detective Agency to say hello to William Pinkerton.

Pinkerton wasn't sure what Burke had up his sleeve, but he was certain that he hadn't given up being a sneak thief. In spite of their friendship, after Burke left the office, Pinkerton drafted a letter to send to other offices in the company.

Yesterday I met in this city with William Burke, alias "Billy" Burke, alias "Billy the Kid," bank sneak and all around crook. I do not know whether Burke is out with a mob at the present time or not, but thought it advisable to send out an all office letter for the benefit of our offices only, describing this man as he looks now. There are pictures of him in all the [rogues'] galleries. He is now 53 years of age, stout build, florid complexion, brown hair, slightly mixed with gray, gray mustache, closely cropped chin beard, rather on the Van Dyke order; no beard on the side of the face. He looks like a prosperous saloon keeper or wholesale liquor man and would readily pass for a business man to anybody who sees him. He is very stout and heavy in his build, and, while his height is only about 5 feet 5 inches, he really weighs about 175 pounds, neatly dressed in dark clothes, wearing a brown flat top telescope hat, loose dark overcoat with very large pockets on the side.[9]

Burke struck again on July 22, 1911. That day he was arrested in Stockholm, Sweden, alongside Alfred "Frenchie" Duprey, a thief from Montreal, for "sneaking" 31,000 kronur (at the time worth about $8,000 in U.S. dollars) from a Stockholm bank. Authorities discovered another 11,000 stolen kronur in Burke's possession when they arrested him. He'd apparently employed a walking stick outfitted with pincers on the bottom to grab the money through a bank cage.[10] As it turns out, Burke wasn't in Sweden just to pull heists—he was busy entertaining himself in the company of a woman who was *not* his new wife.

When news of Burke's arrest reached Detroit, a *Free Press* reporter was sent to interview Sophie. In an age when sex was almost never discussed in the media (or anyplace else, for that matter), she gave him some choice quotes for his article, which was printed on the front page:

This talk about my Billy being arrested in Sweden, in company with another woman, does not disturb me in the slightest. My ideas of love and family devotion may differ widely from those which other people hold, but I firmly believe every man should have two or three affinities.

What is an affinity, anyway? It is only a passion, a temporary infatuation. And I think that a man can be just as good a husband and family man if he does lavish a little affection on other ladies occasionally. After all, there are several Billie Burkes and there may be several Mrs. Billie Burkes, but there is only one Sophie Lyons.[11]

After making these curious remarks, Sophie launched into her usual lecture about how she and Burke had been "chums" for years, and she exclaimed about what a "great man" he was. She said she had planned to go to Sweden to see for herself whether it was "her Billy" who was in jail there, but her doctor had advised her not to travel. She ended the interview by stating that Burke had recently sent her $500 from Chicago, telling her to buy a new dress and hat with the money, but instead she'd done the responsible thing and paid her property taxes.

Burke and Duprey were found guilty of the bank robbery and imprisoned in Långholmen Central Prison on Långholmen Island near
Stockholm. Sophie sailed to Europe in February 1912 to try to see Burke,
but she wasn't allowed to enter the prison.[12] Rather than waste the trip,
Sophie visited some of the large stores in Stockholm that sold jewelry,
furs, and other luxury goods. She spent a lot of time looking at things and
asking questions (likely in German, her native tongue, which she spoke
fluently), though she didn't buy anything.

Meanwhile, Swedish police suspected there were American criminals on their turf researching opportunities to exploit during the up-
coming Summer Olympics in Stockholm. Sophie's behavior caught their
attention, because they believed she was scoping out shoplifting prospects
in order to sell the information to criminals. They arrested her and had
her deported from the country.[13]

Before leaving Europe, Sophie stopped in Paris to do some shopping and pay a visit to her daughter, Madeline, who was living there at
the time. In addition to getting reacquainted with her daughter, who she
hadn't seen in almost 10 years, Sophie had an important document that
required Madeline's signature.

From Criminal to Published Author

In 1913, Sophie's book, a memoir of her life and crimes titled *Why
Crime Does Not Pay*, was finally completed. In it, Sophie claimed to have
seen the error of her ways and reformed from her life of crime. "There is
something I want more than property," she said. "That is the respect of
good people. Maybe I can get some of it by showing that I am not all bad
and am sincere."[14]

The book was a mishmash of truth and fiction written in an entertaining style. Some of her stories were more or less copied from newspaper
articles and other books, such as *Professional Criminals of America*. She
threw in some recollections of real events for good measure but changed
most participants' names and left out the dates of most of the crimes discussed. Naturally, all of this frightened and angered some members of
the professional criminal community, but not Burke. Sophie was careful
to mention neither the name nor the criminal adventures of her current
husband or, for that matter, any of her husbands other than Ned Lyons.

Some of the spicier sections of the book were published as stand-alone articles in American newspapers before J.S. Ogilvie Publishing Co. of New York released the full volume in paper and hardback versions. J.S. Ogilvie primarily published dime novels, inexpensive books that told stories of adventure and romance. Although *Why Crime Does Not Pay* was far from high-class literature, Sophie apparently savored the publication of its much-embellished tales of true crime. She handed the book out to her friends and even to some of her tenants in Detroit.

For a brief time Sophie Lyons was known more for her writing than for her criminal career, but one man in particular was unimpressed. Writing to a

Sophie, looking every bit the prosperous matron, posed for a professional photograph for her 1913 memoir. For once she was not in front of a police camera.

colleague in New York, William Pinkerton had this to say: "The stories which she published and which are now in book form, under the title of *Why Crime Does Not Pay* are a lot of the veriest rot ever published and are untrue in every particular." He referred to Sophie as a "hop fiend" who used morphine and was "very sensational."[15]

Although Detroit police had suspected Sophie of using morphine in the late 1870s, that suspicion was never proven, and there was no evidence that she was using street drugs in the 20th century. There's also no evidence that Pinkerton and Sophie ever actually met. What's more likely is that Pinkerton had a sexist hatred for any woman who didn't conform to the feminine ideals of the day, and Sophie clearly didn't fit that mold.

Final Trips and Tales Before the War

Buoyed by the publication of her book, Sophie sailed to Europe on July 25, 1913.[16] After she arrived, she traveled to Kiev hoping to interview Mendel Beilis, a Russian Jew who had recently been tried for the murder of a Ukrainian Christian boy named Andrei Yushchinsky. Yushchinsky's body was mutilated after his death, and the Czarist government circulated anti–Semitic rumors that the murderer must have been a Jew. A witness, who was later found to be lying, implicated Beilis, and he was charged with the boy's murder. Although Beilis was acquitted of the crime in November 1913 upon discovery that he had an alibi for the day of the murder, the story had made international headlines.[17]

Sophie met with Beilis and falsely claimed that she was a reporter with the Hearst newspaper chain in the United States. She requested that he hand over his memoirs to her. Beilis was suspicious of her story and refused to give her anything. The following day, the actual Hearst agent met Sophie and told her that if she didn't leave Russia he would have her arrested. She replied that she had no fear of jail. He fired back that he would report her as a Jew who had entered Russia without a passport, which meant she could be imprisoned and would have no way of proving she was an American citizen.[18]

Sophie, who had never before gotten a passport for overseas travel, was frightened enough by the threat that she immediately went to the American Embassy in Berlin to apply for an emergency passport.[19] On the passport application, she claimed she planned to return to Russia, as well as visit Turkey and Persia, but she was so rattled by the episode with the Hearst agent that instead she returned to New York. She sailed home in January 1914 aboard the French ocean liner *La Lorraine*.[20]

While Sophie was away, Burke was released from prison in Sweden. He returned to Detroit to find the house at 42 23rd Street in darkness with a key that no longer fit the lock on the front door.[21] Was it just a mix-up with the locks, or was Sophie sending him a message that, despite public comments to the contrary, she'd had enough of his "affinities" with other ladies? Burke didn't hang around to ponder the question; he headed west to Chicago to visit family and friends.

Eight months later, W.H. Jenkins, head of the Pinkerton Detective Agency's Detroit office, received an anonymous letter. It accused Burke and his pal Freddie Smith of carrying out the nighttime robbery of a jewelry shop in Alexandria, Egypt, in April 1914. A safe inside the store had been opened by blowtorch and emptied of cash, and £5000 of jewelry had been stolen from the premises. Jenkins knew that Burke had never been part of a robbery involving a break-in or the opening of a safe by force, but he checked the story with the Detroit Police Department's detective bureau. Detective Jacob Golden requested information on the robbery from Egyptian police and learned that they already had a group of French safebreakers in custody for the crime.

Jenkins suspected Sophie had written the letter implicating her husband in the crime, so he sent a copy of it to William Pinkerton to get his opinion. The Chicago office had a sample of Sophie's handwriting, and Pinkerton confirmed that she had written the letter. "You can take it from me that the story of hers is a lie, and that her husband is not guilty of the offense, but has run away from her and she takes this means of getting him back."[22]

Sophie told a reporter who stopped by her house that she had no idea as to Burke's whereabouts. The reporter wasn't allowed inside, but he thought he spotted the "elusive William" sitting at a table in the dining room. If the man the reporter glimpsed was indeed Burke, was it Sophie's threat that brought him home, or was it the fact that World War I had begun in Europe?

The world was changing rapidly, and Sophie had gotten a taste of some of the changes during her visit to Russia. For example, overseas travel was now unadvisable for Americans, particularly for those who might land in jail. Soon the Great War would alter Sophie's world in ways she could never have imagined.

17

Fighting for Her Legacy

From the moment when he commits his first crime the profes-
sional criminal never knows what it is to enjoy real peace of
mind. His crimes hang over him like the sword of Damocles,
and, unless he reforms, he can never be free from the fear of
some day being found out and sent away to prison for a long
term.
— Sophie Lyons, *Why Crime Does Not Pay*

On January 22, 1915, Madeline Belmont appeared in the Surrogate's Court in Newark, New Jersey, to stake her claim to a small legacy left by her aunt, Mary Ann Brady. Garbed in what the press described as "a long drab cape and chic black hat," the young woman told the court about her life.

I spent my girlhood days in a convent in Paris, little knowing or dreaming what sort of woman my mother had been. Life was very happy there. I often inquired about my mother, but could find out little. Then, many years ago, it seems, she came over. It was the first time I had seen her since I was a little girl and, of course, I scarcely remembered her.

She asked me about myself and told me that I was to be educated in England and Germany. Then she went away. I left the convent and returned to London. I went to school there and later went to Germany, studying art and music. It was several years ago that my mother brought me over here, and I spent a short time in your country. But I was glad to get back to Paris.

I became a governess and then a stenographer. Then the war started and I was out of work.[1]

The Emergence of an Inheritance

Mary Ann Brady was the sister of Madeline's father, Jim Brady, King of the Bank Burglars. She was born in Ireland and came to America with her parents and sisters while still a child.[2]

The Bradys were among many families escaping the terrible famine that struck the Emerald Isle in the mid–1840s. Their first home in the United States was Troy, New York, a prosperous city on the east side of the Hudson River, north of Albany, the state capital. By 1860 the Bradys had relocated to the village of Cohoes, a mill town on the west side of the Hudson River.[3] Around 1847, Mary Ann's only brother, James, was born; he was also the family's first child to be born in America.[4]

Mary Ann never married. She spent her life working as a seamstress, often living in the homes of the people for whom she sewed. Her mother and sisters remained in Cohoes, but she moved to Newark in the 1870s. By then her brother was a notorious bank robber who'd been in and out of prison several times.

Late in life, Mary Ann suffered a debilitating stroke that left her paralyzed. One of the families she sewed for took her in, and she died in their home on February 22, 1900. Though not a wealthy woman, Mary Ann had been thrifty and inclined toward saving any money that came her way. She left an estate of about $1,068 (worth more than $30,000 in 2018 dollars) with instructions that the money was to be split equally among her widowed mother, a sister, and two nieces: Marion Slavin, daughter of her sister Julia, and Sophia Brady, daughter of her brother Jim. The three women collected their legacies, but none of them had ever met Jim's daughter and didn't know how to get in touch with Sophia (who was now, unbeknownst to Marion, going by the name Madeline Belmont) or her mother.[5] Leave it to Sophie to solve that problem.

Marion Slavin Johnson exchanged letters with Sophie in an effort to help her cousin, Madeline, obtain the small inheritance left by their aunt, Mary Ann Brady. The cousins never met because Marion died of tuberculosis before Madeline arrived in the United States to stake her claim to the money. Courtesy Ruth Colozza.

Sophie, possibly through the grapevine of the criminal fraternity, learned of the money Mary Ann had left her daughter. She wrote to the Cohoes police department asking for more information about the legacy. Marion Slavin Johnson lived in Cohoes and was married to a Cohoes police officer named Lewis Johnson, who was asked to investigate the matter. He in turn requested that his wife write to Sophie and get more details about her marriage to Jim Brady and their daughter. If Sophie's story was true, then the daughter was Marion's cousin.

The women exchanged letters, and Sophie convinced Marion that Madeline was her uncle Jim's daughter. Marion responded to Sophie, whom she addressed as "Auntie," and told her she agreed that Madeline had a right to the money. "I feel that my cousin in Paris is just as much entitled to her father's (my Uncle James) share as I was to mama's," Marion wrote.[6] Marion explained that if Sophie or her daughter didn't show up to court with proof the money should go to Madeline, it would go to the State of New Jersey by process of escheatment.[7] Sophie wasn't about to let that happen.

A High-Stakes Court Appearance

When Sophie traveled to Europe in February 1912 to try to visit Billy Burke in the Swedish prison where he was being held, she stopped in London and located Thomas Turner, the vicar who had married her and Jim Brady and christened their daughter two months after she was born. Sophie got him to make official copies of the marriage and baptism records. She then met with Madeline in Paris and had her sign a power of attorney at the American consulate, giving Sophie the right to collect Madeline's inheritance on her behalf.[8] Sophie's motivation for wanting to collect the money rather than letting Madeline go to court herself may have been because she feared Madeline would discover information about her parents' criminal backgrounds during the hearing. As with her other children, Sophie wanted to avoid this at all costs. It's also possible that she was motivated by self-interest and planned to keep the money for herself.

Upon returning to America, Sophie went to Newark, where she got a hearing at the Essex County Surrogate's Office, where probate matters were handled, to apply to collect the money Mary Ann had left for her daughter. As evidence of her claim, she brought the marriage and baptism records as well as the power of attorney she'd had Madeline sign. She also brought along her sister, Mary Rohrs, who lived in Brooklyn, to serve as a witness.

Sophie testified that she had once met Mary Ann but had never met the other Brady sisters or mother because they all lived in Cohoes, 165 miles north of New York City, somewhere she hadn't been. She also used poor grammar, such as "I never met them people," a number of times in her testimony, probably to give the incorrect impression that she wasn't very well educated or sophisticated.

Some of Sophie's responses to the court's questions were outright lies. For example, when asked whether she knew Brady had been incarcerated in Auburn Prison for a number of years, she claimed she had no idea he'd been in prison. Her response to a question about being personally convicted of a crime in the United States was downright puzzling: "Well, I have no recollection of it." She also swore she'd never pleaded guilty to a crime.

Another confusing string of questions revolved around the number of times Sophie had been married. "Well, I think twice." "Twice?" inquired the court, surprised that her memory about how many husbands she'd had was hazy. Sophie quickly revised her answer. "No, three times," she said firmly. Her answer still left out her first husband, Morry Harris, but who's counting? When asked the name of her husband before Brady, she answered, "Man by the name of Lyons."

Next she was asked whether Jim Brady had children other than her daughter. "Not to my knowledge," Sophie replied. She went on to claim that the last time she saw Brady was in late November 1890, two months before their baby was born.

Sophie claimed that in late March 1891, when Madeline was eight weeks old, she got a cable informing her of Brady's death at New York Hospital under the alias Charles White. She testified that she returned to America as soon as possible and went straight to New York City where she paid a friend, Michael Murray, $100 to cover the cost of Brady's burial, which had already occurred. She wasn't told what caused his death and evidently wasn't interested enough to go to the hospital to investigate. When asked by the court why Brady had changed his name before he died, she answered that she didn't know.

Sophie's sister, Mary, testified that she had met Brady in March 1888, before he and Sophie were married. She recalled the meeting because of the Great Blizzard of 1888, a devastating snowstorm that hit New York City in March of '88. But this was a lie, because he wasn't released from prison until August. She stated that she knew about her niece's birth because she had "the announcement of it in the paper. European paper," though she admitted she'd neither met her niece nor written to her (or any of Sophie's daughters, for that matter). Mary also testified that Sophie and "some other friend" had told her Brady was dead.

The one-time Queen of the Burglars had good reason to be evasive when answering questions about her marriage to Jim Brady. Her divorce from Ned Lyons wasn't granted until January 1892, which meant her marriage to Brady on December 11, 1888, wasn't technically legal, despite the documents proving it had occurred.[9] Sophie had committed bigamy, but fortunately for her, that fact didn't come out at the hearing. If it had, the court would have had to assume Madeline was Ned's child even though Sophie hadn't seen Ned for years, and Sophie wouldn't have been able to legally claim Madeline's inheritance (nor would Madeline have been able to claim it).

Jim Brady's Mysterious Exit

Sophie's confusing testimony also raises questions about when Jim Brady died. No one named Charles White appears in New York death records for March 1891. A man named James Brady did die in New York on April 20, 1891, but he was born about 1861 and was 14 years younger than Jim Brady. Of course, lack of a death record doesn't prove Sophie lied, because there were almost certainly deaths during that era that went unrecorded.

One that *was* documented was the death of a Jim Brady on May 27, 1903, in New Rochelle, New York. He was in poor health and had lost every penny he'd ever stolen. After being released from a local poorhouse, he'd wandered onto train tracks and been hit and killed by a passing train.[10] The man who died was described as being about 78 years old, but the Jim Brady who was once married to Sophie would have been more than 20 years younger. Police eventually determined that the man killed on the train tracks was a horse thief who just so happened to also be named Jim Brady. He apparently passed himself off as the other Jim Brady because he enjoyed the attention he got when he bragged about his days as a famous burglar.[11]

A compelling reason to believe that Brady did indeed die around 1891 is that after 1890 he wasn't involved in any crimes—at least none that were reported in the news. Brady was a career criminal who, when he wasn't in prison, was actively involved in crimes. Why would he suddenly give up his career? Added evidence of his death around 1891 comes from an interview Sophie gave to the *St. Louis Post-Dispatch* in 1898. In it she was quoted as saying "my baby Madeline came to me just at the time her father died."[12]

Brady may have left London in a hurry to avoid being arrested. After all, he'd spent a large chunk of his life in prison and certainly would have been desperate to avoid another incarceration. He was also a master of disguise. It's worth noting that no police department ever got a decent rogues' gallery photo of him. If his death couldn't be established, the court would have had to investigate the possibility that he was still alive and determine whether he'd had any other children.

Regardless, the fact remains that there is no record of Jim Brady's existence after 1891, when Vicar Turner listed his name on Madeline's christening record as the child's father.

Making Her Case

Ultimately, the Surrogate's Court wasn't persuaded by Sophie and Mary's testimony to hand over Mary Ann Brady's money. It would be up to Madeline herself to answer the court's questions.

Prior to sailing from Le Havre, France, and arriving in the United States in late December 1914, Madeline signed and filed a petition revoking Sophie's power of attorney.[13] When she later appeared before the court, she explained that she hadn't understood what she was signing when Sophie presented it to her.[14]

Madeline then went on to tell the court how she'd grown up without a family. She tried her best to describe her strange, fragmented childhood, but for the most part she could only repeat what she'd been told by Sophie, plus a few disjointed early memories, none of which involved her father.

She knew from Sophie that she was born in London on January 28, 1891, and shuttled around to boarding schools in Paris, London, and Montreal as a young child. When Madeline was seven years old, Sophie showed up without warning in France. This woman whom she didn't know told Madeline she was her mother, then brought her to Detroit and changed her name from Sophia Brady to Madeline Belmont. Her mother told her that the reason for the name change was because her half sister, Lottie, went by the surname Belmont, and things would be easier if they had the same last name (though the reason for changing her first name wasn't made clear). Sophie also told Madeline that her father was dead.[15]

After Madeline turned 12, Sophie took her back to France and put her in yet another boarding school. At age 17, Sophie stopped paying for her education, so Madeline was forced to find a job. She first worked as a governess and then as a stenographer. By the time Sophie showed up in Paris with the power-of-attorney document, Madeline hadn't seen her mother in nearly 10 years.

Madeline's situation changed dramatically after the Great War began in July 1914. She lost her stenographer job and had no other recourse for financial support. With no income and essentially no family, Madeline desperately needed the money left to her by her aunt. The court agreed that she'd proven her case and released her inheritance to her. With accumulated interest, the total amount had grown to about $400 (slightly more than $10,000 in 2018 dollars).[16] Sadly, Madeline never got the chance to thank her cousin for helping make this moment possible—Marion Slavin Johnson had died in May 1913 at the age of 32.[17]

As for Madeline's relationship with Sophie, the lies her mother had told her as a child and the disturbing knowledge she'd gained about her parents' lives had strained their connection. Madeline likely didn't stop to visit her mother in Detroit before returning to Europe aboard the steamboat *City of New York* as a third-class steerage passenger. The ship arrived in Liverpool on February 14, 1915.[18] Shortly afterward, Madeline made a decision that would have a devastating effect on her future.[19]

18

A Downward Spiral
of Loss and Grief

*While this generosity is almost universal in the underworld,
those unfamiliar with the workings of the criminal heart
would give it very little credit for such impulses.*
—Sophie Lyons, *Why Crime Does Not Pay*

As the year 1916 dawned, Sophie announced plans to donate a vacant lot she owned at Lafayette and 24th streets in Detroit to an organization called the Pathfinders' Club of America that had been created to provide moral education to young people in public schools and to young men in prison. (Later the group changed its name to "Pathfinders of America" to avoid being confused with a group run by the Seventh-day Adventist Church.[1]) Though its founder, James Franklin Wright, wasn't trained as a teacher or sociologist, he discovered his calling as a social-welfare advocate. Sophie may have met Wright at Belle Isle, a park located in the Detroit River, between Michigan and Ontario, Canada. She often spent time there during the warmer months and may have learned about the group by observing one of its initial councils on the ferry dock at Belle Isle.

The idea of teaching young people to stay on a moral path or helping them leave a life of crime so appealed to Sophie that she began visiting the Detroit House of Correction and sharing stories from her past criminal exploits to encourage the inmates to follow a better life path after they were released. To sweeten her message, she handed out small amounts of cash to the prisoners so that each one would have a little spending money.[2]

An Attempted Act of Goodwill Goes Awry

Sophie's desire to provide property to Wright's group may have been motivated by good intentions, but she also knew the act would generate the kind of newspaper headlines and attention she reveled in. Wright put it succinctly when he later told the *Detroit Free Press*: "You could be sure she'd take up a case if it would bring her publicity. Not that she did it for the sake of publicity, for much of her work will never be known, but the limelight seemed to fascinate her."[3]

Regardless, there were strings attached to Sophie's donation. She wanted a charity home built on the site, but she wasn't willing to put any cash toward the project. The money to pay for constructing the home and running it would have to be raised by the Pathfinders' Club. She certainly had opinions about whom the home should serve, however, and she wasn't shy about sharing them.

First, Sophie said it should be for the "reclamation of children with criminal tendencies."[4] Then she remarked that young men should be accepted at the home and it should be very large—able to house as many as 500 residents.[5] Then in March 1916 she gave a speech at a banquet held by the Pathfinders' Club in which she pleaded that the home be used as a refuge for unwed mothers: "I speak from 40 years experience. I have seen, during the years of my former career, many women who have gone through all in order that they might clasp their babies to their breast, shunning the murderous idea which would have been the easiest way for them."[6]

Although the club members applauded Sophie enthusiastically, they knew a substantial amount of cash would have to be raised to put a plan like hers into action, and providing housing wasn't part of the group's mission. Additionally, the publicity the group received about the potential donation from a woman labeled by the press as "the ex-queen of swindlers" wasn't wholly positive.[7] Ultimately the group decided not to accept her property offer.

The Con Woman Gets Conned

Later that spring, Sophie had something other than charity on her mind. She'd been in negotiations with a supposed Hungarian nobleman who told her he directed motion pictures. The young man said he wanted to make a movie of Sophie's life based on her memoir. If Sophie would just give him $600 for "preliminary expenses," he would write the screenplay and use his industry connections to get a movie deal. He assured her there would be a role for her in the film and she'd get a percentage of the profits.[8] Sophie was flattered by the attention and thrilled with the idea. She promptly handed over the cash.

The "Hungarian nobleman" turned out to be a swindler who ran off with her money. It was a devastating moment for Sophie—the former con woman had been conned. Police in Buffalo, New York, arrested a man they thought might be the crook, but when Sophie was unable to pick him out of a group of men in a courtroom, they let him go.[9]

To ease her embarrassment over the episode, Sophie bragged to the press as she left the courthouse that she was the only woman ever to escape from Sing Sing. She told reporters that she now devoted herself to charity work for soldiers.

Losing Her Love

Meanwhile, Sophie and Billy Burke had ironed out their differences, and Burke was back living with Sophie in Detroit. However, his days as a sneak thief were over. By 1917, Burke was suffering from kidney problems related to nephritis. The following year he had a stroke and had to be hospitalized. He experienced another cerebral hemorrhage while he was in the hospital and wound up dying there on October 25, 1919, at age 61.[10]

Unwilling to shell out for her husband's burial, Sophie had Burke's body sent to his family in Chicago. She missed her old pal Billy the Kid, with whom she'd shared so many adventures, but she did no public weeping over his death at the time. Later, however, she told a friend that she wished she hadn't let his body go because it meant she couldn't visit his grave and pour out her problems to him there.[11]

To commemorate her first holiday season without Burke, Sophie donated $100 to the Detroit House of Correction to pay for a nice dinner for the inmates. She also sent $500 to Sing Sing to purchase presents for the prisoners there. She used the donations, which attracted press attention, as an opportunity to complain about how violent crime in America had become.

JAMES WILLIAM TAYLOR, ALIAS CHARLES BATES, BILLY THE KID, BILLIE BURKE

By the time Bertillon (side and front) mug shots were taken of Billy Burke he'd been imprisoned many times and was in poor health.

> In all the years I trained with the best criminals in this country, and in Europe, I never saw one of them carry a gun. Such stuff as robbing poor men in the streets and stripping homes of their meager possessions was too low and mean for the kind of criminals I knew and worked with.[12]

Evidently Sophie chose not to recall that she'd threatened people, including her own daughter, with a pistol, and had even gone so far as to shoot at Detroit City Railway Company executive George Hendrie back in 1881.

A Mother Outlives Her Son Once More

Another loss struck Sophie when her beloved son, Carleton, died in Spokane, Washington, on March 5, 1922. Carleton had never married and had lived in Washington since about 1910, working in both Spokane and Seattle as a customs inspector.[13] He lived with arteriosclerosis for seven years before dying from kidney disease at age 44.[14]

Carleton's body was cremated, and his ashes were placed in an urn and sent to his mother. Sophie cried over them and carried the urn from room to room, never wanting to leave the remains of her favorite son alone. Sometimes she even slept with the urn cradled in her arms.[15]

Finally one of her tenants, Mrs. William Snell, became so concerned about Sophie's depression over her son's death that she came up with a plan. She suggested they contact the United Spanish American War Veterans, a group Carleton had belonged to, for assistance burying his ashes.[16] The group agreed, and by October 1922 Fireman First Class Carleton C. Mason was in his final resting place at Detroit's Woodmere Cemetery. A military headstone even decorated his grave.[17] Now Sophie had somewhere to go to talk over her troubles. She often visited her son's grave.

The Thief Gets Robbed

While Sophie was still mourning the death of Carleton in the summer of 1922, her home was broken into and robbed. Sophie discovered the theft upon her return from a stay at a resort in Put-in-Bay, an Ohio village on South Bass Island in Lake Erie. She claimed the burglars made off with $13,000 in diamonds and $6,000 to $7,000 in bonds.[18]

The next robbers to steal from Sophie were bolder. In late March 1924 three "nattily-dressed young" men entered a lunchroom on Fort Street, near Sophie's home. They forced her under a table and proceeded to rob her and the lunchroom's proprietor of their cash. Somehow the thieves overlooked the several valuable rings Sophie was wearing beneath her gloves. "Those poor deluded boys," she commented to a *Detroit Free Press* reporter a few weeks later. "I pity them so." Seriously frightened but not otherwise injured in the attack, Sophie vowed never to wear her rings again and leave them permanently in her safe-deposit box at the bank.[19]

Detroit authorities later arrested Gene Murray and Charles Howe for the crime. They were members of a criminal gang known as Robbers' Roost, named for its headquarters in a boathouse of that name in Ecorse, south of Detroit. This time Sophie was able to identify the accused men.[20]

Both robberies Sophie experienced were part of a growing wave of professional criminal activity in the United States that sprang out of Prohibition. This activity escalated into the violent gangster era and contributed to the birth of the Federal Bureau of Investigation. Social changes were also afoot, including women winning the right to vote in 1920. Younger women were cutting their hair, shortening their skirts, and entering the workforce in larger numbers.

Sophie Lyons, the woman once known as a master criminal, felt out of touch and very tired. She was 76 years old, nearing the end of her life, and in need of assistance doing things she could no longer manage herself. Because there was only one person to whom she could turn, she swallowed her pride and called Florence.

A Bittersweet Reunion

Mother and daughter met on April 30, 1924, at the swanky Hotel Statler across from Grand Circus Park in downtown Detroit. If Florence recalled how she'd been thrown out of her mother's house and left to wander on her own near the park 30 years before, she didn't mention it.

Surely many other things were discussed, though. After not speaking to each other for years, the two women talked for four hours before heading to the nearby Hotel Tuller, where they enjoyed dinner together.[21]

Florence's only child, Esther, was now an independent young woman of 19. Florence had remarried Joseph Bauer in 1917, but he hadn't changed his ways, and the marriage was headed toward a second divorce. While they ate, Sophie asked whether Florence would consider giving up her job at a flower shop to move back home and care for her. She also told her that she'd recently changed her will and Florence stood to inherit a substantial amount of property and some valuable jewelry when she died.

Then Sophie dropped the biggest bombshell of all: She told Florence that her half-sister, Madeline, had gone insane. She said that after Madeline returned to France, she had volunteered to be an ambulance driver during the war. While doing her duty, she received an injury that had affected her mind. Sophie didn't know the precise nature of the injury, whether it was shell shock or a blow to the head, but she did know Madeline was now unable to live on her own.

Sophie told Florence that Madeline was being treated at a mental asylum in London. She'd looked into moving Madeline to either Canada or America, but the law didn't allow mentally ill people to be brought into either country. She'd paid a woman traveling to England to visit Madeline, but the woman had been unable to locate her. Sophie wanted to go look for Madeline herself, but she felt too sick and old to make the journey. She begged Florence to go, find her sister, and make sure she was being well cared for, all on Sophie's dime.[22]

Florence was shocked and upset to hear about Madeline's illness. She hadn't seen her sister since she was a young child. Would she even recognize her when she saw her again? Florence wanted to help, but she needed time to digest the devastating information.

Mother and daughter parted company on good terms, agreeing to meet again soon. But exactly one week later, Sophie was dead.

19

Controversial to the End

A life of crime is a life of hard work, great risk, and, comparatively speaking, small pay.
—Sophie Lyons, *Why Crime Does Not Pay*

On May 7, 1924, Sophie Lyons generated the kinds of headlines she hadn't gotten in years, and all she had to do was die.

From coast to coast, newspapers told the story of her life, with a focus on her career as a female criminal when such a thing was rare. Some articles even published three photos of her face (all based on the same photo): one normal; one divided in half and flipped, showing her "good angel" side; and one divided and flipped, showing her "bad angel" side. The photos supposedly proved that she had a split personality similar to the fictional Dr. Jekyll and Mr. Hyde.

Old stories from Sophie's past were dredged up, many of which drew upon the tales she'd written, which were full of lies. Reporters weren't overly concerned about accurately portraying Sophie's life, however. After all, who was going to complain?

Attacked in Her Own Home—or Not

Sophie's death wasn't without mystery. Gertrude Antle, the woman who lived in the rear of Sophie's duplex building, told a *Detroit Free Press* reporter that shortly before Sophie collapsed she (Antle) had opened the door of the home to three men. She said the men had told her they wanted to speak to Mrs. Burke about renting one of her houses. Antle, who didn't question the legitimacy of the men's request, let them in.

A few minutes later, Antle, who'd gone back to her apartment, claimed she heard Sophie cry out, "Quit! Don't! Let me alone!" Antle didn't check

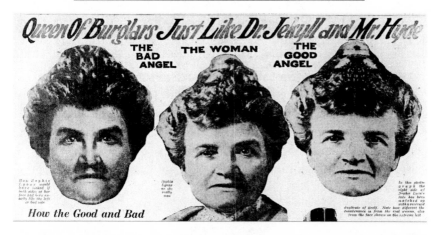

Queen Of Burglars Just Like Dr. Jekyll and Mr. Hyde

THE BAD ANGEL   THE WOMAN   THE GOOD ANGEL

How the Good and Bad

After Sophie's death a newspaper published this photomontage supposedly showing the "good" and "bad" sides of her personality. The original photograph (center) was divided in half, flipped, and duplicated to create the manipulated portraits.

to see what had happened but instead ran off to find a doctor. When she returned (without a doctor), Dr. G.H. Campau was already in the apartment with Sophie, who had collapsed, and an ambulance was waiting outside. The three men had called Campau and the ambulance and then waited for both to arrive. After making sure Sophie was taken care of, they left.[1]

A rumor spread that the men were associates of Robbers' Roost gang members Gene Murray and Charles Howe, whom Sophie had recently identified as two of the three men who'd held her up at the lunchroom. The trio's visit to Sophie was supposedly to threaten her so she wouldn't testify against Murray and Howe, who'd been arrested a month earlier following a shoot-out with police and were under lock and key at the jail.[2]

Antle's story had a number of problems, though. If the men were gang members hoping to scare Sophie into keeping her mouth shut and she was so frightened she fainted, then hadn't they accomplished their task? Why not leave quickly? Violent criminals don't usually call a doctor and ambulance to provide medical attention to their victim. Perhaps they were kind-hearted villains who wanted to make sure the old lady they'd just threatened within an inch of her life survived. If so, why not call for help and then leave? Why wait around for the doctor and ambulance to arrive, letting witnesses see their faces? One could also wonder why Antle didn't go for the police rather than a doctor if she feared the men were up to no good.

The answers to all of these questions likely involve Antle being a publicity seeker. Seeing a chance to get some news attention from the excitement surrounding Sophie's collapse, she spun a good yarn around the visit of three men who were probably there to talk to Sophie about renting one of her houses. This theory is less sensational than what was reported, but it makes far more sense. It wasn't the kind of tale that would sell newspapers, though, which is why many publications ran with the story about the Queen of the Burglars being attacked by criminals. The far-fetched scenario was reprinted multiple times in future decades whenever the press rekindled and retold Sophie's life story.

The Queen Succumbs to Old Age

What *was* documented correctly was that Sophie was taken by ambulance to Grace Annex Hospital. She failed to regain consciousness and died at 4:30 p.m. Florence arrived just moments before her mother took her last breath.

Dr. Campau believed Sophie had died of natural causes. "I didn't see any marks on her that would indicate violence," he said, "nor did I pay any attention to the men who summoned me and who stood about until the ambulance came and then disappeared." He added that Sophie was 76 years old and suffered from high blood pressure. "Possibly she had a shock, but her death had all the appearances of being natural." The coroner, James Burgess, agreed and noted death due to cerebral hemorrhage on her death certificate.[3] The police did a cursory investigation and confirmed what Dr. Campau and the coroner had said: Sophie Lyons died of natural causes.

Florence, dressed in deep black, wept softly in a corner of the Hilliker Undertaking Parlor while curious Detroiters walked by her mother's open casket. Most of them had never met Sophie Lyons but they'd been drawn to the funeral parlor by the stories, good and bad, they'd heard and read about her life.

Following the viewing Sophie's casket was taken by hearse to Woodmere Cemetery, where a service was held in the cemetery's chapel. Florence and Esther were the only family members present for the service. They were joined by a small group of Sophie's closest friends, including Ira Jayne, a justice of the Wayne County Circuit Court known for his work on behalf of troubled children.[4]

The service included two of Sophie's favorite hymns, "Sometime We'll Understand" and "Beautiful Isle Somewhere."[5] Several members of the United Spanish American War Veterans and two of Sophie's male tenants acted as pallbearers. A *Detroit Free Press* reporter documented the scene.

> Hundreds of sensation hunters crowded into the quiet chapel of Woodmere Cemetery Friday afternoon to mingle with the little group of mourners gathered there to witness the simple rites which marked the long and amazing career of Sophie Lyons Burke.[6]

Meanwhile, inmates at the Detroit House of Correction participated in a memorial service in Sophie's honor led by her old friend, Pathfinders' Club founder J.W. Wright.

After the service was over and the mourners and gawkers had left, Sophie's body was cremated. Her ashes were buried in the grave of her son, Carleton Mason.

Florence Lyons Bower, pictured here in a May 1924 edition of the *St. Louis Post Dispatch*, was the oldest daughter of Ned and Sophie Lyons. She was also their only child to spend most of her life in Detroit. The *Detroit Free Press* described her as the daughter who looked the most like Sophie. She certainly shared her mother's taste in extravagant hats.

Sophie's Value

The question of how much wealth Sophie Lyons left behind was on the minds of many in Detroit and elsewhere in the country. When her book was published in 1913, she claimed she was worth half a million dollars. People also wondered who would inherit it all. Would the reformed pickpocket and con artist leave her ill-gotten gains to criminals and prison inmates? Or would the funds go to a more appropriate charitable cause? And what of her family, whom she was rumored not to be on good terms with? Would they get anything?

Esther Bower, for one, expected to inherit a sizable chunk of her grandmother's estate, and she already had plans for how to spend the money. "I would like to go east to a finishing school now. I want to develop my mind as I know my grandmother would have liked me to do. I want to learn how to manage the estate we expect to have and give my mother an opportunity to regain her health," she commented to a reporter from *The Detroit News*.[7]

The day after the funeral, Florence and Judge Jayne, as executor of Sophie's estate, joined an officer of the Union Trust Company for the opening of Sophie's safe-deposit boxes and the reading of her will. The document began with this statement: "I hope for my sake there will be no litigation over this, my last will and testament."[8]

The will directed that after her debts and funeral expenses were paid, her "beloved son" Carleton was to receive a house on 23rd Street for use during his life, plus the proceeds from several of her properties that had been mortgaged. He was also given household items as well as a diamond stud. Her "dear daughter" Florence was bequeathed a cottage on 23rd Street and a nearby vacant lot. She also received household items, jewelry, and the rental income from several other houses. Lottie, who was listed as a resident of the Hotel De Parce in Geneva, Switzerland, got $2,000 (just

SOPHIE LYONS' GRANDDAUGHTER

MISS ESTHER BOWER

This photograph of Esther Bower appeared in a 1924 *Detroit News* article after Sophie's death.

under $30,000 in 2018 dollars). Madeline was also to receive $2,000. Esther was in for a disappointment. She and Sophie's sister, Mary Rohrs, each got a measly $100, whereas Jayne and another friend, Detroit real-estate investor and politician Sherman Littlefield, were each bequeathed $2,000.

She left other small bequests to friends and acquaintances as well as a gift of $50 to Jesse Pomeroy, an infamous inmate of the Charlestown State Prison in Massachusetts. When he was a young teen, Pomeroy was convicted of brutally murdering two children, a 10-year-old girl and a four-year-old boy. He'd been in prison for almost 50 years when Sophie died and would soon be declared insane. It's doubtful Sophie ever met Pomeroy; her legacy to the notorious murderer was more likely her attempt to spit in the eye of polite society than to help Pomeroy, who died in 1932.[9]

The inmates at Sing Sing, the Detroit House of Correction, and several other prisons were to receive yearly gifts of magazines and holiday treats. Additionally, $1,000 was earmarked to purchase a new Steinway piano for the House of Correction.

Another specification of Sophie's will was that the estate's trustees weren't to sell any of her real estate for a period of 50 years after her death. But that wasn't all: Sophie wanted two of her properties to be converted into a home for children "between the ages of two to four years, regardless of color, religion or nationality, one or both of whose parents are inmates of some prisons." The balance of the estate was to be used to create the Sophia Lyons Memorial Trust Fund, with income from the fund going to pay the children's home's expenses. A playroom in the home was to be outfitted with toys, and the children were to be taken four times a year to Sophie's favorite vacation spot, Belle Isle Park. Each year the home was to have a Christmas tree, and holiday gifts were to be purchased for every child who lived there. Through her charity, Sophie reckoned her name would live on in Detroit.

Sophie wrote her will in 1920 with the assistance of her attorney, John Gafill. The will was not filed in the Wayne County Probate Court until February 1922, a month before Carleton died.[10] She hadn't updated her will after her son's death, however Carleton, who never married, apparently knew which properties he was due to inherit from his mother. Before he died he'd deeded the properties to Florence.[11]

The total value of Sophie's estate fell far short of the rumored half million dollars, but it was still an impressive amount: $241,766 (more than

Judge Ira W. Jayne (center) reading Sophie Burke's will to Mrs. Bower, one of the eldest of her nine children

In this photograph published in a May 1924 edition of the St. Louis Post Dispatch, Judge Ira Jayne (center), Florence Lyons Bower (right), and a bank official are shown with the contents of Sophie's open safe deposit box. Jayne, a respected Detroit judge, was the executor of Sophie's estate.

$3.5 million in 2018 dollars). After her debts and the cash legacies were paid, the estate was worth $167,135.[12] Sophie Lyons had, in the long run, proved herself an astute businesswoman. Unlike many of her criminal colleagues, most of whom had died paupers, Sophie had ended life a financial success.

A Challenge Is Raised

The ink was barely dry on the probate documents when a lawsuit to reopen Sophie's estate was brought in Wayne County Probate Court on behalf of Madeline Belmont. The basis of the suit was that Sophie wasn't of sound mind when she wrote her will and that "she was abnormal in all her relations with her children and if any of them showed a disposition to live a respectable life she cast them out."[13] The argument was that Madeline, the "pauper lunatic," deserved a larger portion of Sophie's estate than she had received.

Florence was a major force in bringing the lawsuit. The Detroit Trust Company was appointed as guardian to represent Madeline's rights and interests, given that she was mentally incompetent and unable to leave England to appear in court. Florence, however, was able to testify that Judge Jayne had told her that "after the estate was closed they would disregard the will and not carry out its provisions" to create the trust fund and build the children's home because he and the other trustees considered it an unworkable plan.[14] She also insisted her sister Lottie was still alive and that the executor and trustees hadn't made any real efforts to locate her.

Executor Jayne and the trustees, Sherman Littlefield, a businessman, and two attorney friends of Sophie's, brothers Fred and Leo Butzel, represented the estate in the lawsuit. Though none of them had psychiatric training, they argued that Sophie *was* of sound mind when she made her will and insisted the document had been properly probated. Accordingly, the estate should remain closed. Jayne insisted that Madeline wasn't a pauper and was "being furnished with whatever was needed for her care." He said he believed Florence supported the lawsuit in hopes of getting control of a larger chunk of the estate in Madeline's name for her own use.[15]

A lot of Sophie's dirty laundry was aired in the course of the lawsuit, which went all the way to the Michigan Supreme Court. Sophie possibly anticipated something like this, based on her stated desire that there be no litigation over her will. Nonetheless, many of her friends and tenants willingly testified on behalf of reopening of her estate. They provided descriptions of Sophie's bizarre behavior over the course of many years. Many of them said she had treated Florence cruelly for decades and spoke often of a strong preference for two of her children, Carleton and Madeline.

Emma Betzing had particular experience with Sophie's mood swings and treatment of her children. Betzing worked as a matron at the Detroit House of Correction when Sophie was a prisoner there in the 1880s. They became friends and stayed in touch for years afterward. Betzing testified that Sophie starved herself while she was in prison in order to get her own way and fell into violent fits of temper. After she got out of prison, Sophie once asked Betzing to send a doll to Madeline's boarding school in Europe as a Christmas present. Instead of sending one doll, Betzing sent two. When Sophie heard about this, she was so furious that she wrote Betzing a 14-page letter containing nothing but abuse.[16]

Mrs. William Snell, Sophie's longtime tenant and friend, testified that sometimes when she went to pay her rent, Sophie wouldn't let her into the house, saying, "Go away, go away, I can't see anybody today." After three or four days, Sophie would emerge from her house and behave normally again. "She was of very changeable disposition, telling one thing today and the opposite tomorrow," Snell said. She also claimed that rents on Sophie's properties would go unpaid for months at a time because no one knew where she was or how to contact her. She also recounted an occasion when Sophie became angry with a tenant and chased the man around his yard, beating him with a broom handle.[17]

Minna Carpenter, a neighbor who'd known Sophie for nearly 50 years, testified that Sophie was "accustomed to take a very pronounced dislike to people and to maintain that dislike stubbornly." She added that Sophie enjoyed talking about crime to the extent that she "gloried in crime and criminals."[18]

Elizabeth Somerville, wife of the late William Somerville, a Detroit police officer who'd befriended Sophie in the early 1880s, swore that she'd known Sophie since 1883 and that her family had taken in Sophie's children while she was imprisoned in the Detroit House of Correction. She testified that Sophie was subject to "frequent, violent fits of melancholy, when she would be extremely despondent, saying that she felt like throwing herself in the river, saying she had no friends, no home, no money and on some of these occasions she would speak about some of her criminal exploits."[19]

Another of Sophie's longtime tenants, a contractor named Duncan Graham, testified that the buildings allocated for use as the children's home were in very poor condition. One had a leaky roof, and the other had mostly broken windows. Neither building had plumbing facilities inside. He stated that it would, in his opinion, be cheaper to tear them down and build a new structure for the children's home.[20]

Dr. Arnold Jacoby, a psychiatrist who ran the Psychiatric Clinic of the Detroit Recorder's Court, gave his opinion on the soundness of Sophie's mind when she prepared her will. In his job with the court, Jacoby evaluated the minds of people accused of serious crimes. Jacoby hadn't known Sophie personally, so he based his opinion on a reading of her memoir and her will. His testimony echoed that of her friends and neighbors: He stated that her will was a "product of a deranged, disordered, abnormal and unsound mind, having no conceptions of her duties or relations to her own children and possessed of abnormal, deranged and unbalanced ideas respecting crimes and criminals."[21]

The Michigan Supreme Court announced its decision on October 3, 1927. The arguments presented by the plaintiffs had convinced the court to allow Sophie's estate to be reopened.[22] The Wayne County Probate Court didn't take the decision to disregard a person's last wishes lightly, even if that person was Sophie Lyons.

Resolution finally came in January 1929 when the probate court announced its decision: Madeline would receive $42,500 in cash and a $10,000 mortgage through her representative, the Detroit Trust Company.[23] The court also ruled that if Lotta Belmont couldn't be located, Madeline and Florence would split her $2,000 legacy equally. Florence had already received real estate, jewelry, and other personal items valued at almost $45,000.

Approximately $120,000 was set aside to carry out the establishment of a memorial fund in Sophie's name and to create a home for the small children of convicted criminals who had nowhere else to live.[24] After a four-year battle, the probate court's decision seemed like a reasonable compromise. Those who had testified on Madeline's behalf, particularly Florence, were satisfied with the outcome.

Three Sisters

"I do not want to see you. You are a thief! Go away, please!"
Those words cut me to the heart—from my own precious
daughter.
                            —Sophie Lyons, *Why Crime Does Not Pay*

Peace at Last for Florence

In the battle over her mother's estate, Florence proved she had more of Sophie's tenacity and spirit than anyone gave her credit for. She'd gone up against highly respected Detroit attorneys and businessmen and won the fight.

After receiving her inheritance, Florence stopped working and bought a comfortable home in suburban Detroit, where she lived with her daughter. By 1930 Esther was married to William Johnson, who worked as an auditor for an automobile manufacturer. By this point Florence was once again divorced from Joseph Bauer.[1]

Perhaps because her childhood was so traumatic and there was so much she wanted to forget, Florence went through life claiming to be substantially younger than she actually was. Case in point: The age on her death certificate was recorded as 59, but she was actually 67 years old when she died on January 8, 1935.[2] Like her mother, Florence passed away after suffering a cerebral hemorrhage.

Lottie's Lonely Life in London

Florence had told the trustees of Sophie's estate that her sister, Lottie, was still alive when their mother died. They evidently paid no attention, but Florence was correct.

Lottie had enjoyed a moderately successful career as a comic actress in England in the late 1890s, performing regularly under the name Lotta Belmont at London's Prince of Wales Theatre.[3] After 1899 her name no longer appeared in ads for stage productions. When the census was taken in England in 1901, Lottie was living in a London boarding house. The census taker recorded that she was involved in "stage/art," so she still had hopes for a return to work in theatre.[4] Lottie was not recorded on the 1911 census in England or Canada, nor does her name appear on the 1910 U.S. census.

Sophie's friend Emma Betzing testified in the appeal to reopen Sophie's estate that Lottie and her mother had become estranged. Betzing didn't mention a date when the falling-out began, but she did report that Sophie had said "Lotta was beautiful and proud and too good for her," implying they'd had an argument about Sophie's criminal history.

When Sophie made her will in 1922, she apparently believed that her middle daughter lived at a hotel in Geneva, Switzerland, but by then Lottie was living in poverty in London. Lottie, going by the name Charlotte Belmont, entered the Fulham Road Workhouse in the city's Westminster district in late November 1921, noting her occupation as "teacher of languages" on the workhouse admission form.[5] She was discharged one day later but entered the workhouse again for a three-day stay in early December. Lottie was released on December 5, 1921, and admitted to another workhouse on Britten Street in Chelsea the following day "at her own request." She stayed there just a single night.[6]

Between the 18th and early 20th centuries in England, people who were unemployed, homeless, poor, and without family support often ended up in one of the workhouses scattered across London. Although they offered shelter and food, one of the purposes of a workhouse was to punish a poor soul desperate enough to end up in one, because needing public charity in order to survive was viewed as shameful. Workhouse residents were generally considered lazy and unwilling to perform paid work, so they were put to work doing jobs in the workhouse.

Conditions in English workhouses improved a little by the 20th century, but even then they were degrading, disagreeable places to live with many rules and few comforts. A description of the Newington Workhouse paints a depressing picture of life in the workhouse:

> By as late as the 1920s, there were no curtains at ward windows or rugs for day rooms. All chairs were made from wood without upholstery. Inmates were not free not come

and go as they pleased: men under the age of 60 could only leave the workhouse on the first Friday of the month from noon until 7 pm and alternate Sundays from 11 am to 7 pm, women could leave for the first Wednesday of the month and alternate Sundays. Those over 60 were allowed more frequent leave. Inmates still had to wear "house clothes" and their own clothing and small possessions were kept in store for them while they were resident.[7]

Lottie, who'd been living in Spitalfields, a poor section of London, became homeless again in January 1924. As a result of losing her housing, she was admitted to the St. Pancras Workhouse.[8] She refused to give the admission staff any information about herself, including the name and address of a friend or relative. The staff was later able to determine that she was an unmarried English teacher in her late 40s. She was listed in their records as being a Roman Catholic who'd been born in Canada and "resettled" in England. It's impossible to know how long she stayed, though, because her discharge record from St. Pancras hasn't survived.

The news of Sophie's death was published in several British newspapers, including in *The Guardian* in London.[9] Either Lottie didn't see the articles or, if she did read about her mother's death, she chose to ignore it.

Ira Jayne, the executor of Sophie's estate, apparently never fully investigated Florence's assertion that Lottie was alive, so she never received her much-needed $2,000 inheritance from her mother. Presumably Jayne contacted the Swiss hotel where Sophie thought her daughter lived and found no trace of her there. With no other clues as to her whereabouts, he and the estate's trustees assumed she was dead and split her legacy equally between her sisters.

They never discovered that Lottie didn't die until April 11, 1935. She passed away at the Chelsea Workhouse infirmary just four months after her older sister. The cause of death was the same as both Florence and Sophie: a cerebral hemorrhage. Her death record lists her as Charlotte Belmont, a 59-year-old spinster and former schoolteacher with no fixed address. She was buried in a pauper's grave, the location of which went unrecorded.[10]

Apparently after her stage career faded, Lottie made use of her boarding-school training in languages and embarked on a new career as a teacher. World War I may well have thrown her temporarily out of work and into poverty. Existing information about Lottie doesn't indicate that she suffered from mental illness, but the large gaps in the records mean much of her life remains hidden in the shadows, including insight into her mental state. One fact, however, is certain: Although she and her sister, Madeline, both lived in London, they weren't in touch with each other.

Madeline's Illness Takes Its Toll

Madeline, who'd been evacuated from Paris to London by the American Red Cross during the war, was behaving strangely by May 1918. She hadn't eaten much or changed her clothes in several weeks and was infested with lice as a result. A friend finally convinced her to seek medical attention, so she saw a doctor at St. Thomas' Hospital. He agreed that she was ill and recommended she be treated at Royal Bethlem Hospital.[11]

Originally named the Priory of St. Mary of Bethlehem, the building was constructed in 1247 to help care for London's homeless population. Around 1400 it began to accept "insane" patients, and it was the only public hospital to "treat" the mentally ill in England until the 1800s.[12]

By the 1600s people were allowed to visit the facility to gaze at the patients. Guided tours were even offered as a way for the institution to raise money. The tours are described in a history of the hospital.

> At a time when the effects of scarring diseases, deformity, wounding and other medical problems were all considered valid forms of fee-paying entertainment, word of the wondrous cavorting of the inmates of Bethlem spread across London as promise of good, cheap entertainment—an image that the institution (or indeed asylums in general) would not really even try to shake off for more than 150 years to come, as such visitors tended to bring money with them.[13]

Due to the disturbing and bizarre behavior exhibited by many of the hospital's patients, it acquired the nickname Bedlam in the 1600s. By the time Madeline was a patient there, the public was no longer allowed to wander the hospital's halls and corridors, but its nickname had stuck.

During her initial exam at Bethlem, Madeline told the physician she hadn't undressed because she was "suspicious of everything." He then put her under hypnosis (this was apparently not an unusual thing for an admitting physician to do), and she confessed to him that her fears had something to do with air raids in Paris. She also expressed worries that her food was poisoned and that poisonous fumes had been pumped into her room. These statements were enough to warrant Madeline's official admission on May 24, 1918, as well as a tentative diagnosis of "dementia praecox," or precocious (early) dementia, an outdated term for schizophrenia.

Bethlem Hospital, on Lambeth Road in Southwark, in an 1896 photograph. Madeline was suffering from schizophrenia when she was admitted as a patient to Bethlem in 1918-1919. The hospital was relocated in 1930 and currently the building houses the Imperial War Museum. The Queen's London: a Pictorial and Descriptive Record of the Streets

As part of its process of establishing background information on new patients, the hospital located a woman, Mademoiselle Crisafulli, who had known Madeline for about a year and could speak to at least some of her past.

Crisafulli said she'd become acquainted with Madeline in Paris and said she occasionally "had delusions that someone whistled and made signals when she was in the street." Crisafulli believed Madeline had experienced "some sort of disappointment" and told the hospital authorities she'd heard Madeline had gone to an expensive school in Paris and was reputed to be very rich, as was her mother. However, Madeline's mother had withdrawn her financial support when her daughter reached the age of 17. "Her whole case was very mysterious," said Crisafulli. She also noted that Madeline was "very learned and intellectual." She spoke French and German and had studied logic.

According to Crisafulli's narrative, after Madeline arrived in England from her trip to America in 1915, she found work as secretary to the Lady Pembroke at Wilton House, a country estate in Wiltshire, England. Madeline stayed in the job for about 18 months before leaving for Paris in the hopes of volunteering in the war effort.

She walked into a horrendous situation. Paris wasn't far from the front lines during World War I. Air raids were frequent, as were food and fuel shortages.[14] The winter of 1916–1917 was bitterly cold, and Parisians suffered because the city was cut off from coal supplies in northern France by the German lines. It was a terrible place for a young woman with no family or emotional support to end up.

Sophie told her friends and family that Madeline's insanity was the result of an injury she sustained while driving an ambulance during the war. Crisafulli didn't mention that Madeline had driven an ambulance, but she may not have known that part of her history. Regardless, serving as an ambulance driver was a dangerous and traumatic job that would have placed Madeline in prime position to witness horrendous casualties of the war. Neither "Madeline Belmont" nor "Sophia Brady," her birth name, appears in the records of British Red Cross First World War volunteers, but it's possible she served with another volunteer group.[15]

Madeline's case notes at Bethlem indicate that although she was apprehensive and suspicious and appeared to have experienced hallucinations, she was well nourished and quiet in her first weeks. Doctors were initially hopeful she could be cured; at the very least, they thought her condition might improve. Their outlook on Madeline's prospects changed in August 1918 when she became emotionally excited and put her hand through a window, resulting in a cut that required stitches. When asked why she did it, she replied, "I want to go to the front" (meaning the Western Front, the main site of fighting in Europe during the Great War). The following month she cut her hand again, explaining, "I want to shed blood for my country."

By January 1919, Madeline was spending much of her time trying to injure herself. She punched herself in the eyes and beneath the jaw, causing severe bruising. She repeatedly jumped in the air and landed on her knees. She spent hours turning somersaults in an unsuccessful effort to break her neck. She tore her lower lip away from her jaw, requiring stitches to sew it back in place. Occasionally she was able to converse rationally, but more often than not she was confused, noisy, and unwilling to eat.

She became obsessed with the idea of going to the front and headed for a window whenever she got the chance. To keep her from harming herself when she was in the grip of strong hallucinations she was occasionally put into a straightjacket. She lost weight and had to be fed via a tube. Bethlem staff stated that she enjoyed having the tube put down her throat and being fed through it. By spring 1919 she'd lost 20 pounds from her pre-hospitalization weight of 106 pounds and was dangerously underweight. Hospital staff also noted that she was often incoherent and had "a persistent inane smile."

Other than tube feeding and restraints, Madeline's treatment consisted of various drugs, including "Sulphonal" (a hypnotic), "Veronal" (a barbiturate used as a sleep aid), and cod liver oil. Although the Veronal knocked her out at night, none of these pharmaceuticals improved her mental condition, and she continued to deteriorate.

In a moment of clarity in April 1919, Madeline told the staff she wanted to write a letter to her fiancé. Did he actually exist? Had he died in the war? Was his death what caused Madeline's descent into madness? If anyone on staff wondered about him enough to ask, they either didn't get answers or didn't write down the information because this was the only time in the patient notes it was mentioned that Madeline might have had a lover.

Two months later, Madeline tore up all of her clothing and was restrained in her bed because she had nothing to wear. At this point, her behavior was described as "childish." In September she threw herself on the floor and cut her chin below the jaw, causing another wound that needed stitches. She was also experiencing regular auditory hallucinations. She'd now been institutionalized for 16 months and was more confused than ever.

Thrown Out on the Streets of London

By the 1850s, doctors at Bethlem preferred to treat only acutely ill patients, an approach to mental health treatment that continued into the 20th century. The tragic result of the policy was that those who remained "uncured" after they'd been at the hospital for about a year were discharged.[16] By fall 1919, Madeline had been at Bethlem nearly 17 months and she had overstayed her welcome. After the wound under her jaw healed, she was discharged as "uncured." She left the hospital on October 15, 1919, in a much worse state than she'd arrived: weak, underweight, and hearing things.

Without friends or family, sick and dumped on the streets of London as winter approached, what did Madeline do? Where did she go? Answering these questions is impossible. No record of her exists until spring 1920, when she was admitted to Newington Workhouse in the London borough of Southwark.[17] According to her admission record, she was an unmarried, "able-bodied woman" whose profession was "typist" and religion was "Church of England." Given this description, the workhouse authorities may not have known she'd been in a mental hospital. They must have noticed something wrong, though, because Madeline was given a "class 4 infirm diet," which was a more meat-based diet than the typical woman received in the workhouse.[18]

Madeline's mental illness must have become apparent to Newington staff quickly, because she was sent to Manor Asylum, a mental hospital, just 10 days after entering the workhouse.[19] She stayed at Manor Asylum for a few months, but her condition failed to improve. In late December 1920 she was transferred to nearby Horton Hospital.[20] Both facilities were part of a group of five large psychiatric hospitals called the Epsom Cluster in the town of Epsom, south of London. They'd been built to ease overcrowding in London's existing mental hospitals. Unfortunately many of the patient records and case notes from the Epsom Cluster hospitals, including Madeline's, haven't survived.

Details of Madeline's condition after she was sent to Horton come from records of the appeal of her mother's estate. Dr. Strode, Horton's medical superintendent, followed Madeline from her first days at the hospital. Almost nothing was known about her life when she entered the institution. All the staff knew was that she was a 28-year-old single woman who'd been born in England and worked as a clerk and typist. The names and addresses of her next of kin were unknown. She was described as being suicidal upon arrival.[21]

In March 1925, Dr. Strode gave a deposition for the appeal of Sophie's will. Like the doctors at Bethlem, he described Madeline as suffering from "dementia praecox." He went on to note: "Little sense or reason can be extracted from her. She is quite devoid of insight into her condition, is faulty in her habits, and requires constant care and attention." He explained that she was in moderate physical health but that her prospects of recovering her mental faculties were "very poor." He thought she might be capable of enjoying the "small comforts" that could be purchased for her with the money left by her mother's estate, which may have been a self-serving observation: By this point the Southwark Guardians, an elected administrative board responsible for patients' bills, were owed £381.13.6 for the nearly five years Madeline had been hospitalized.[22]

On August 28, 1939, just before the outbreak of World War II, Madeline was transferred to her fourth mental hospital. She was sent to Banstead Hospital, located 12 miles southeast of Horton Hospital, in Banstead, Surrey.[23] Her care was listed on hospital documents as "chargeable to London County," which raises the question of whether the Detroit Trust Company ever sent any of her inheritance to pay for her care in England or only allowed it to be used for "small comforts."

In September 1939 the England and Wales Register was compiled to keep records of British citizens in order to produce identity cards. Madeline was listed on the register as a patient of Banstead Hospital.[24] She apparently never recovered enough to leave there because the facility was listed as her place of death. Madeline was 72 years old when she passed away of cardiovascular degeneration on August 27, 1963.[25]

She was buried in Hundred Acres, a cemetery named for the farm that was on the site before the hospital was built there in 1873. Banstead Hospital closed its doors 23 years after Madeline died, and the building was torn down. It was replaced by HM Prison High Down in 1991.[26] So the daughter of two infamous American criminals now lies buried beneath an English prison.

Closing Sophie's Books "in the approved manner"

In 1946 executor Ira Jayne finally announced that he would disregard Sophie's requirement not to sell her Detroit properties until 50 years after her death. Nothing is left now of the houses she owned or the neighborhood that was her refuge for almost 50 years. Warehouses and truck lots have replaced her old community near Fort and 23rd streets. Nearby is the convergence of two interstate freeways that were built in the 1950s: I-75 runs north to south between Sault Ste. Marie in Michigan's Upper Peninsula and Miami, Florida, and I-96 runs from the nearby Ambassador Bridge across the state almost to Lake Michigan.

Also in 1946, Jayne made clear that the home for criminals' children that Sophie wanted so much would never be built. "Modern sociological thought agrees that such institutions are never beneficial," he told the *Detroit Free Press*. He claimed Sophie's estate had decreased in value by $70,000 from 1929, possibly due in part to the hefty fees he and the Detroit Trust Company had been taking over the years to manage it. Jayne said the money from the property sale would be "turned over to established social agencies for distribution in the approved manner."[27]

Sophie Lyons never did anything in "the approved manner." No doubt she would have been furious about Jayne ignoring her last wishes, not to mention giving away her hard-earned fortune. But by then Sophie's children were all deceased except for Madeline, who was incapable of understanding or objecting to Jayne's decision.

Epilogue

But instances of noble deeds among criminals whose souls are generally believed to be wholly black might be narrated without end. These men and women who declare war against society only to find that CRIME DOES NOT PAY are not without their redeeming qualities. Their evil deeds are published far and wide, but the good that they do seldom comes to light.

—Sophie Lyons, *Why Crime Does Not Pay*

After she published her memoir, Sophie said that what she wanted in life more than money was the "respect of good people."[1] She thought she might be able to win their respect by showing that she was not "all bad" and proving that she was sincere in her desire to help others. She certainly understood the difficulties people faced finding honest work, due to discrimination, after they left prison. She also knew from personal experience how easy it was to fall back into bad habits. She found it very hard, however, to live down her notorious past because she took perverse pride in it. In addition, serious mental health issues plagued Sophie to the end of her life.

Although he never met her, Dr. Arnold Jacoby, the University of Michigan–trained psychiatrist who testified in the appeal of Sophie's will, stated that "her processes of feeling, thinking and reasoning were manifestly and clearly diseased and the judgments reached by her were pathological and rendered the person in question incompetent in all matters when the rights of others were under consideration." Based on Jacoby's medical opinion, along with the personal descriptions provided by the acquaintances, friends, and family members who also testified, as well as newspaper accounts of her actions, it's possible to conclude Sophie had one or more mental disorders.

Deciphering Sophie's Mental State

Was Sophie schizophrenic? Her daughter Madeline suffered for most of her adult life with schizophrenia, a condition that can run in families. Yet Sophie didn't display the illness' hallmark symptoms: delusions (beliefs not based in reality), hallucinations (seeing and hearing things that don't exist), disorganized thinking and speech (difficulty with verbal communication), abnormal motor behavior (a wide range of problems that manifest themselves physically), and negative symptoms (inability to function normally). She did present what might have been a negative symptom—periodic social withdrawal—but one symptom alone wouldn't be enough to indicate she had schizophrenia.

A more likely possibility is that Sophie had a bipolar disorder. These are brain disorders that cause shifts in mood, energy and ability to function leading to extreme highs and lows in the sufferer's emotional states. Sophie displayed both manic and depressive tendencies. In terms of manic symptoms, at times she was extremely self-confident, bragging to her tenants and friends about her criminal accomplishments. She once boasted to her tenant Mrs. Snell about her ability to get away with crimes. In describing this ability in herself, she also told her old friend Minna Carpenter "that's what it is to be smart." Sophie didn't recognize that her pride in the crimes she'd committed was repulsive to her friends who weren't criminals.

Other manic symptoms Sophie exhibited included risk-taking and promiscuity. She was unable to stop herself from shoplifting, even when she knew she'd be caught. She was also sexually uninhibited and made a living from her multiple sexual partners by blackmailing some of them.

On the depressive end of the emotional spectrum, Sophie experienced periods when she was unable to leave her home, suggesting she had bouts of deep melancholy. She also expressed suicidal thoughts to some of her friends. For example, she told her friend Elizabeth Somerville that she sometimes felt like throwing herself in the river. Additionally, when she was jailed in Detroit in December 1877, she went so far as to attempt suicide not once but twice.

Sophie also behaved in ways that could indicate she had a personality disorder. Personality disorders include a wide range of symptoms in which the individual has trouble perceiving and relating to situations and people. The person doesn't realize they aren't thinking or acting in a normal way and blames their problems on other people. Sophie had a history of becoming violently angry, to the point of engaging in physical fights. She vented her anger not only at her enemies, such as Theresa Lewis, but also her family members, friends, neighbors, and tenants. She held grudges for years; lied compulsively; and was often incapable of recognizing others' feelings, particularly those of her children.

As a child, Sophie suffered serious, prolonged abuse, both psychological and physical, at the hands of her family members, people she should have been able to trust. There was no way for her to escape the abuse, which may have led her to relive those events and suffer from post-traumatic stress disorder as an adult. Her inability to maintain close and loving relationships with her children, and in particular her tendency to abuse Florence, suggests she may indeed have struggled with PTSD.

Another possibility is that when she was abused as a child, Sophie suffered a blow to her head that damaged her brain. A brain injury could explain why she was emotionally labile—angry one minute and calm the next. Her tendency to engage in impulsive behavior could also have been due to a traumatic brain injury.

It's even possible that, due to the mistreatment she endured as a child, Sophie later developed a serious psychological problem known as dissociative identity disorder (DID). Previously known as multiple personality disorder, DID often presents in individuals who've suffered severe emotional or physical abuse in childhood. Years later, the person with DID develops two or more distinct personalities and can switch between them quite suddenly. When an alternate personality takes over from the main, or core, personality, memory lapses often occur. Other symptoms, such as suicidal tendencies, mood swings, and depression, can also be present with DID.

Both George Ellis and Emma Betzing, two of the people who provided testimony during the will appeal, described events that could indicate Sophie suffered from DID.

Ellis was a plumber who often worked on Sophie's rental properties in Detroit. He recalled going to Sophie's home one day to collect on a plumbing bill. She let him in and was very courteous toward him. Then she excused herself and went upstairs for a few minutes. After she came back down, her manner toward him had changed completely. She expressed surprise to see him in her home and then became violent and abusive toward him. She gave Ellis the impression that she thought he was someone else. He claimed she yelled curses at him and literally drove him from her house. In a flash, Sophie had gone from being calm and polite to angry and belligerent. Not surprisingly, Ellis found the experience confusing and extremely disturbing.

Betzing, the former matron at the Detroit House of Correction, told a story about an incident so peculiar it still stood out in her mind years later. She and Sophie had been good friends for decades, ever since they met while Sophie was an inmate at the Detroit House of Correction. Betzing had telephoned Sophie to invite her and Billy Burke over to her home for dinner, and Sophie had accepted the invitation. Betzing told Sophie she would come over in her car, pick them up, and take them to her house. (Although she didn't mention when this scenario occurred, it was probably around 1916. Betzing wasn't a wealthy woman, and by this point in time, automobiles were less expensive and more common.) After she arrived at the house, Sophie and Burke were just leaving. Sophie saw Betzing drive up but declined to look at her or acknowledge her in any way. She did, however, turn to Burke and say loudly, "Come on, Billy, our time is valuable." Burke tried to reason with her, saying "this is Mrs. Betzing," as if he thought Sophie didn't know who Betzing was. Sophie ignored him. Burke then turned to Betzing and said, "Don't pay any attention to her, Mrs. Betzing. She is on one of her crazy spells today." Sophie and Betzing had always gotten along well, even when she'd been a prisoner and Betzing had been her guard. Yet it was as if Sophie had become another person and didn't even recognize her.

We'll never know what mental illness or combination of ailments plagued Sophie. But the fact that she lived with untreated mental illness makes it all the more remarkable that she eventually turned away from a life of crime and began to make a living by honest means. Such a change was a substantial achievement for someone who had very little formal schooling, hadn't previously held an honest job, and had spent decades involved in illegal activities.

Protecting Her Children as Best She Could

Because Sophie grew up with parents and older cousins who were criminals, she was forced to participate in criminal activities from a young age. She knew from her own experiences that children learn from the adults around them, and she realized there was a strong possibility that her children would follow in her footsteps and the footsteps of their fathers.

As a result, she tried to keep her children away from crime, though these efforts came too late for her son George. According to his records from the Elmira Reformatory, George spent some of the year 1876, when he turned 10, living solely with his father. Presumably Ned didn't share Sophie's worries about the children becoming criminals, and he spent that time teaching his oldest child the craft of burglary. George admired his father and soon started down the criminal path. Asking a New York City judge to send George to the House of Refuge was Sophie's misguided way of trying to halt his progression into crime. It also speaks volumes about her childhood that she thought being sent to a reformatory would help George change his ways, but at least she tried to do her job as a parent.

Sophie told anyone who would listen that she loved her children and was concerned about their welfare. Although her behavior didn't always reflect this sentiment, there's no reason to think it wasn't, at its core, something she truly believed. There is, however, reason to accept that Sophie didn't know how to love her children because she'd never been loved herself as a child. She was convinced she needed to lie to them in order to keep them in the dark about her criminal background. She also knew she needed to hide their identities so society wouldn't paint them with the same brush it had used on her. However, her goal of protecting her children was at odds with her desire for fame, and she made the situation worse by talking, lecturing, and writing about her criminal exploits. Thanks to her wishes and actions, it was impossible for Sophie's children to ever *not* find out about her notorious life.

The Price of Sophie's Love and Those Who Paid It

Believing that if her children didn't know about her criminal past they'd be protected from it, Sophie hated her daughter Florence for revealing her secrets to the younger children. But instead of accepting any blame for the choices she herself had made, Sophie foisted it all onto Florence.

Sophie's decision to keep the children separated from each other also hurt them, because it meant they had no support system to fall back on when times got tough, and there were *many* tough times in the lives of Sophie's children. For George it meant dying in prison before he'd even really lived. For Florence it meant years of rejection and poverty. For Carleton it meant changing his name and moving as far away from his family as possible. For Lottie it meant refusing to admit who her family was and spending part of her life in workhouses. For Madeline it meant a lonely life in mental institutions.

Of Sophie's children, only Florence—the child most mistreated by her mother—chose to stay in Detroit. In her desperation for maternal acceptance, Florence never gave up trying to crack Sophie's hard shell. She fought hard to make a decent life for herself and her daughter. She also helped her disabled half sister get a larger part of their mother's estate.

Tucked between the pages of my worn copy of *Professional Criminals of America*, I discovered a note Florence left. Written in her round, feminine hand, it reads: "Wrong will right itself, dear." Was this meant as an optimistic message for Esther, her daughter and Sophie's only grandchild? Or was it something Sophie told Florence she hoped people would say about her life after she was gone? The answer will forever remain a mystery, as will the different paths Sophie's children might have taken in life, if their mother had not been the "Queen of the Burglars."

Chapter Notes

Introduction

1. "Sophia Burke," 1910 United States Federal Census, Census Place: Detroit Ward 12, Wayne, Michigan; Roll: T624_685; Page: 6A; Enumeration District: 0174; FHL microfilm: 1374698. Ancestry.com.

2. "Marion L. La Touche," 1900 United States Federal Census, Census Place: Chicago Ward 4, Cook, Illinois; Page: 4; Enumeration District: 0097. Ancestry.com.

3. Sophie Lyons, *Why Crimes Does Not Pay* (New York: J. S. Ogilvie, 1913), 90–93.

4. "Decades Before They Had the Vote, Women Launched Their Own Stock Exchange," by Mary Pilon, www.History. com, https://www.history.com/news/decades-before-they-had-the-vote-women-launched-their-own-stock-exchange.

5. Lyons, *Why Crimes Does Not Pay*, 95–98.

6. *Ibid.*, 102–103.

7. "Miss Morse Convicted," *The Sun* (New York, NY), June 12, 1884.

8. "A Poor Woman's Speculation," *New York Times*, October 18, 1882.

9. "Sophie Lyons," *Detroit Free Press*, March 17, 1882.

10. "Sophie Lyons, Philanthropist at 70," *Brooklyn Daily Eagle*, February 3, 1916.

Chapter 1

1. "Sophie Elkan," New York, Passenger Lists, 1820–1957, Year: 1855; Arrival: New York, New York; Microfilm Serial: M237, 1820–1897; Microfilm Roll: Roll 159; Line: 4; List Number: 1248. Ancestry.com.

2. "Castle Garden: Where Immigrants Came Before Ellis Island," by Jaya Saxena, New York Historical Society Museum & Library, last modified August 8, 2013, http://behindthescenes.nyhistory.org/castle-garden-where-immigrants-first-came-to-america.

3. "Castle Garden: America's First Immigration Center," www.castlegarden.org.

4. Lisa Kuhlmann, Beate L. Weiland, and Erich Woehlkens, *Beiträge zur Geschichte der Juden in Uelzen und in Nordostniedersachsen* (Oldenburg, Germany: Isensee, Florian, GmbH, 1996), Family #281.

5. *Ibid.*

6. *Ibid.*

7. "Schutzjude," by Joseph Jacobs, www. jewishencyclopedia.com/articles/13333-schutzjude.

8. "J. I. Van Elkan," New York, Passenger Lists, 1820–1957, Year: 1854; Arrival: New York, New York; Microfilm Serial: M237, 1820–1897; Microfilm Roll: Roll 139; Line: 36; List Number: 524. Ancestry.com.

9. Kuhlmann, Weiland, and Woehlkens, *Beiträge zur Geschichte*, Family #281.

10. "Elkan, Jacob," 1857, New York, New York, U.S. City Directories, 1822–1995. Ancestry.com.

11. "Kleindeutschland: The History of the East Village's Little Germany," by Dana Schultz, last modified October 2, 2014, https://www.6sqft.com/kleindeutschland-the-history-of-the-east-villages-little-germany/.

12. Tyler Anbinder, *Five Points: The 19th-Century New York City Neighborhood That Invented Tap Dance, Stole Elections, and Became the World's Most Notorious Slum* (New York: Free Press, 2001), 85.

13. "Public Baths: East Village/Lower

East Side, Manhattan, Historic District Council, accessed October 19, 2019, http://6tocelebrate.org/site/former-free-public-baths-of-the-city-of-new-york/.

14. "Friedr. Van Elkan," New York, Passenger Lists, 1820–1957, Year: 1854; Arrival: New York, New York; Microfilm Serial: M237, 1820–1897; Microfilm Roll: Roll 139; Line: 36; List Number: 524. Ancestry.com.

15. "Mary Alken," 1860 United States Federal Census: Census Place: New York Ward 8 District 4, New York, New York; Roll: M653_795; Page: 562; Image: 43; Family History Library Film: 803795. Ancestry.com.

16. "Sophie Lyons's Plea for Mother-Love," *The World* (New York, NY), June 28, 1896.

17. *Ibid.*

18. Sophie Lyons, *Why Crime Does Not Pay* (New York: J. S. Ogilvie, 1913), 11–12.

19. "Sophie Lyons's Plea for Mother-Love," *The World* (New York, NY), June 28, 1896.

20. *Ibid.*

21. "Jacob Alken," 1860 United States Federal Census: Census Place: New York Ward 8 District 4, New York, New York; Roll: M653_795; Page: 562; Image: 43; Family History Library Film: 803795. Ancestry.com.

22. *Ibid.*

23. "Mary Rohis," New York City Municipal Deaths, Ancestry.com.

24. "Alleged Perjury," *New York Tribune*, September 24, 1859.

25. "Jacob Alken," 1860 United States Federal Census: Census Place: New York Ward 8 District 4, New York, New York; Roll: M653_795; Page: 562; Image: 43; Family History Library Film: 803795. Ancestry.com.

26. "Miscellaneous News," *New York Daily Herald*, March 2, 1862.

27. "Jacob Elkins," U.S. Civil War Soldier Records and Profiles, 1861–1865 database, Ancestry.com.

28. "Miscellaneous News," *New York Daily Herald*, February 21, 1864.

29. "Pauline Walton," New York Governor's Registers of Commitments to Prisons, 1842–1908, Ancestry.com.

30. "Mary Elkin," New York Governor's Registers of Commitments to Prisons, 1842–1908, Ancestry.com.

31. "Dealings in Diamonds," *New York Daily Herald*, April 29, 1872.

32. "Mary Elkin" and "Julia Keller," New York Governor's Registers of Commitments to Prisons, 1842–1908, Ancestry.com.

33. "Sophia Elkin," 1860 United States Federal Census: Census Place: Randalls Island, New York, New York; Roll: M653_802; Page: 180; Image: 774; Family History Library Film: 803802. Ancestry.com.

34. "Our City Charities," *New York Times*, January 23, 1860.

35. "House of Refuge," 1860 United States Federal Census: Census Place: Randalls Island, New York, New York; Roll: M653_802; Pages: 168–184; Image: 774; Family History Library Film: 803802. Ancestry.com.

36. "Our City Charities," *New York Times*, January 23, 1860.

37. "House of Refuge," 1860 United States Federal Census: Census Place: Randalls Island, New York, New York; Roll: M653_802; Pages: 168–184; Image: 774; Family History Library Film: 803802. Ancestry.com.

38. *Ibid.*

39. "Our City Charities," *New York Times*, January 23, 1860.

40. "Court of General Sessions," *New York Times*, September 21, 1861.

41. "Miscellaneous," *New York Times*, October 3, 1866.

42. "Sylvan-Lyons. Review of the Revere House Blackmail Case," *Boston Globe*, June 27, 1880.

43. "Maurice Harris," 1860 United States Federal Census: New York Ward 6 District 4, New York, New York; Roll: M653_791; Page: 221; Image: 635; Family History Library Film: 803791. Ancestry.com.

44. "Noted Pick-Pocket in Custody," *New York Times*, September 12, 1860.

45. "Wolf Levy," New York Governor's Registers of Commitments to Prisons, 1842–1908. Ancestry.com.

46. "Charged With Pocket Picking," *New York Times*, April 1, 1866.

47. "Sylvan-Lyons. Review of the Revere House Blackmail Case," *Boston Globe*, June 27, 1880.

Chapter 2

1. "Fredericka Henriette Auguste Wiesener," accessed October 18, 2019, http://

www.findagrave.com/memorial/130475634/fredericka-henriette_auguste-mandelbaum.

2. "Fredericka Mandlebaum," 1870 United States Federal Census: *New York Ward 13 District 2, New York, New York;* Roll: *M593_991;* Page: *96A;* Family History Library Film: *552490. Ancestry.com*

3. George Washington Walling, *Recollections of a New York Chief of Police* (New York: Caxton Book Concern, 1887), 286–287.

4. "Death of Mother Mandlebaum," *The Sun* (New York, NY), February 27, 1894.

5. *Ibid.*, 281.

6. *Ibid.*, 286–287.

7. *Ibid.*

8. *Ibid.*, 281.

9. *Ibid.*, 197.

10. Sophie Van Elkan Lyons, *Why Crime Does Not Pay* (New York: J. S. Ogilvie, 1913), 191.

11. Ben Macintyre, *The Napoleon of Crime: The Life and Times of Adam Worth, Master Thief* (New York: Dell Publishing, 1997), 30–31.

12. "Buying Out of Sing Sing," *The Sun* (New York, NY), July 11, 1873.

13. *Ibid.*

14. "A Notorious Female Pickpocket," *New York Daily Herald*, February 23, 1865.

15. "Reddy the Blacksmith," *The Sun* (New York, NY), September 7, 1869.

16. "Sophie Lyons Divorced," *Detroit Free Press*, January 5, 1892.

17. *Documents of the Assembly of the State of New York, One Hundred and Fifth Session* (Albany: Weed Parsons, Legislative Printers, 1882), 140. Google Books.

18. "Bridget Lyons," Massachusetts Passenger and Crew Lists, 1820–1963. Ancestry.com

19. "Edward Lyons," 1850 United States Federal Census: Census Place: Lowell Ward 5, Middlesex, Massachusetts; Roll: M432_326; Page: 146B; Image: 525. Ancestry.com

20. "Edward Lyons," Massachusetts Town and Vital Records, 1620–1988 database. Ancestry.com.

21. "#70 Edward Lyons," Professional Criminals of America–REVISED, by Jerry Kuntz, last modified December 16, 2018, https://criminalsrevised.blog/2018/12/16/70-edward-lyons/.

22. Thomas Byrnes, *Professional Criminals of America* (New York: Cassell, 1886), 139.

23. "Edward Lyons," 1860 United States Federal Census: Census Place: New York Ward 7 District 1, New York, New York; Roll: M653_792; Page: 523; Image: 530; Family History Library Film: 803792

24. *Ibid.*

25. "Buying Out of Sing Sing," *The Sun* (New York, NY), July 11, 1873.

26. *Ibid.*

27. *Ibid.*, 140.

28. Sophie Van Elkan Lyons, *Why Crime Does Not Pay* (New York: J.S. Ogilvie, 1913) 15–16.

29. "Edmund Lyons," 1870 United States Federal Census: Census Place: New York Ward 12 District 6, New York, New York; Roll: M593_989; Page: 154A; Family History Library Film: 552488. Ancestry.com.

30. "Bold Bank Robbery," *New York Times*, June 29, 1869.

31. *Ibid.*

32. "Fire Recalls an Old Crime," *The Sun* (New York, NY), May 18, 1900.

33. "Further Particulars in Regard to the Losses," *New York Times*, June 30, 1869.

34. "Buying Out of Sing Sing," *The Sun* (New York, NY), July 11, 1873.

35. "Edmund Lyons," 1870 United States Federal Census: Census Place: New York Ward 12 District 6, New York, New York; Roll: M593_989; Page: 154A; Family History Library Film: 552488. Ancestry.com.

Chapter 3

1. "Death of a Desperado," *Harrisburg Telegraph*, January 27, 1871.

2. "#20 James Hope," Professional Criminals of America–REVISED by Jerry Kuntz, last modified May 24, 2018, https://criminalsrevised.blog/2018/05/24/20-james-hope/.

3. "The Arrest of Lyons," *Philadelphia Inquirer*, October 8, 1870.

4. "Robert E. Hapgood," New York Governor's Registers of Commitments to Prisons, 1842–1908 database. Ancestry.com.

5. "Buying Out of Sing Sing," *The Sun* (New York, NY), July 11, 1873.

6. *Ibid.*

7. "Criminal Courts," *New York Tribune*, September 25, 1871.

8. "Buying Out of Sing Sing," *The Sun* (New York, NY), July 11, 1873.

9. *Ibid.*

10. "Susan Lockwood," New York Governor's Registers of Commitments to Prisons, 1842–1908 database. Ancestry.com.

11. "Dealings in Diamonds," *New York Daily Herald,* April 29, 1872.

12. "First Prison for Women in the U.S.?" Prison Public Memory by PPMP Editor, last modified August 12, 2011, https://prisonpublicmemory.us/first-prison-for-women/.

13. "Our State Institutions," *The New York Times,* December 25, 1871.

14. "Buying Out of Sing Sing," *The Sun* (New York, NY), July 11, 1873.

15. "John Reilly," New York Governor's Registers of Commitments to Prisons, 1842–1908 database. Ancestry.com.

16. "Horace Greeley," *New York Times,* December 4, 1872.

17. "Buying Out of Sing Sing," *The Sun* (New York, NY), July 11, 1873.

18. "Not Indicated in the Features," *Daily Gazette* (Wilmington, DE), March 18, 1881.

19. "Buying Out of Sing Sing," *The Sun* (New York, NY), July 11, 1873.

20. *Ibid.*

21. *Ibid.*

Chapter 4

1. "Buying Out of Sing Sing," *The Sun* (New York, NY), July 11, 1873.

2. "Bank Robbers Captured," *New York Times,* October 25, 1877.

3. "Rebecca Sturge," London Metropolitan Archives; London, England; Reference Number: *p92/geo/157;* Board of Guardian Records and Church of England Parish Registers. London Metropolitan Archives, London. Ancestry.com.

4. "Rebecca Sturge," *New York, Passenger and Crew Lists (including Castle Garden and Ellis Island), 1820–1957; 1855;* Arrival: *New York, New York;* Microfilm Serial: *M237, 1820–1897;* Microfilm Roll: *Roll 152;* Line: *17;* List Number: *351. Ancestry.com.*

5. "Bank Robbers Captured," *New York Times,* October 25, 1877.

6. "Burglars Sentenced," *Detroit Free Press,* October 1, 1870.

7. Langdon Moore, *Langdon W. Moore: His Own Story of His Eventful Life* (Boston: Langdon W. Moore, 1893), 386–388.

8. *Ibid.*

9. "Langdon W. Moore Bailed," *New York Daily Herald,* January 4, 1878.

10. "Buying Out of Sing Sing," *The Sun* (New York, NY), July 11, 1873.

11. *Ibid.*

12. "Sophia English," 1880 United States Federal Census; Census Place: Detroit, Wayne, Michigan; Roll: 614; Page: 478A; Enumeration District: 310. Ancestry.com.

13. "An Awful Record," *Ottawa Daily Citizen,* October 30, 1880.

14. *Ibid.*

15. "Ned and Sophy Lyons," *Brooklyn Daily Eagle,* December 29, 1876.

16. "Important to Escaped Convicts," *New York Daily Herald,* December 28, 1876.

17. "Sophia Lyons' Future," *New York Daily Herald,* January 8, 1877.

Chapter 5

1. "The Sad Unknown," *Detroit Free Press,* December 23, 1877.

2. *Ibid.*

3. *Ibid.*

4. "Police Court Garnerings," *Detroit Free Press,* December 27, 1877.

5. "Room Eleven," *Boston Weekly Globe,* July 29, 1879.

6. *Ibid.*

7. *Ibid.*

8. *Ibid.*

9. *Ibid.*

10. *Ibid.*

11. "Police Intelligence," *The New York Times,* June 4, 1858.

12. "The 'Duchess of California,'" *Times Herald* (Port Huron, MI), February 25, 1886.

13. "Mrs. Lucas," *Cincinnati Daily Star,* June 22, 1878.

14. *Ibid.*

15. *Ibid.*

16. "Room Eleven," *Boston Weekly Globe,* July, 29, 1879.

17. "Suspected Sophie," *The Boston Globe,* October 27, 1880.

18. "Room Eleven," *Boston Weekly Globe,* July, 29, 1879.

19. *Ibid.*

20. *Ibid.*

21. "Postscript. Room No. 11," *The Boston Globe,* August 16, 1878.

22. "Room Eleven," *Boston Weekly Globe*, July, 29, 1879.

23. "Postscript. Room No. 11," *The Boston Globe*, August 16, 1878.

24. "Jumped Bail," *The Boston Globe*, August 10, 1878.

25. "Room Eleven," *Boston Weekly Globe*, July, 29, 1879.

26. "Before the Recorder," *Detroit Free Press*, July 30, 1878.

Chapter 6

1. "75 Years After It Pushed Out the Pushcarts, Essex Street Market Presses Forward," by Alexandra Hall, Bedford + Bowery, last modified Decemeber 28, 2015, https://bedfordandbowery.com/2015/12/75-years-after-it-pushed-out-the-pushcarts-essex-street-market-presses-forward/.

2. "Accusing His Mother," *The Sun* (New York, NY), February 1, 1880.

3. *Ibid.*

4. *Ibid.*

5. "George Lyons," Elmira Reformatory Biographical Registers and Receiving Blotters, Series: B0141, vol. 1; New York State Archives, Albany, New York.

6. "Accusing His Mother," *The Sun* (New York, NY), February 1, 1880.

7. "The Son of the King of the Burglars," *Cincinnati Daily Star*, February 4, 1880.

8. "Accusing His Mother," *The Sun* (New York, NY), February 1, 1880.

9. "Sophia English," 1880 Federal Census, Census Place: *Detroit, Wayne, Michigan*; Roll: *614*; Page: *478A*; Enumeration District: *310. Ancestry.com.*

10. "New York Court of Sessions," *Brooklyn Daily Eagle*, July 5, 1871.

11. "Recent Deaths. Brock," *St. Johnsbury Caledonian* (St. Johnsbury, VT), March 26, 1897.

12. "Fooling with a Horse-Pistol," *The Boston Globe*, January 23, 1878.

13. *Ibid.*

14. "Louise Sylvan," *Boston Post*, August 13, 1878.

15. "M. Frank Paige," *Boston Post*, April 5, 1879.

16. "Items," *Chicago Tribune*, October 23, 1879.

17. "The Shooting of E. J. Lyons," *New York Times*, October 27, 1880.

18. "Shot While Intent on Murder," *New York Times*, October 25, 1880.

19. *Ibid.*

20. *Ibid.*

21. *Ibid.*

22. "Ned J. Lyons, Burglar," *The Sun* (New York, NY), October 27, 1880.

23. "Shot At," *Detroit Free Press*, March 19, 1881, p.1.

24. "Ned J. Lyons, Burglar," *The Sun* (New York, NY) October 27, 1880.

25. "Which?" *Boston Post*, October 28, 1880.

26. *Ibid.*

27. *Ibid.*

28. John D. Lawson, LLD, editor, *American State Trials*, Vol. XI (St. Louis: F. H. Thomas Law Book, 1919), 532.

29. "The Veiled Murderess Dies, An Insane Woman," *Buffalo Times*, July 16, 1905.

30. Jeanne Winston Adler, *The Affair of the Veiled Murderess* (Albany: State University of New York Press, 2011), 226–227.

31. "The Jury Disagrees," *The Boston Weekly Globe*, November 3, 1880.

32. "Hamilton Brock" Groom, November 6, 1882, Vermont, Vital Records, 1720–1908. Ancestry.com.

33. "Recent Deaths. Brock," *The St. Johnsbury Caledonian* (St. Johnsbury, VT), March 26, 1897.

Chapter 7

1. "Shot At," *Detroit Free Press*, March 19, 1881.

2. *Ibid.*

3. "In the Matter of the Estate of Sophie Lyons Burke, Deceased," State of Michigan Supreme Court Records, Case 33,402. Box 54; Library of Michigan, Lansing, Michigan.

4. "Shot At," *Detroit Free Press*, March 19, 1881.

5. "George Hendrie," Michigan, Death Records, 1867–1950, Michigan Department of Community Health, Division for Vital Records and Health Statistics; Lansing, Michigan. Ancestry.com.

6. "George Hendrie," by R. D. Jones, Michigan Transportation History, last modified October 9, 2019, www.michtranshist.info/pmwiki/pmwiki.php/Main/GeorgeHendrie.

7. "George Hendre," 1900 United States Federal Census: Census Place: Grosse Pointe

Farms, Wayne, Michigan; Page: 3; Enumeration District: 0188; FHL microfilm: 1240754. Ancestry.com.

8. "George Hendrie," by R. D. Jones

9. "George Hendrie," 1880 United States Federal Census: Census Place: Detroit, Wayne, Michigan; Roll: 613; Page: 200A; Enumeration District: 301. Ancestry.com.

10. "Sophie Lyons-Sylvan," *Boston Weekly Globe*, March 23, 1881.

11. "Assault With Intent to Kill," *Detroit Free Press*, March 20, 1881.

12. "The People of the State of Michigan vs. Sophie Lyons," The Recorder's Court in and for the City of Detroit, Case file 3104, March–May, 1881; Library of Michigan, Lansing, Michigan.

13. *Ibid.*

14. "Sophie Lyons," *Detroit Free Press*, April 16, 1881.

15. "Sayings and Doings," *Detroit Free Press*, May 14, 1881.

16. *Ibid.*

17. *Detroit Free Press*, May 25, 1881.

18. "Sophie Lyons on the War Path Again," *Detroit Free Press*, May 28, 1881.

19. "The People of the State of Michigan vs. Sophie Lyons," The Recorder's Court in and for the City of Detroit, Case file 3104, March–May, 1881; Library of Michigan, Lansing, Michigan.

20. "'Red' Lyons," *Detroit Free Press*, August 13, 1881.

21. "A Strange Will," *Evening News* (Detroit, MI), January 27, 1900.

22. "Mrs. Kate Loranger...," *Evening News* (Detroit, MI), March 20, 1880.

23. "Savage Sophie," *Detroit Free Press*, August 4, 1881.

24. *Ibid.*

25. "Once More Sophie Lyons," *Boston Globe*, August 4, 1881.

26. "Sophie Lyons," *Detroit Free Press*, August 26, 1881.

27. "Where Is Sophie Lyons," *Detroit Free Press*, November 6, 1881.

28. "Michigan News," *Times Herald* (Port Huron, MI), August 8, 1882.

29. "Lydia Patterson..." *St. Joseph Saturday Herald* (Saint Joseph, MI), December 31, 1892.

30. "Said to Be a Son of Ned and Sophie Lyons," *The Sun* (New York, NY), August 31, 1884.

31. "Heredity," *Detroit Free Press*, September 25, 1881.

Chapter 8

1. "Theresa Lewis," *Detroit Free Press*, December 29, 1881.

2. Untitled, *Detroit Free Press*, May 25, 1881.

3. "A Story of Crime," *Detroit Free Press*, December 10, 1881.

4. "Teresa A. White," Kentucky, County Marriage Records, 1783–1965. Ancestry.com.

5. "Theresia Lewis," Michigan, Death Records, 1867–1950. Ancestry.com.

6. *Ibid.*

7. "The Lyons-Lewis Case," *Detroit Free Press*, December 20, 1881.

8. "Stolen Property Recovered," *Detroit Free Press*, November 19, 1881; "The Lyons-Lewis Case," *Detroit Free Press*, December 28, 1881.

9. "Sophie Lyons in Court" *Detroit Free Press*, December 3, 1881.

10. *Ibid.*

11. *Ibid.*

12. "The Lyons-Lewis Case," *Detroit Free Press*, December 8, 1881.

13. *Ibid.*

14. "The Lyons-Lewis Case," *Detroit Free Press*, December 20, 1881.

15. *Ibid.*

16. "A Story of Crime," *Detroit Free Press*, December 10, 1881.

17. Thomas Byrnes, *Professional Criminals of America*, 67.

18. "Bob McKinney," *Detroit Free Press*, November 14, 1882.

19. "A Story of Crime," *Detroit Free Press*, December 10, 1881.

20. *Ibid.*

21. *Ibid.*

22. "Theresa Lewis," *Detroit Free Press*, December 29, 1881.

23. *Ibid.*

24. "Two Celebrated Cases," *Detroit Free Press*, February 11, 1882.

25. "The Superintendent Of Police Tenders His Resignation...," *Detroit Free Press*, February 1, 1882.

26. "Growing in Interest," *Detroit Free Press*, December 30, 1881.

27. "Guarded Detroit 56 Years; Retired to

Deserved Rest," *Detroit Free Press*, December 17, 1920; "Rogers Resigns," *Detroit Free Press*, February 1, 1882.

28. "Sophie Lyons' Ann Arbor Case," *Detroit Free Press*, December 9, 1881.

29. "Washtenaw County Fair," *Detroit Free Press*, October 8, 1881.

30. Charles B. Howell, editor and compiler, *Michigan Nisi Prius Cases, Decided by the State and Federal Courts in Michigan* (Detroit: Richmond, Backus, 1884), 212, 214, 222, https://archive.org/details/michigannisipri00howegoog/page/n6.

31. "Sophie Lyons' Ann Arbor Case," *Detroit Free Press*, December 9, 1881.

32. Howell, *Michigan Nisi Prius Cases*, 207.

33. *Ibid.*, 219.

34. *Ibid.*, 220.

35. "A Depot Episode," *Detroit Free Press*, February 7, 1882.

36. "Guilty," *Detroit Free Press*, February 3, 1883.

37. "Sophie Lyons," Register of Prisoners, Oct. 1, 1877–Dec. 26, 1883, Detroit House of Correction, Burton Historical Collection, Detroit Public Library, Detroit, Michigan.

38. "Sophie Lyons," *Detroit Free Press*, May 6, 1883.

39. *Ibid.*

40. *Ibid.*

41. "In the Matter of the Estate of Sophie Lyons Burke, Deceased," State of Michigan Supreme Court Records. Library of Michigan, Lansing, Michigan; Case 33,402. Box 54.

42. "Sophie vs. Theresa," *Detroit Free Press*, March 26, 1884.

43. "More Trouble for Sophie Lyons," *Detroit Free Press*, March 28, 1884.

Chapter 9

1. "In the Matter of the Estate of Sophie Lyons Burke, Deceased," State of Michigan Supreme Court Records. Library of Michigan, Lansing, Michigan; Case 33,402. Box 54.

2. "Mable Lyons," FamilySearch, Ontario Deaths, 1869–1937 and Overseas Deaths, 1939–1947, December 30, 1881, accessed October 21, 2019, https://www.familysearch.org/ark:/61903/1:1:JNTC-1PT.

3. "In the Matter of the Estate of Sophie Lyons Burke, Deceased," State of Michigan Supreme Court Records. Library of Michigan, Lansing, Michigan; Case 33,402. Box 54.

4. Sophie Lyons, *Why Crime Does Not Pay* (New York: J. S. Ogilvie, 1913), 23.

5. *Ibid.*, 24.

6. *Ibid.*, 24–25.

7. "Guilty," *Detroit Free Press*, February 3, 1883.

8. "In the Matter of the Estate of Sophie Lyons Burke, Deceased," State of Michigan Supreme Court Records. Library of Michigan, Lansing, Michigan; Case 33,402. Box 54.

9. Silas Farmer, *The History of Detroit and Michigan* ([Detroit, MI?]: Silas Farmer, 1884), 659–660, https://catalog.hathitrust.org/Record/100248511.

10. *Ibid.*, 660.

11. "In the Matter of the Estate of Sophie Lyons Burke, Deceased," State of Michigan Supreme Court Records. Library of Michigan, Lansing, Michigan; Case 33,402. Box 54.

12. "Grinds Organ for Pennies," *Detroit Free Press*, November 17, 1908.

13. "In the Matter of the Estate of Sophie Lyons Burke, Deceased," State of Michigan Supreme Court Records. Library of Michigan, Lansing, Michigan; Case 33,402. Box 54.

14. "Grinds Organ for Pennies," *Detroit Free Press*, November 17, 1908.

15. "Sophie Lyons," *Detroit Free Press*, April 26, 1884.

16. *Ibid.*

17. *Ibid.*

18. "The Higher Criminal Court," *Detroit Free Press*, May 9, 1884.

19. "Amusements," *Detroit Free Press*, May 28, 1884.

20. "A Sophistical Lecture," *Detroit Free Press*, May 29, 1884.

21. "Death of Theresa Lewis," *Detroit Free Press*, May 12, 1886.

22. "George Lyons," Elmira Reformatory Biographical Registers and Receiving Blotters, New York State Archives, Albany, New York; Series: B0141, vol. 1.

23. *Documents of the Assembly of the State of New York, One Hundred and Fifth Session* (Albany: Weed Parsons, Legislative Printers, 1882), 149–151. https://babel.hathitrust.org/cgi/pt?id=coo.3192410602613 5&view=1up&seq=7.

24. *Ibid.*, 143.

25. "George Lyons," Elmira Reformatory Biographical Registers and Receiving Blotters, New York State Archives, Albany, New York; Series: B0141, vol. 1.

26. "Zebulon Brockway: A Controversial Figure in Prison Reform," last modified January 2, 2014, https://connecticuthistory. org/zebulon-brockway-a-controversial-figure-in-prison-reform/.

27. *Ibid.*

28. "George Lyons," Elmira Reformatory Biographical Registers and Receiving Blotters, New York State Archives, Albany, New York; Series: B0141, vol. 1.

29. *Ibid.*

30. "George Lyons," New York Department of Health; Albany, NY; NY State Death Index; Certificate Number: 2813. Ancestry. com.

31. Thomas Byrnes, *Professional Criminals of America* (New York: Cassell, 1886), 141.

32. "George Lyons," Find A Grave database and images, page maintained by LMV, last modified July 21, 2004, https://www. findagrave.com/memorial/9152664/george-lyons.

Chapter 10

1. "Mary A. Brady," New Jersey, Wills and Probate Records, 1739–1991; Author: New Jersey. Surrogate's Court (Essex); Probate Place: Essex, New Jersey. Ancestry.com.

2. "Sophie Lyons Found," *The Sun* (New York, NY), June 10, 1886.

3. *Ibid.*

4. Shayne Davidson, *Captured and Exposed: The First Police Rogues' Gallery in America* (St. Louis: Missouri History Museum Press, 2017), e-book.

5. Thomas Byrnes, *Professional Criminals of America* (New York: Cassell, 1886), 206.

6. "She Can't Help Stealing," *Detroit Free Press*, October 26, 1886.

7. "Billy the Kid," *St. Louis Post-Dispatch*, February 26, 1887.

8. *Ibid.*

9. *Ibid.*

10. "The "Con" Gang," *St. Louis Post-Dispatch*, March 1, 1887.

11. "James W. Burke," 1860 United States Federal Census; Census Place: North

Bridgewater, Plymouth, Massachusetts; Roll: M653_518; Page: 664; Family History Library Film: 803518. Ancestry.com.

12. "William Burke," 1860 United States Federal Census; Census Place: Chicago, Cook, Illinois; Roll: 193; Page: 96C; Enumeration District: 113. Ancestry.com.

13. "Late Local Items," *Chicago Tribune*, September 5, 1879.

14. "The Rogues Gallery," *Detroit Free Press*, January 26, 1890.

15. "Billy Burke," *Detroit Free Press*, December 9, 1881.

16. Byrnes, *Professional Criminals*, 234–235.

17. "The "Con" Gang," *St. Louis Post-Dispatch*, March 1, 1887.

18. "A Gallery of Thieves," *Courier-Journal* (Louisville, KY), March 31, 1887.

19. "Mugs," *Cincinnati Enquirer*, February 26, 1893.

20. "Morris Harris," New York, Governor's Registers of Commitments to Prisons, 1842–1908. Ancestry.com.

21. "Has to Support Herself," *Detroit Free Press*, March 31, 1887.

Chapter 11

1. "James Brady," 1850 United States Federal Census; Census Place: Troy Ward 4, Rensselaer, New York; Roll: M432_584; Page: 137B; Image: 281. Ancestry.com.

2. "Michael Brady," New York, Registers of Officers and Enlisted Men Mustered into Federal Service, 1861–1865. Ancestry.com.

3. Thomas Byrnes, *Professional Criminals of America* (New York: Cassell, 1886), 329.

4. "The Rogues Gallery," *Detroit Free Press*, January 26, 1890.

5. "A Bold Robbery," *Star and Enterprise* (Newville, PA), February 16, 1871.

6. "A Criminal's Varied Life," *New York Times*, August 4, 1877.

7. Byrnes, *Professional Criminals*, 330.

8. *Ibid.*, 329.

9. Thomas Duke, *Celebrated Criminal Cases of America* (San Francisco: The James H. Barry Co., 1910), 674.

10. "A Criminal's Varied Life," *New York Times*, August 4, 1877.

11. Byrnes, *Professional Criminals*, 329.

12. *Ibid.*, 330.

13. "James Brady," New York State

Department of State Lists of Convicts Discharged by Expiration of Sentence or Pardon, New York State Archives, Albany, New York; Series: B0043, Box 3, Folder 9.

14. Sophie Van Elkan Lyons, *Why Crime Does Not Pay* (New York: J.S. Ogilvie, 1913), 258–259.

15. "A Pretty Smart Woman," *Buffalo Courier*, January 6, 1889.

16. "Sophie Lyons," Pinkerton National Detective Agency Records, 1853–1999, Library of Congress, Washington, D.C.; Criminal Case Files, 1861–1992.

17. Lyons, *Why Crime Does Not Pay*, 219–220.

18. Ellen E. Adams, *Forgotten World's Fairs: Detroit, 1889*, The Alice T. Miner Museum, last modified March 25, 2016, http://minermuseum.blogspot.com/2016/03/forgotten-worlds-fairs-detroit-1889.html.

19. "An Important Arrest," *Detroit Free Press*, September 20, 1889.

20. "A Clash of Authority," *Times Herald* (Port Huron, MI), September 27, 1889.

21. "Sophie Brady," London Metropolitan Archives; London, England; Board of Guardian Records, 1834–1906/Church of England Parish Registers, 1754–1906; Reference Number: p90/sav/005. Ancestry.com.

22. "Sophie Brady," "Lotta Belmont," 1891 England Census: The National Archives of the UK (TNA); Kew, Surrey, England; Class: RG12; Piece: 90; Folio: 127; Page: 6. Ancestry.com.

23. Byrnes, *Professional Criminals,* 154.

24. "Tragedy in Court," *Evening World* (New York), January 13, 1888.

25. Byrnes, *Professional Criminals,* 155.

26. "Mary A. Brady," New Jersey, Wills and Probate Records, 1739–1991; Author: New Jersey. Surrogate's Court (Essex); Probate Place: Essex, New Jersey. Ancestry.com.

27. "Miss Lotta Belmont," National Archives and Records Administration (NARA); Washington D.C.; NARA Series: Emergency Passport Applications (Issued Abroad), 1877–1907; Roll #: 35; Volume #: Volume 064: Germany. Ancestry.com.

Chapter 12

1. "King and Queen of Crooks," *Akron Daily Democrat*, May 28, 1892.

2. "Alleged Bank Sneak Released," *Courier-Journal* (Louisville, KYy), May 11, 1892.

3. Thomas Byrnes, *Professional Criminals of America* (New York: G. W. Dillingham, Publisher, successor to G. W. Carleton, 1895),102.

4. "Sophie Lyons in Louisville," *Courier-Journal* (Louisville, KY), December 10, 1892.

5. "Police Intelligence: Guildhall," *The Standard* (London, UK), March 22, 1890.

6. "Frank Lackrose," 1891 England Census, The National Archives of the UK (TNA); Kew, Surrey, England; Class: RG12; Piece: 44; Folio: 158; Page: 33. Ancestry.com.

7. Eddie Guerin, *CRIME: The Autobiography of a Crook* (London: John Murray, 1928), 107–108.

8. "'Super-Crook' Eddie," Daily News (New York, NY), March 20, 1938.

9. "The Funeral of Tom Bigelow," *Chicago Tribune*, December 2, 1886.

10. "Sophie Lyons Divorced," *Detroit Free Press*, January 5, 1892.

11. "Chinese Smugglers Laughing at Detroit Officers," *Detroit Free Press*, April 27, 1893.

12. "Sayings and Doings," *Detroit Free Press*, April 26, 1893.

13. "Waiting for Husbands," *Detroit Free Press*, December 10, 1893.

14. *Ibid.*

15. "Her Life at Home," *St. Louis Post-Dispatch*, January 27, 1895.

16. "Foiled Again Is Sophie Lyons," *Cincinnati Enquirer*, December 9, 1894.

17. "Sophie Lyons, 'Queen of the Pickpockets,'" *Cincinnati Enquirer*, November 19, 1894.

18. "In a Green Goods Lair," *The Sun* (New York, NY) October 9, 1894.

Chapter 13

1. "Found in St. Louis," *Courier-Journal* (Louisville, KY), January 14, 1895.

2. "Detectives in New Jobs," *The New York Times*, July 20, 1895.

3. "Carleton C. Mason," New York, Spanish-American War Military and Naval Service Records, 1898–1902. Ancestry.com.

4. "The People of the State of Michigan vs. Sophie Lyons," The Recorder's Court in

and for the City of Detroit, Library of Michigan, Lansing, Michigan: Case file 3104, March–May, 1881.

5. *Ibid.*

6. "Held at the Line," *Pittsburgh Post-Gazette*, December 16, 1895.

7. "Burke Wants Acquittal," *Detroit Free Press*, December 22, 1895.

8. "Must Come Back," *Pittsburgh Post-Gazette*, December 25, 1895.

9. "William Burke," Pinkerton National Detective Agency Records, 1853–1999, Library of Congress, Washington, D.C.; Criminal Case File, 1861–1992.

10. "Pointed Out as a Thief in a Sixth Avenue Car," *The Sun* (New York, NY), June 22, 1896.

11. *Ibid.*

12. "Sophie Lyons's Plea for Mother-Love," *The World* (New York, NY), June 28, 1896.

13. *Ibid.*

14. "Jacob Elkan," New York, State Census, 1875. Ancestry.com.

15. "Elkins, Jacob (alias) Elkan, Jacob," Civil War Pension Application, National Archives and Records Administration, Washington, D.C.: record # 784847.

16. "Jacob Elkan," New York, Death Index, 1880–1956: New York Department of Health; Albany, NY; NY State Death Index. Ancestry.com.

17. "Mary Elkan," New York, Death Index, 1880–1956: New York Department of Health; Albany, NY; NY State Death Index. Ancestry.com.

18. "Mary Elkan," Probate Records, 1787–1916; Author: New York. Surrogate's Court (Ulster County); Probate Place: Ulster, New York. Ancestry.com.

19. "In the Matter of the Estate of Sophie Lyons Burke, Deceased," State of Michigan Supreme Court Records. Library of Michigan, Lansing, Michigan; Case 33,402. Box 54.

20. "Florence Edwards," 1900 United States Federal Census; Census Place: Detroit Ward 1, Wayne, Michigan; Page: 16; Enumeration District: 0009; FHL microfilm: 1240747. Ancestry.com.

21. "In the Matter of the Estate of Sophie Lyons Burke, Deceased," State of Michigan Supreme Court Records. Library of Michigan, Lansing, Michigan; Case 33,402. Box 54.

22. "Seymour, Identifier for Pinkerton Agency, Dead," *Buffalo Morning Express and Illustrated Buffalo Express*, October 14, 1912.

23. "Sophie Lyons," Pinkerton National Detective Agency Records, 1853–1999, Library of Congress, Washington, D.C.; Criminal Case File, 1861–1992.

24. "Miss Lotta Belmont," U.S. Passport Applications, 1795–1925: National Archives and Records Administration (NARA); Washington, D.C.; NARA Series: Emergency Passport Applications (Issued Abroad), 1877–1907; Roll #: 35; Volume #: Volume 064: Germany. Ancestry.com.

25. "Prince of Wales Theatre," *Pall Mall Gazette* (London, UK), June 16, 1897.

26. "Crooks Daughter Tells Her Life History," *New-York Tribune*, January 23, 1915.

27. "Sophie Lyons, World-Famed Thief, Has Determined Upon Reformation," *St. Louis Post-Dispatch*, November 23, 1898.

28. *Ibid.*

29. "William Burke," Pinkerton National Detective Agency Records, 1853–1999, Library of Congress, Washington, D.C.; Criminal Case File, 1861–1992.

30. "Sophie Lyons," Pinkerton National Detective Agency Records, 1853–1999, Library of Congress, Washington, D.C.; Criminal Case File, 1861–1992.

31. Ben Macintyre, *The Napoleon of Crime: The Life and Times of Adam Worth, Master Thief* (New York: Dell Publishing, 1997), 15.

32. *Ibid.*, 173.

33. *Ibid.*

34. "Billy, the Kid," *The Windsor Star*, July 19, 1899.

Chapter 14

1. "Industrial Detroit (1860–1900)," Detroit Historical Society, accessed October 21, 2019, https://detroithistorical.org/learn/timeline-detroit/industrial-detroit-1860-1900.

2. "William Burke," Pinkerton National Detective Agency Records, 1853–1999, Library of Congress, Washington, D.C.; Criminal Case File, 1861–1992.

3. "Says Pope Blessed Her," *Boston Post*, June 6, 1901.

4. *Ibid.*

5. "Elkins, Jacob (alias) Elkan, Jacob,"

Civil War Pension Application, National Archives and Records Administration, Washington D.C.: Record #784847.

6. "No Expense," *Detroit Free Press*, July 18, 1901.

7. "Sophia Lyons Lost," *Detroit Free Press*, April 9, 1902.

8. "Florence Edwards," 1900 United States Federal Census; Census Place: Detroit Ward 1, Wayne, Michigan; Page: 16; Enumeration District: 0009; FHL microfilm: 1240747. Ancestry.com.

9. "In the Matter of the Estate of Sophie Lyons Burke, Deceased," State of Michigan Supreme Court Records. Library of Michigan, Lansing, Michigan; Case 33,402. Box 54.

10. *Ibid.*

11. "No Expense," *Cincinnati Enquirer*, July 18, 1901.

12. "Troubles of Sophie Lyons," *The Evening News* (Detroit, MI), September 28, 1898.

13. "Mary A. Brady," New Jersey, Wills and Probate Records, 1739–1991; Author: New Jersey. Surrogate's Court (Essex); Probate Place: Essex, New Jersey. Ancestry.com.

14. "Crook's Daughter Tells Life History," *New-York Tribune*, January 23, 1915.

15. "Carleton Charles Mason," Massachusetts, Mason Membership Cards, 1733–1990. Ancestry.com.

16. "Says Pope Blessed Her," *Boston Post*, June 6, 1901.

17. "Two Days Bazaar," *The Morning Post* (London, UK), November 28, 1898.

18. "Lotta Belmont," 1901 England Census, Class: RG13; Piece: 78; Folio: 41; Page: 16, Ancestry.com.

19. "Sophie Lyons Back Home," *Detroit Free Press*, May 5, 1904.

20. "William Burke," Pinkerton National Detective Agency Records, 1853–1999, Library of Congress, Washington, D.C.; Criminal Case File, 1861–1992.

21. "Must Leave Burke Alone," *Detroit Free Press*, July 7, 1904.

22. "'Billy The Kid' Can't Live Here," *Detroit Free Press*, June 30, 1904.

23. "'Billy' Burke's Bail Was Set at $2,000," *Detroit Free Press*, August 13, 1904.

24. "Sophie Lyons Lost Her Happy Home," *Detroit Free Press*, April 14, 1905.

25. "Sophie Lyons-Brady Says She Was Robbed," *Detroit Free Press*, April 8, 1905.

26. "Fake 'Ad' Atributed to Sophie Lyons," *The Detroit News Tribune*, May 14, 1905.

27. "Sophie Will Make Them Pay," *The Evening News* (Detroit, MI), June 2, 1905.

28. "In the Matter of the Estate of Sophie Lyons Burke, Deceased," State of Michigan Supreme Court Records. Library of Michigan, Lansing, Michigan; Case 33,402. Box 54.

Chapter 15

1. "Sophie Lyons Is Glad She's No One Else..." *Detroit Free Press*, August 16, 1908.

2. "Lieut. Lally Discovers that 'Billy' Burke Grabbed Cash," *Detroit Free Press*, October 29, 1907.

3. *Ibid.*

4. "'Billy B' Burke now Confined in Prison Founded by Quakers," *Detroit Free Press*, May 6, 1908.

5. "Sophie Lyons Is Glad She's No One Else..." *Detroit Free Press*, August 16, 1908.

6. "Grinds Organ for Pennies," *Detroit Free Press*, November 17, 1908.

7. *Ibid.*

8. "'Perfumed Vagrant,' Says Sophie Lyons of Child," *Detroit Free Press*, November 20, 1908.

9. "Florence L. Bower," Michigan Department of Community Health, Division for Vital Records and Health Statistics; Lansing, Michigan; Michigan. Divorce records; Ancestry.com.

10. "In the Matter of the Estate of Sophie Lyons Burke, Deceased," State of Michigan Supreme Court Records. Library of Michigan, Lansing, Michigan; Case 33,402. Box 54.

11. "Exiled From Toronto," *The Gazette* (Montreal, Canada), February 3, 1906.

12. "Stole a Million; Now He is Broke," *The Topeka Daily Capital*, January 29, 1906.

13. "Tale of Forty Thieves as Told by the Forty-First," *The Inter Ocean* (Chicago, IL), January 13, 1907.

14. "Grinds Organ for Pennies," *Detroit Free Press*, November 17, 1908.

15. *Ibid.*

16. "'Perfumed Vagrant,' Says Sophie Lyons of Child," *Detroit Free Press*, November 20, 1908.

17. "'Higher Education Bad for Girls':

Sophie Lyons," *The Detroit News*, November 20, 1908.

18. *Ibid.*

19. "In the Matter of the Estate of Sophie Lyons Burke, Deceased," State of Michigan Supreme Court Records. Case 33,402. Box 54. LOM.

20. *Ibid.*

21. "Asks Only for Love and Recognition," *Detroit Free Press*, November 19, 1908.

22. "Grinds Organ for Pennies," *Detroit Free Press*, November 17, 1908.

23. "'Perfumed Vagrant,' Says Sophie Lyons of Child," *Detroit Free Press*, November 20, 1908.

24. "In the Matter of the Estate of Sophie Lyons Burke, Deceased," State of Michigan Supreme Court Records. Library of Michigan, Lansing, Michigan; Case 33,402. Box 54.

25. "'Perfumed Vagrant,' Says Sophie Lyons of Child," *Detroit Free Press*, November 20, 1908.

26. "Frank Lackrose," 1891 England Census, The National Archives of the UK (TNA); Kew, Surrey, England; Class: RG12; Piece: 44; Folio: 158; Page: 33. Ancestry.com.

27. "Asks Only for Love and Recognition," *Detroit Free Press*, November 19, 1908.

Chapter 16

1. "'Billy' Burke Is Back in Detroit," *Detroit Free Press*, February 28, 1910.

2. "Sophia Brady," Ontario, Canada, Marriages, 1801–1928, 1933–1934, Archives of Ontario; Toronto, Ontario, Canada; Registrations of Marriages, 1869–1928; Series: MS932; Reel: 147. Ancestry.com.

3. "Sophie Lyons Is Badly Stung in Recent Real Estate Deal," *Detroit Free Press*, April 25, 1908.

4. *Michigan Manual of Freedmen's Progress*, Compiled by Francis H. Warren, Secretary of Freedman's Progress Commission (Detroit, Michigan, 1915), 31, https://catalog.hathitrust.org/Record/009570585.

5. "Sophie Lyons Wins Out," *The Windsor Star*, June 17, 1909.

6. "Mary McCoy," 1910 United States Federal Census; Census Place: Detroit Ward 12, Wayne, Michigan; Roll: T624_685; Page: 5A; Enumeration District: 0174; FHL microfilm: 1374698. Ancestry.com.

7. "Pickaninnies Will Not Hurt the Garbage Works," *Detroit Free Press*, June 6, 1909.

8. "Not Drawing the Color Line," *Detroit Free Press*, June 9, 1909.

9. "William Burke," Pinkerton National Detective Agency Records, 1853–1999, Library of Congress, Washington, D.C.; Criminal Case File, 1861–1992.

10. *Ibid.*

11. "'I don't care if Billie has an affinity'—Sophie Lyons Burke," *Detroit Free Press*, August 6, 1911.

12. "William Burke," Pinkerton National Detective Agency Records, 1853–1999, Library of Congress, Washington, D.C.; Criminal Case File, 1861–1992.

13. "Stockholm Police Arrest Sophie Lyons," *Detroit Free Press*, June 19, 1912.

14. "Queen of Crooks Reforms," *The Daily Republican* (Rushville, IN), May 10, 1913.

15. "William Burke," Pinkerton National Detective Agency Records, 1853–1999, Library of Congress, Washington, D.C.; Criminal Case File, 1861–1992.

16. "Mrs. Sophia L. Burke," U.S. Passport Applications, 1795–1925; National Archives and Records Administration (NARA); Washington, D.C.; NARA Series: Emergency Passport Applications, Argentina thru Venezuela, 1906–1925; Box #: 4576; Volume #: Volume 159: Berlin. Ancestry.com.

17. "Beilis Acquitted Because Russia Dare Not Commit Official Murder," *The San Francisco Examiner*, Novemver 13, 1913.

18. "William Burke," Pinkerton National Detective Agency Records, 1853–1999, Library of Congress, Washington, D.C.; Criminal Case File, 1861–1992.

19. "Mrs. Sophia L. Burke," U.S. Passport Applications, 1795–1925; National Archives and Records Administration (NARA); Washington, D.C.; NARA Series: Emergency Passport Applications, Argentina thru Venezuela, 1906–1925; Box #: 4576; Volume #: Volume 159: Berlin. Ancestry.com.

20. "Sophie Lyons Returns," *The Sun* (New York, NY), January 11, 1914.

21. "'Billy' Burke Back, But Not For Long," *Detroit Free Press*, October 22, 1913.

22. "Sophie Lyons," Pinkerton National Detective Agency Records, 1853–1999, Library of Congress, Washington, D.C.; Criminal Case File, 1861–1992.

Chapter 17

1. "Crook's Daughter Tells Life Story," *New-York Tribune*, January 23, 1915.

2. "Mary Ann Brady," 1850 United States Federal Census; Census Place: Troy Ward 4, Rensselaer, New York; Roll: M432_584; Page: 137B; Image: 281. Ancestry.com.

3. "Mary A Brady," 1860 United States Federal Census; Census Place: Cohoes, Albany, New York; Roll: M653_721; Page: 887; Family History Library Film: 803721. Ancestry.com.

4. "Michael Brady," U.S., Civil War Pension Index: General Index to Pension Files, 1861–1934; The National Archives at Washington, D.C.; Washington, D.C.; Record Group Title: Records of the Department of Veterans Affairs, 1773–2007; Record Group Number: 15; Series Title: U.S., Civil War Pension Index: General Index to Pension Files, 1861–1934. Ancestry.com.

5. "Mary A. Brady," New Jersey, Wills and Probate Records, 1739–1991; Author: New Jersey. Surrogate's Court (Essex); Probate Place: Essex, New Jersey. Ancestry.com.

6. *Ibid.*

7. *Ibid.*

8. *Ibid.*

9. *Ibid.*

10. "One-Time King of Bank Thieves Killed by Train," *Buffalo Courier*, May 28, 1903.

11. "Dead Jim Brady Not 'The' Jim," *Evening World* (New York, NY), June 5, 1903.

12. "Sophie Lyons, World-Famed Thief, Has Determined Upon Reformation," *St. Louis Post-Dispatch*, November 23, 1898.

13. "Madeline Belmont," New York, Passenger Lists, 1820–1957; Year: 1914; Arrival: New York, New York; Microfilm Serial: T715, 1897–1957; Microfilm Roll: Roll 2391; Line: 3; Page Number: 65. Ancestry.com.

14. "Mary A. Brady," New Jersey, Wills and Probate Records, 1739–1991; Author: New Jersey. Surrogate's Court (Essex); Probate Place: Essex, New Jersey. Ancestry.com.

15. *Ibid.*

16. "Crook's Daughter Tells Life Story," *New-York Tribune*, January 23, 1915.

17. "Marion V. Johnson," New York, Death Index, 1880–1956; New York Department of Health; Albany, NY; NY State Death Index. Ancestry.com.

18. "Madeline Belmond," UK, Incoming Passenger Lists, 1878–1960; The National Archives of the UK; Kew, Surrey, England; Board of Trade: Commercial and Statistical Department and successors: Inwards Passenger Lists.; Class: BT26; Piece: 604. Ancestry.com.

19. "In the Matter of the Estate of Sophie Lyons Burke, Deceased," State of Michigan Supreme Court Records. Library of Michigan, Lansing, Michigan; Case 33,402. Box 54.

Chapter 18

1. "Voice of the People," *Detroit Free Press*, July 12, 1918.

2. "In the Matter of the Estate of Sophie Lyons Burke, Deceased," State of Michigan Supreme Court Records. Library of Michigan, Lansing, Michigan; Case 33,402. Box 54.

3. "Sophie Lyons Will Endows Orphans' Home," *Detroit Free Press*, May 11, 1924.

4. "Children's Home Site Is Donated By Sophie Lyons," *Detroit Free Press*, May 11, 1924.

5. "Home Planned By Woman Ex-Crook," *Leader-Post* (Regina, Saskatchewan, Canada), March 25, 1916.

6. "Sophie Lyons Is Banquet Speaker," *Detroit Free Press*, March 24, 1916.

7. "Children's Home Site Is Donated By Sophie Lyons," *Detroit Free Press*, February 2, 1916.

8. "Ex-Queen of Slickers Gets Stung for $600," *Chicago Tribune*, July 29, 1916.

9. "Behner Is Discharged," *Detroit Free Press*, August 4, 1916.

10. "William James Burke," Michigan, Death Records, 1867–1950. Ancestry.com.

11. "In the Matter of the Estate of Sophie Lyons Burke, Deceased," State of Michigan Supreme Court Records. Library of Michigan, Lansing, Michigan; Case 33,402. Box 54.

12. "Conscience Clear, Says Sophie Lyons," *Detroit Free Press*, December 21, 1919.

13. "Carleton Mason," 1910 United States Federal Census; Census Place: Seattle Ward 4, King, Washington; Roll: T624_1659; Page: 14A; Enumeration District: 0103; FHL microfilm: 1375672. Ancestry.com.

14. "Carleton Mason," Washinton State Board of Health, Certificate of Death #1627.

15. "In the Matter of the Estate of Sophie Lyons Burke, Deceased," State of Michigan Supreme Court Records. Library of Michigan, Lansing, Michigan; Case 33,402. Box 54.

16. *Ibid.*

17. "Military Funeral Given C.C. Mason," *Detroit Free Press*, October 1, 1922.

18. "Rob Ex-Confidence Woman," New York Times, July 6, 1922.

19. "Holdups Beat Sophie Lyons," *Detroit Free Press*, March 26, 1924.

20. "Sophie Lyons Identifies Bandits Who Slugged Her," *Lansing State Journal*, April 4, 1924.

21. "In the Matter of the Estate of Sophie Lyons Burke, Deceased," State of Michigan Supreme Court Records. Library of Michigan, Lansing, Michigan; Case 33,402. Box 54.

22. *Ibid.*

Chapter 19

1. "Mystery Shrouds Mrs. Burke's Death," *Detroit Free Press*, May 8, 1924.

2. "Bullet Kills Two in Battle with Outlaws," *Detroit Free Press*, April 1, 1924.

3. "Sophia Lyons Burke," Michigan, Death Records, 1867–1950. Ancestry.com.

4. "Ira Jayne, Top Jurist, Dies at 78," *Detroit Free Press* (Detroit, Michigan), January 23, 1961, p.1.

5. "Huge Crowd Attends Sophie Lyons Funeral," *Detroit Free Press*, May 10, 1924.

6. *Ibid.*

7. "Sophie Lyons Goes to Tomb," *The Detroit News*, May 10, 1924.

8. "In the Matter of the Estate of Sophie Lyons Burke, Deceased," State of Michigan Supreme Court Records. Library of Michigan, Lansing, Michigan; Case 33,402. Box 54.

9. "Strange and Sinister Secrets of Our Champion Prison Breaker," *Star Tribune* (Minneapolis, MN), November 20, 1932.

10. "In the Matter of the Estate of Sophie Lyons Burke, Deceased," State of Michigan Supreme Court Records. Library of Michigan, Lansing, Michigan; Case 33,402. Box 54.

11. *Ibid.*

12. "Sophie Lyons' Estate Fails to Show Millions," *Detroit Free Press*, October 28, 1925.

13. "Lyons Appeal Right Granted," *Detroit Free Press*, October 4, 1927.

14. "In the Matter of the Estate of Sophie Lyons Burke, Deceased," State of Michigan Supreme Court Records. Library of Michigan, Lansing, Michigan; Case 33,402. Box 54.

15. *Ibid.*

16. *Ibid.*

17. *Ibid.*

18. *Ibid.*

19. *Ibid.*

20. *Ibid.*

21. *Ibid.*

22. "Lyons Appeal Right Granted," *Detroit Free Press*, October 4, 1927.

23. "End of Sophie Lyons' Will Reveal Mercy," *Detroit Free Press*, January 24, 1929.

24. *Ibid.*, 3.

Chapter 20

1. "Florence L. Bower," Michigan, Divorce Records, 1897–1952; Michigan Department of Community Health, Division for Vital Records and Health Statistics; Lansing, Michigan; Michigan. Divorce records. Ancestry.com.

2. "Florence L. Bower," Michigan, Death Records, 1867–1950. Ancestry.com.

3. "Prince of Wales Theatre," *Pall Mall Gazette* (London, UK), 1897, various editions.

4. "Lotta Belmont," 1901 England Census; Class: RG13; Piece: 78; Folio: 41; Page: 16. Ancestry.com.

5. "Charlotte Belmont," London, England, Workhouse Admission and Discharge Records, 1764–1930; London Metropolitan Archives; London, England; Reference Number: WEBG/CW/049/04. Ancestry.com.

6. "Charlotte Belmont," London, England, Workhouse Admission and Discharge Records, 1764–1930; London Metropolitan Archives; London, England; Reference Number: CHBG/188/075. Ancestry.com.

7. "Newington Workhouse (later Newington Lodge)," by Zoe Lyons, accessed October 21, 2019, Exploring Southwark and Discovering its History, http://www.exploringsouthwark.co.uk/newington-workhouse/4593930744.

8. "Charlotte Belmont," London, England, Workhouse Admission and Discharge

Records, 1764–1930; London Metropolitan Archives; London, England; Reference Number: STPBG/275. Ancestry.com.

9. "Miscellany," *The Guardian* (London, UK) June 6, 1924.

10. "Charlotte Belmont," England GRO, Death Record in District of Chelsea, Metropolitan Borough of Chelsea.

11. "Madeline Belmont," London, Bethlem Hospital Patient Admission Registers And Casebooks 1683–1932, Patient casebook. FindMyPast.com.

12. Bethlem: History, accessed October 21, 2019, https://www.countyasylums.co.uk/bethlem-royal-hospital/.

13. *Ibid.*

14. "Air Raid on Paris," *The Observer* (London, UK), March 10, 1918.

15. British Red Cross, First World War, accessed October 21, 2019, https://vad.redcross.org.uk/Search

16. Bethlem Museum of the Mind, Bethlem Royal Hospital (1247-), accessed October 21, 2019, https://museumofthemind.org.uk/projects/european-journeys/asylums/bethlem-royal-hospital.

17. "Madeline Belmon," London, England, Workhouse Admission and Discharge Records, 1764–1930; London Metropolitan Archives; London, England; Reference Number: SOBG/111/75. Ancestry.com.

18. "Workhouse Food," The Workhouse, The story of an Institution, accessed October 21, 2019, www.workhouses.org.uk.

19. "Madeline Belmon," London, England, Workhouse Admission and Discharge Records, 1764–1930; London Metropolitan Archives; London, England;

Reference Number: SOBG/111/75. Ancestry.com.

20. "Madeline Belmont," Manor Hospital Epsom, Patient Records; Alphabetical Register of Female Patients, 1899–c.1921; History Centre Surrey; Woking, Surrey, England; Reference Number: 6282/13/30.

21. "In the Matter of the Estate of Sophie Lyons Burke, Deceased," State of Michigan Supreme Court Records. Library of Michigan, Lansing, Michigan; Case 33,402. Box 54.

22. *Ibid.*

23. "Madeline Belmont," Banstead Asylum Records, London Metropolitan Archives; London, England; Reference Number: H22/BAN/B/01/094.

24. "Madeline Belmont," 1939 England and Wales Register; The National Archives; Kew, London, England; 1939 Register; Reference: RG 101/1407J. Ancestry.com.

25. "Madeline Belmont, otherwise Sophy Brady," England GRO, Death Record in Surrey Mid-Eastern, County of Surrey.

26. Banstead Hospital History, Asylum Projects, last modified May 9, 2014, http://www.asylumprojects.org/index.php/Banstead_Hospital.

27. "Convicts: Sophie Lyons' Will Still Gives Them Aid," *Detroit Free Press*, August 4, 1946.

Epilogue

1. Sophie Lyons, *Why Crime Does Not Pay* (New York: J. Ogilvie Publishing, 1913), 264.

Selected Bibliography

American Psychiatric Association. *Understanding Mental Disorders: Your Guide to DSM-5.* Washington, D.C.: American Psychiatric Publishing, 2015.

Anbinder, Tyler. *Five Points: The Nineteenth-Century New York City Neighborhood.* New York: Free Press, 2001.

Asbury, Herbert. *The Gangs of New York: An Informal History of the Underworld.* New York: Alfred A. Knopf, 1928.

Butterfiled, Fox. *In My Father's House: A New View of How Crime Runs in the Family.* New York: Knopf, 2018.

Byrnes, Thomas. *Professional Criminals of America.* New York: G.W. Dillingham, 1886.

Byrnes, Thomas. *Professional Criminals of America: New and Revised Edition.* New York: Cassell & Company, 1895.

Cole, Simon A. *Suspect Identities: A History of Fingerprinting and Criminal Identification.* Cambridge: Harvard University Press, 2001.

De Grave, Kathleen. *Swindler, Spy, Rebel: The Confidence Woman in Nineteenth Century America.* Columbia: University of Missouri Press, 1995.

Eldridge, Benjamin P., and William B. Watts. *Our Rival, the Rascal: A Faithful Portrayal of the Conflict Between the Criminals of this Age and the Defenders of Society, the Police.* Boston: Pemberton Publishing Company, 1897.

Farley, Phil. *Criminals of America, Or, Tales of the Lives of Thieves: Enabling Every One to be His Own Detective.* New York: Author's Edition, 1876.

Gilfoyle, Timothy J. *A Pickpocket's Tale: The Underworld of Nineteenth-Century New York.* New York: W.W. Norton & Company, 2006.

Grannan, Joseph. *Grannan's pocket gallery of noted criminals of the present day, containing portraits of noted and dangerous criminals ...* Cincinnati: Grannan Detective Bureau Co., 1890.

Grannan, Joseph. *Grannan's warning against fraud and valuable information. A treatise upon subjects relating to crime and business and also embracing many practical suggestions for everyday life.* Akron: The Werner Ptg. & Litho. Co., 1890.

Guerin, Eddie. *Crime: The Autobiography of a Crook.* London: John Murray, 1928.

Horn, Stacy. *Damnation Island: Poor, Sick, Mad, and Criminal in 19th-Century New York.* Chapel Hill: Algonquin Books, 2018.

Konnikova, Maria. *The Confidence Game: Why We Fall for It...Every Time.* New York: Viking, 2016.

Kuntz, Jerry. *Professional Criminals of America—Revised.* Last Modified July 22, 2019. https://criminalsrevised.blog/.

Lucas, Netley. *Ladies of the Underworld.* Cleveland: Goldsmith Publishing, 1927.

Macintyre, Ben. *The Napoleon of Crime: The Life and Times of Adam Worth, Master Thief.* New York: Farrar, Straus & Giroux, 1997.

Martelle, Scott. *Detroit: A Biography.* Chicago: Chicago Review Press, 2012.

Miller, Patricia. *Bringing Down the Colonel: A Sex Scandal of the Gilded Age, and the "Powerless" Woman Who Took on Washington.* New York: Farrar, Straus & Giroux, 2018.

Moore, Langdon. *Langdon W. Moore: His Own Story of His Eventful Life.* Boston: L.W. Moore, 1893.

Roth, Alisa. *Insane: America's Criminal Treatment of Mental Illness*. New York: Basic Books, 2018.

Rovere, Richard H. *Howe & Hummel: Their True and Scandalous History*. New York: Farrar, Straus and Company, 1947.

Sante, Luc. *Low Life: Lures and Snares of Old New York*. New York: Farrar, Straus & Giroux, 1991.

Schteir, Rachel. *The Steal: A Cultural History of Shoplifting*. New York: The Penguin Press, 2011.

Segrave, Kerry. *Women Swindlers in America, 1860–1920*. Jefferson, NC: McFarland, 2007.

Van Elkan Lyons, Sophie. *Why Crime Does Not Pay*. New York: J. S. Ogilvie, 1913.

Walling, George. *Recollections of a New York Chief of Police*. New York: Caxton Book Concern, 1887.

Index